THE TRUTH ABOUT DEMONS

A MEMOIR

C.A.GILCHRIST

THE TRUTH ABOUT DEMONS

A MEMOIR

C.A. GILCHRIST

COPYRIGHT

The Truth About Demons

The Truth About Demons depicts actual events in the life of the author as truthfully as recollection permits and/or can be verified by research. For privacy reasons, some names, locations, identifying characteristics and dates may have been changed.

979-8-9914029-0-3 Ebook

979-8-9914029-1-0 Kindle

979-8-9914029-2-7 Paperback

979-8-9914029-3-4. Hardcover

979-8-9914029-4-1 Audiobook

Library of Congress CIPD has been applied for.

First Edition: January 2025 10 9 8 7 6 5 4 3 2 1

True Ink Press

San Diego, Ca

To contact the author or to book an event:

www.CamGilchrist.com

CONTENT NOTE

This is my story and I've told it to the best of my memory corroborated with interviews and research. Names have been changed to protect the innocent and the not-so-innocent.

My story includes events that depict violence, child and animal harm, suicidal thoughts, mental illness, racism, sexism, homophobia, drug and alcohol abuse, grief, and loss.

Some of the dialogue contain racial slurs. In order to tell my story honestly within its historic setting, I have included examples of the hate speech.

Reader discretion is advised. It was a rough ride at times.

C.A. Gilchrist

A RECORD OF EVENTS IN 40 PARTS

Genesis 1
1. Tree of Knowledge 2
2. The Angels Above 10
3. Sacrifice 18
4. Manor Born 23
5. The Death of Heroes 33
6. aixelsyD 39
7. Inheritance 48
8. On the Origin of The Problem 54
9. Crayon Yellow Sun 60
10. Truth or Consequences 67
11. Blue Sky 74
Exodus 81
12. Bereft 82
13. A New Hope 87
14. Resolution of Happiness 94
15. The King of Wishful Thinking 101
16. Worn Books, New Shoes 107
17. Meet Cute 115
18. The Grand Gesture 123
19. Monikers 132
20. Yellow Brick Road Trip 140
21. Court Jesters 150
22. Sledgehammer 158
23. Dance Hall Days 166
Job 175
24. What He Takes Away 176
25. Advice for the Recently Displaced 181
26. Respite 186
27. Whiskey Lullaby 192
28. Cardboard 200
29. Kyrie Eleison 207
30. Pasta and Herb 218
31. Deus ex Machina 225
Revelation 231
32. Friday the 13th 232
33. Friends 236
34. Last Call 243
35. My Empire of Dirt 251

36. Between the Soul and Soft Machine 260
37. A Banquet of Consequences 267
38. Armageddon 274
39. Execution of Bitterness 284
40. San Francisco - Monday, August 16, 2021, 2:12 pm 291

After 293
Thank you 295
Acknowledgments 297
About the Author 299

For Sid

"The only thing you absolutely have to know, is the location of the library." - *Albert Einstein*

GENESIS

1

TREE OF KNOWLEDGE

I pulled the baggie of coke out of my pocket. It was empty, just like me. How was I still alive? I probably wouldn't be for long. You can't just walk away from these people, no matter who you know. They would find me. *Who cares anyway*? Everyone I loved was dead or gone. Maybe it was time to join them.

My car turned onto my old street, as if guided by spirit magnets. The gas tank gave up the last of its fumes and the engine stalled, coasting to a stop across the street from my childhood home. I got out to confront the locus of my early construction. The gravity of the place made me too heavy to stand. I slumped back against the car door.

I'd survived a lot in the years since I'd called this my home, more than anyone had a right to. Maybe I had used up all my allotted luck, for this life at least. Was there a trace of me to be found in its old wood? Something good, something redeemable? Something I could use?

Where was the boy who was going to be an astronaut, a doctor, a scientist?

Where was the boy who'd vibrated with plans birthed from a flashlight-lit book under a blanket?

Where was the boy who swam in rivers of words and danced under the light of a thousand distant suns?

Was there anything left of that me besides an echo?

No, there was nothing of him in the old house. Not even an echo. Its wood and brick were long purged of him, given over to new families full of life and love. There were no answers to be found on Chestnut Lane.

I abandoned my car and started walking the familiar route to the library. My feet remembered the way and I let them take me. My walk turned into a run. I let my legs go faster, trusting them to remember the shortcuts between houses, across lawns. I flew, the wind drying the wetness of tears and sweat, leaving behind a film of salt like a rouge of all pains past and present.

The murmur tried to distract me with memories and promises of the drink, the drugs, the adoration.

Where are you going? Nothing there for you.

I wanted a drink. I wanted a line.

You are alone, so alone.

My legs pumped, the burn helping to quiet the ever-present murmur.

It's no use. It's too late.

The library looked smaller yet felt larger than I remembered. I leaned against one of its walls to catch my breath, feeling the coarse brick under my fingers. I willed my heart to slow, lest it explode in my chest. I gripped the door handle like it was the first rung of a ladder out of a fire. The coolness of the aluminum felt like home against my hot hand. It had been so long. Maybe too long.

How had it come to this? I guess it all started with books. And the demons of course.

I burst through the library door and slammed the book, *Something Wicked This Way Comes,* onto the counter with a smack, startling Miss Elizabeth, the serious-faced librarian.

"Easy with the book Mr. Gilchrist." Miss Elizabeth pursed her thin lips, adjusted her John Lennon style glasses, and gave me a shaming head shake. "Returning it already? Didn't you like it? I thought Ray Bradbury was your latest favorite."

"It's my mom. She won't let me read this one. She says it's chock-full of demons."

"What does that mean?"

"Mom says she can see 'em and hear 'em. The demons, I mean."

"Hmm. What does your dad think of that?"

"Mom told Dad and me that the demons were out to get all of us, but especially smart-mouthed, rebellious boys like me that have a willful mind of their own."

"Did she now," she said, her comment more a judgment than a question.

"Gotta go now, thank you, bye." I pushed open the door. "Tomorrow I'll check out a different Bradbury book with a safer title."

"Maybe *Fahrenheit 451*?"

I had to be careful. If the mom caught me reading a book she didn't like one more time, punishment would be swift and painful.

"What's that one about?"

"Trust me, you'll love it." She gave me one of her smiles she reserved for special occasions. "It's required reading for all rebellious, strong-willed eight-year-olds."

"I'm not eight yet, I'm seven and a half."

"You're so tall for your age. You're almost as tall as my nephew, and he's turning eleven next month."

"Yea, everyone says that, gotta go, bye!"

It was time to ride. The big, glorious weekend was splayed out before me like a buffet. A pre-dinner bike ride was the best kind of weekend appetizer. My riding crew was else-wise occupied, so after the book return, I was a lone bike warrior. No worries, I thought, I would spend some quality time zipping up and down the streets on The Green Monster, my Schwinn Stingray bike, making sure everything in the neighborhood was as it should be.

The air had a stillness that only happens a few times a year. The reassuring smells of chicken and meatloaf dinners being prepared floated to my nose as I pedaled through the Crabtree section of Levittown, Pennsylvania. The air carried the sounds from even the quietest occupants to my ears as I rode past the happy families snug in the Ranchers, Jubilees, and Colonials doing their happy family things. Giggles of young girls and snippets of playful banter escaped from open windows as I zoomed past. The warm air helped wash away the school week and the mom's latest lecture.

"You will take this book back to the library right this second!" she'd said only an hour before.

"But—"

"But, but, but. When will you learn that they are always watching, waiting. If you let down your guard, the demons will get you," the mom said.

I released the handlebars, sat up on the banana seat, and closed my eyes, forgetting, cleansing, extending my arms out like the wings of a jet airplane. My mouth opened to an O, letting the air find my tongue. It made a rushing sound in my mouth, drying my teeth and hanging up my lip. I chomped down, capturing a chunk of the wind, swallowing it, letting it join with my DNA.

All was good. All was right. Every atom was where it was supposed to be. Almost.

In my town, there were no homeowners' associations to ensure everything stayed tidy. There was, however, a measurable blue-collar pride that made sure grass was cut, edges were edged, cars were washed, and hedges were trimmed.

Except for one house. You know the house. Every neighborhood has one. The yard is overgrown and dead in spots. The house needs a coat of paint. There is at least one broken down vehicle in the driveway. Trash cans are never put out or taken in on time, if at all. The front yard is a magnet for loose trash, dead leaves, and old tires. Kids' legs quicken as they walk past. The mailman shakes his head as he faces the daily challenge of fitting mail into the already stuffed mailbox and the threatening barks of an unseen dog. When folks hear of a problem in the neighborhood, they immediately think of "that family" that lives in "that house."

In my neighborhood that house belonged to the Jensens. They had a kid a year older than me named Kaleb. I wasn't friends with Kaleb, and from what I saw, he didn't have any. I'd see him around on occasion. His dirty clothes, shoulder length greasy hair and angry pinprick eyes made me feel unsettled. He always had bruises on his legs, arms, and sometimes his face. I hoped it was from the rough play that kids do and not something else.

I gave the Jensen house a side-eye glance as I passed. Best be careful. You never know what might happen if you look too long.

Lightning bugs were taunting each other with pops of sun yellow light and the streetlights were clicking on by themselves as the first long shadows of dusk hatched. Streetlights gave first notice to kids that it was time to head home, because the rule was, *Be Home by Dark*. This rule was universally known and there were no exceptions. Repeated violations of this rule resulted in the most severe punishment known to a kid: *No Bike for A Week* – Unthinkable!

I decided to flirt with danger and do one more spin before heading home. Dad would be home by the time I was done and these days, the less time alone with the mom, the better. I peddled hard, determined to complete the ride before the light moved across the midline between dusk and "I told you to be home by dark." I rounded the corner near my school. Kaleb Jensen was standing by the Big Pine Tree.

The Big Pine Tree was one of the known trees. It wasn't the biggest tree in the neighborhood. That honor belonged to the Giant Tree near the library. The branches of the Big Pine Tree were so heavy that the lower branches formed a dome-like space underneath the tree. Word was, the older kids made a fort under the tree, safe from prying eyes, where all manner of teenager things occurred.

The under-tree fort was a no-go place for the likes of me, but I was intrigued when Kaleb Jensen pointed to me, pointed to the tree, then asked me in an uneven voice, "Can you help me for a minute?" as I rode within earshot.

It was universally agreed that I was a helpful child. I was a Cub Scout on a solid track to becoming a Boy Scout, fully badged to help old ladies across the street and quite the accomplished knot maker. Despite beatings at the mom's hands for the most trivial transgressions, and despite the fumbling attempts of the last Cub Scout den leader to get me alone, I was a trusting sort.

Sure, we all knew the stories that popped up around Halloween about razorblades in apples. We kids heard repeatedly how there were roving bands of men offering free candy from vans, and how they would steal us away. Despite those warnings and more like them, I believed that people were basically good.

I dropped my bike. "Sure, what's up?" I said.

"In here." Kaleb motioned to the tree with his chin, rubbing the back of his hand over his thick lips. "I need some help."

With a sway, the branches opened like a curtain opening at a school play. Kaleb was swallowed into the under-tree. My curiosity combined with my helpful nature pushed aside any concerns I had. I followed him through the boughs of the pine branches to the under-tree.

The branches fell back into place with a rustle and darkness descended, lit only by stray beams of light between the pine needles. Smells of dirt, stale beer, pine, cigarettes, and a dirty-person smell that may have been Kaleb filled my nose. On the ground was a pit about three-feet wide and a few feet deep. The bottom of the pit contained a collection of cigarette butts, crushed cans, and one lone sock. How could someone lose one sock under here? Could this be the place where lost socks ended their socky lives?

My pupils adjusted to the dim. The bottom of the tree trunk was mostly bark-less and carved with initials and names. I read through them to see if I knew any of the carvers. I thought that it was quite a mean thing to do to a tree.

My eyes found Kaleb's.

Perhaps you have seen the face of a child about to open a birthday present when they know the box holds exactly what they always wanted. Perhaps you've seen the face of a child when they are punching their brother or sister while thinking no one is looking. Kaleb's expression was a mutated blend of both.

"Sit down," he said in a weird lilting voice like a cut-rate magician before performing a trick.

I sat down, my feet in the hole.

"What do you need me to do?"

"Just stay right there and don't move."

He brought a hand from behind his back. As if pulled from an alternate universe, a rock about the size of a cantaloupe appeared in it. He raised it over his head, lifting it up as high as it would go under the canopy of branches. He paused.

What was this? Was he showing me the rock? Was this a display of strength to impress me? To scare me?

No, it was something else, something darker. On his face was anticipation, excitement. His knobby kneed, thin-framed body was quivering with it. He wasn't pausing for any sort of display or effect. No. He was savoring!

He brought the rock down in an arc designed to split my head. I snapped my head back, the rock just missing my head and scraping the tip of my nose. The rock smacked into the ground at my feet with a muddy thud. I looked up to see the joy in his face changing to rage.

"No, no, no!" he said, his voice dropping octaves.

No, he wasn't showing off or trying to scare me. He wanted to hurt me, kill me even. Why? Had I done something to him? Would he have tried this with any kid that agreed to go under the tree, or was I his target?

He bent down to pick up the rock, probably for try number two. I snapped out of my confused state. This was no time for questions. He was a predator and I was the prey, and it was time to…RUN!

I launched out from under the tree like a Saturn Five rocket, abandoning The Green Monster, pumping my skinny legs for all they were worth. An agonized "Noooo" came from the under tree.

Smashing open the screen door, I screamed, "Dad!"

"He's not home yet. Calm down. What is your problem smacking the door open and yelling like that?" the mom said.

In between breaths I coughed out, "Kaleb Jensen... tried... kill me... rock. Ohnomybike."

"What are you on about?"

"Kaleb tried to kill me with a rock over by the school! We need to call the police!"

She looked at me like I had two heads. "You shouldn't be playing with that boy. Something's not right with him."

For once, I agreed with the mom.

"Wasn't Mom, promise. He tried to kill me. He—"

"Stop exaggerating. Boys will be boys."

"No, really. He tricked me under the Big Pine Tree and lifted a—"

"You and your stories. Stop exaggerating. No one tried to kill you. Now let me be and go wash up for dinner."

"But he did. Mom, he did."

"Stop talking nonsense. He did not try to kill you. This is just one of your stories."

"Look at my nose. The rock hit me right here, see?"

She grabbed me by the cheeks and pinched. "You have a tiny scratch," she said. "It's nothing."

"But—"

"No buts. Go wash up."

"Can you go with me to get my bike? Please?"

"You left your bike at the school?"

"Yes, I—"

"That bike cost good money, what is wrong with you?!"

I don't know whether she finally believed me or, more likely, she was worried she'd have to pony up for a new bike, but she relented and went with me to the playground. She wouldn't hear another word on the rock matter and spent the walk talking to herself about the indignities of having a child that made up stories for attention.

With a wary eye on the playground and the Big Pine Tree, I collected my bike and walked it back in silence, following her just out of lecture range, fearful of getting in front of her and her anger and catching a slap.

"Don't you dare say anything to your father about this. He works hard all day and doesn't need to hear your made-up stories."

"I didn't make it up."

She turned and slapped my face. "Not a word, do you hear me?"

For days and weeks that followed, I was filled with dread, fearing I would run into Kaleb Jensen for round two of the I'll-bash-your-brains-out-with-a-rock game. I walked to school early and left late to avoid any chance of crossing his path.

I didn't see Kaleb at school or in the neighborhood. He seemed to have disappeared so completely that I was starting to believe that the mom was right. Perhaps I did invent the entire thing, including Kaleb himself.

But she was wrong, I hadn't invented anything. She was right about one thing. Demons do exist, just not the kind she believed in. And Kaleb? He was all too real and he was not done with me. Neither was the mom.

Not by a long shot.

2

THE ANGELS ABOVE

"No, Mom, I don't think I can go. My belly and head hurt real bad."

"Well, you don't have a fever." She felt my forehead with the back of her hand.

"Maybe if I sleep some more, I'll feel better."

"Um, hmm, okay, but no books. You probably have a headache from all the reading."

"I don't think so, Mom. Reading is good for you."

"I don't read and I don't get headaches. You should read your Bible instead of that space garbage. Pray to Jesus. Maybe he will take away your headache."

No way to argue with that logic, so I didn't. Besides, I accomplished my goal of avoiding a Monday's worth of school, so best to stay still and quiet lest she change her mind.

Pretending to be sick to get out of school is a trick best used sparingly. Use it too much, and it loses its power, or worse yet, you end up at the doctor's office with a thermometer stuck in your mouth and a cold stethoscope on your chest. The trick was to appear sick, but not too sick. It was a fine line that required a delicate touch.

I didn't like to fake it, but every so often I needed an extra day to do the special stuff. On Mondays, the mom had her ladies' church thing from 12:00 to 5:00, and Dad wouldn't be home until 5:30 or so, leaving me home alone for five glorious hours. I had plans.

A few more hours of sleep, and a reading of the final chapters of Ray

Bradbury's *Fahrenheit 451*, and it was rounding 11:30. Miss Elizabeth was right; it was a great book and I understood why she recommended it. In the story, books were banned and burned. To save the stories, people memorized their favorite books and became walking, talking books. If that future ever happened, I wondered what book would I become?

"I'm leaving soon. Do you feel well enough to eat?" the mom asked.

"Yes, please. Can I have a peanut butter and jelly sandwich, lots of chips, iced tea, and maybe an orange?"

"I guess your belly is better."

My response was way too enthusiastic. *Careful, Cam, you're blowing it.*

"Maybe not the orange."

"Umm hmm. But chips though, huh?"

"Maybe not the chips."

Ah, the luxury of lunch in bed on a Monday. All those poor suckers sitting down to a chaotic cafeteria lunch while I dined, snug in pajamas, novel in hand.

With a final: "Are you feeling well enough for me to go?" and: "I'll be a few streets away at the church, the number's by the phone," the house was empty.

First up, some TV to ease into the day. *Password* and *Let's Make a Deal* scratched the itch. Next up, I had some science I'd been wanting to do. My current obsession was taking things apart to see how they worked. I fed it a steady diet of broken electronics. Last week's sacrifice to the workbench was Dad's old drill. I had dissected it into a pile of copper wire and gears, drawing each piece in my notebook. A trash-picked Panasonic clock radio itched to be broken down into its component parts, and this was its lucky day.

I loved the shed. It was eight feet by four feet with a tall workbench and one of those chairs that architects sit in when they design buildings. Above the workbench was a brown pegboard full of all the tools necessary to disassemble my victims. Surrounding me were shelves filled with my dad's electronic test gear and a narrow cedar closet that held our winter coats. The smell of the cedar, gasoline from the lawn tools, and hints of my father's aftershave combined to smell like adventure.

The shed was attached to the house at the end of our carport. There was no walking access from the shed into the house, but above the shelves and closet there was direct access into the house's attic. Lately, I wondered what treasures it contained, and while it didn't make the official day-off plan, the thought of adding it to the list was enticing.

Under the precise use of my father's hand tools, the Panasonic clock radio gave up its secrets over the next few hours. Part of my process was to place each part on the workbench to create an exploded layout of the object under dissection. I examined each part carefully and discovered why the clock radio was discarded.

One of the cables that turned a dial was snapped in half. I bet I could fix it with a properly sized rubber band. One of Dad's parts bins yielded just what I needed. Band installed, I reassembled it and plugged it in. It hummed to life. I tuned it to 93.3 WMMR, a new rock station in Philadelphia. Mick Jagger told me that "You can't always get what you want." He was right, I thought, as I eyed the attic "But sometimes…"

I grabbed Dad's flashlight and cleared off the top of the cedar closet. Using the chair as a ladder, I hoisted myself up into the attic. It spanned the length of the house, and it was filled with boxes packed with secrets.

Time to explore. The first boxes held our Christmas and Halloween decorations. I opened the boxes behind those to find baby clothes. Another set of boxes was filled to the brim with boring old paperwork. I wanted treasures, something cool from my dad's time in the Korean War or some stuff I could take apart.

Careful to only walk on the roof beams, I made my way further back to a valley between stacks of boxes. Sitting down, I stretched across a series of beams and opened the closest box. Looking up from inside of the box, bathed in the glow of the Eveready, was an angel. She was blonde with blue eyes, and her sweater was open, showing quite a bit of her chest.

I'd never seen a Playboy in the flesh, but kids at school talked about them constantly. Many a kid had promised to smuggle a copy of their dad's Playboy, or at least a centerfold, into school to be shared around. Despite rumors of success, to the best of my knowledge, no one had pulled it off. Here I was with a boxful. Sometimes, you do get what you want.

One by one, I took out the Playboys and went through them cover to cover. So many lovely ladies and so much smooth, glowing skin. My head swam. I liked the boobies, but my favorite pictures were the ones of ladies in stockings. Those made me feel funny in a tingly way.

I became so engrossed in looking through the Playboys that I lost track of time. The sound of a car pulling into the carport pulled me out of my delirium. The car door opened and shut. The shed door opened.

"Cam?"

Oh no! Dad had come home early. He clicked off the radio, closed the shed door, and went into the house.

"Cam, where are you?" he asked the empty house.

I could get away with this, but I had to move fast. I gathered up the Playboys, sticking them back in the box. Hurry, hurry, I told myself. I stood up on a ceiling beam to get my hands on a few I had tossed just out of reach. My right foot slipped off the beam and, with a crunch, I went clear through the drywall ceiling and into the dining room below, up to my mid-thigh.

"Cam? Don't move. I'm coming," Dad said from below me.

In a flash, he was up in the attic, like a monkey escaping a lion.

"Are you okay? Does anything hurt?" He took the flashlight from me and shined it around my leg.

"No, but I'm stuck."

"I'll get you out."

He leveraged in and helped me get my leg out of the hole, but my sneaker wasn't so lucky. It fell onto the dining room table below. When I was safely down and out of the shed, I got the quick inspection for injuries.

"You were lucky you didn't break anything, sport." His concern faded. "What in the hell were you doing in the attic?"

"I was exploring and then I found the magazines and I slipped. I'm sorry."

He led me inside. The dining room table was covered in ceiling parts and drywall dust. My solitary Converse lay on the table like a surrealist entree. Realizing the damage I caused, I cried.

"Hey, hey, it's okay. No crying. Let's get you and this mess cleaned up before Mom gets home. Go change, then get the vacuum and get as much of it up as you can. Okay, pal?"

"Okay, Dad."

"I'll go clean up the attic."

I changed and cleaned up as best I could. Dad came in behind me to finish the task. By the time he was finished, there were no signs of the hole besides the hole itself. He had placed some cardboard over it from the top.

I sniffled, on the verge of crying again. Dad knelt in front of me.

"Okay, champ. Mom will be home any minute. You did a great job cleaning up. Mom will never know what happened and we don't need to tell her, right sport?"

"You won't tell Mom?"

"You know how she can get. This one is our secret."

I threw my arms around him and gave him a hug. Beating averted.

"Why don't you go read your books until dinner."

"Okay, Dad. And Dad?"

"Yes?"

"You're the best dad ever for not punishing me for finding your—"

"Don't say it. In fact, never say that word, ever."

"Sure," I said. I wondered why he didn't want me to say the word magazines.

"Dinner," the mom announced.

I made my way to my usual spot at the table. I couldn't help but snatch a look at the hole in the ceiling, but I averted my eyes before the mom could follow my gaze.

"Cam stayed home from school today, didn't you Cam?" she said.

"He did, did he?"

"Yes, he did. Belly ache and headache, but it may have been Mondayitis," she said.

"Is that true sport? Was it Mondayitis?"

"No," I said, feeling the tears returning. Why were the dining room lights so bright? Maybe they would let me turn them off so I could eat in the dark.

"What did you do while I was at church? Did you say your prayers?" she asked.

"I uh, I read and I..." That darn hole had the gravity of the sun. My eyes were powerless to its pull.

The mom followed my gaze.

"Good lord, what is that?" she said standing up. "When did that happen? Was that there yesterday?"

A tiny sob escaped me.

"It was just a small attic accident. A box shifted or something," Dad said.

My sob multiplied into sobbing.

They both stared at me. The mom, questioningly and Dad, menacingly.

My sobbing completed its journey to crying.

"What is wrong with him? Cam, why are you crying?" she asked.

My crying escalated into blubbering.

"Maybe he's still sick. Why don't you go lay down, sport." Dad stood up.

"Cam, look at me. Why are you crying?"

"I'm sorry, I didn't mean to do it." I stood up. "It was an accident. I was just exploring…"

"Don't…" Dad whispered from between clenched teeth.

"…in the attic…"

"Cam…" Dad said.

"…and I found a box of…"

Dad pounded the dining room table with his fist.

I remembered not to say *magazines,* just like he told me.

"Playboys."

"Playboys?" the mom shouted. "You found Playboys? What Playboys? Al, what Playboys?"

My father deflated like a beach ball after Labor Day. He looked down at the hand he'd used to pound the table and considered it as if his palm held the lost secrets of the universe. I was busy filling my plate with tears, terrified of the dual beatings I was sure to receive.

"Al, did you put those Playboys in the attic instead of throwing them away like you promised?"

My father leaned over me. "Sport, we had an agreement." The look of disappointment on his face twisted me up.

The mom slapped his arm and then slapped me on the back of my head.

"Dirty birds, the two of you. God has taken his protection from us. I am disgusted to be in the same house with you both."

She dragged me into the bathroom and turned on the sink until the water was steaming hot.

"Wash your filthy hands," she commanded.

"It's too hot."

"It will teach you not to touch dirty things."

She grabbed me by the wrist and put my hands under the scalding water. I screamed.

Dad pushed into the bathroom. "Pat, that's enough. Stop."

Arguing and screaming went on through the night. Ranting, Bible-verse reading, and praying went on for a full week. The next time the mom got me alone, my hands went under the hot water and she spanked me for a solid thirty minutes. She also grounded me for two weeks and threatened harsher penalties if I ever even thought of "touching that filth again." You woulda thought I ate dinner with Satan himself instead of seeing some boobies.

Just when I thought the fallout was over, the mom dragged me to church to meet with the minister.

"Your mother told me what happened. Would you like to talk about it?" Minister Mike asked.

Heck no, I didn't want to talk about it.

I gave him an "I'm sorry." I hoped it would suffice.

"Well, Cam, I'm sure you are, but your mother wanted me to talk with you about what you did and why it was a sin," he said.

"I shouldn't look at Playboys," I volunteered.

"Well, yes." He laughed. "There is that, but what God cares about is lustful thoughts and the bigger sins it leads to."

"What are you talking about?" I asked.

He leaned in across his wooden desk. "I'm glad you asked. In Mathew, Jesus tells us that if 'your right hand causes you to sin, cut it off and throw it away.'" He sat back smugly as if that answered everything.

"I don't know what that means."

"Let's do this another way. In Genesis, God tells us that spilling your seed on the ground is a sin." Again, with the smirky sit back. This time he added a little nod.

"What seed?"

His brow wrinkled over his glasses. "The Lord is telling us that it is better to cut off your own hand than let lustful thoughts lead you to masturbate. Masturbation is a sin, do you see?"

"No, not really. What is massenterbate?"

"Masturbate," he corrected. "That's the sinful act of rubbing yourself, you know, down there, until it feels good."

I still didn't get it. He looked to the mom. "Have you had the talk with him yet?"

"Not yet. He's tall for his age."

"Hmmm. Cam, when you looked at the Playboys, did you feel lust in your heart?" he asked.

"I don't think so," I said.

"Okay, then, did you rub your, um, your pee pee?"

"No. Why?" I asked.

"Because, young man, it's a sin. That's what masturbate means, and it will lead you to Hell. Okay?" he said with a big smile.

"Oh. Okay," I said, still confused but anxious for it to be over.

"Pat, we're good here. Cam, obey your mother and father in all things and say your prayers. We will see you on Sunday." He got up abruptly and left the office.

Lying in bed that night remembering the pictures in the Playboys, I felt tingly. I tried what the minister said I shouldn't.

Wow. Who knew you could do that? Now I did, thanks to Minister Mike.

Welp. Looks like I'm going to Hell, I thought. As good as that felt, I was sure everyone in the whole entire world was going to Hell with me.

3

SACRIFICE

Four am and Dad was asleep on the couch. I woke him with repeated arm poking.

"Daddaddad."

"What's going on? You okay?"

"I can't find Buttons. He always sleeps with me. I don't think he came home last night."

"Maybe he found a girlfriend cat."

"I hope he is alright."

"I'm sure he is, pal. He'll be home before you know it."

It's funny how certain words put us at ease. Dad calling me *pal* or *sport* or *ace* always did the trick. I headed back to bed. I felt bad for waking up my poor dad. The night before, we all barely slept because he and the mom were at it. It was a level 10 fight. A real down and dirty one. The crying of the mom was always horrible, but the clenched-mouth silence was the worst part of after.

In the morning, doors slammed as Dad went to work. The house let out its breath as if to say, *We must collect ourselves before the next battle.* The mom, red eyed, yelled at me for not getting up on time.

I was exhausted. I nodded off in social studies class, and of course the teacher called on me mid-head-nod. I had no idea what the question was, so I blurted out "The Constitution," since that was the answer to 75% of the questions in the class. Nope. Not this time. The class erupted into laughter.

I came home to find the mom sitting at the kitchen table smoking and drinking. The type of glass was how I knew to keep my distance. It wasn't water or tea, so off to my room and into a book I went.

Dinner was a solemn affair.

"Did you find Buttons, sport?" Dad said.

"No."

I looked to his food bowl. It was full.

Buttons usually came home to ravage his bowl around 6:00. If he ate at Restaurant a la Wild, he would be home by 8:30 at the latest. By 9:00, I couldn't hold out anymore and I dozed off. At 11:30, I woke up. Buttons was not in bed. There was no way he would miss two nights. I checked his bowl. Still full.

I woke up early the next morning with Saturday plans on my mind. Washing The Green Monster was one of my favorite weekend events, and I also had a tree in mind that desperately needed climbing. As I planned my day, warm under the covers, my heart froze. Buttons was not in bed. A quick search through the house confirmed that he hadn't come home.

"Dad, Mom! Buttons still hasn't come home."

Dad looked at me with a not-this-again glance.

"I'm sure he's okay. Go outside and shake the Friskies box. He'll come running," the mom said.

Out I went, Friskies box in hand. I shook the box, making the noise that all cats know while yelling "Buttons!" at the top of my lungs. I shook it in the back yard, I shook it in the front yard, and then again in the back yard. I made the *pss pss* noise as loud as I could. I walked up and down my street shaking for all I was worth. No Buttons. I hopped onto my bike and rode the neighborhood streets, stopping and repeating the shake, shake, *pss pss,* every half block.

Passing telephone and light poles and seeing missing-pet flyers attached to the poles increased the fervor of my search. More and more handmade flyers had been showing up recently. Sammy the cat and Jinx the puppy cried out from the flyers, hoping to be found. I wouldn't let Buttons end up on the poles, not while I breathed.

Shake, shake. "*Pss, pss.* Buttons!" Ride fast. Stop. Repeat.

Past the Saturday mornings cacophony of lawnmowers I went, amid the smell of fresh cuttings and the chunk-hiss of oscillating sprinklers. Sweat-soaked men in white T-shirts were having cross hedge conversations about the best length to cut the lawn, the latest mower at Sears, and those damn Phillies, oblivious to my panic. My father was just finishing his yard ritual by wrapping up the garden hose with mathematical precision when I arrived back at the house. I was exhausted, right arm and both legs burning, throat sore, heart heavy.

"No luck, champ?"

"No."

"Where did you check?"

"Everywhere."

He paused mid-wrap and looked at me closer. He released the hose, letting it uncoil into a python of curls amid the grass.

"Let's go," he said, getting the car keys out of his yard-work chinos. In that moment I loved him more than he would ever know. Dad had this.

We loaded in and drove around our neighborhood and the surrounding neighborhoods. I shook the Friskies box while we both called "BUTTONS!" out the windows of his Ford Fairlane 500. We silently agreed that the *pss pss* sound was not something that men should do in each other's company.

Two hours of shaking and calling brought out a few cats, none of them Buttons.

"How about we break for some lunch?"

"Can we look more after?"

"Of course. He might even be home now."

The mom made us turkey and American cheese on white bread with mayo, a side of chips, and homemade iced tea. She served her hard-working men on flowered, pleated-rim paper plates.

There was a knock at the door and Dad got up to answer. A familiar kid's voice was talking with Dad, and I got up to see what was what. As I approached the door, my friend Mario's curly-haired head popped into view. He gave me a hesitant wave around my father's intervening frame.

"What's up, Dad?"

"Nothing. Go back and eat." He put an arm out to keep me back, the way he did when his car came to an abrupt stop because a "damn idiot driver" cut us off.

"I'll be right back." He stepped out and closed the door behind himself.

An hour later he came home. He sat alone in the car for a long time. I watched him out the front window.

What was he doing? Where did he go? What did Mario say? What was going on?

My desire for answers overrode my feeling of trepidation. I went outside and approached the car. My father, a veteran of two wars, a steel worker, the toughest man I knew, was crying. He wiped his cheeks and got out of the car holding a cardboard box.

"What's in the box, Dad?

"I'm so sorry."

"Is it Buttons, Dad?"

"Yes. I'm sorry."

"What happened?"

"It's bad. Someone killed him."

"What happened to him? I want to see."

"Mario found him in the park by the school. There was a rock. A rock with blood. It's best not to—"

"I want to see!"

"No, Cam."

"Show me. I need to see."

A father did what his son asked. I saw a horror.

My father hammered together a box from wood scraps. I insisted on digging the hole myself. Together, we buried Buttons in the back yard under a tree he loved to climb. As I shoveled the dirt into the hole, my father placed his hand on my shoulder. No words were spoken. His hand on my shoulder was almost enough.

We only spoke about what happened once after the events of that day. We were sitting side by side on the couch. I was reading *I, Robot,* by Isaac Asimov, and wondering if a robot could have a soul. My father was reading the newspaper, wondering the same about politicians.

"Dad, who could do a thing like that?"

"I don't know, sport. A person with no conscience, no feelings, soulless."

"Dad, where did Buttons go when he died?"

My father was a man of few words. But not that time.

"You will hear many things in your life about where we come from and where we go when we die. Your teachers will have some things to say about it. The pastor will have some things to say about it. Your mother will have many, many things to say about it. The truth is, Cam, we don't know. And that's okay to say because no one does."

"No matter who tells you that they have it figured out, they don't," he continued. "They may sound certain, and you will want to believe them.

Sometimes, they will try to force their belief on you about the meaning of life, God, and the universe. Don't let them. Go out there and find out for yourself. The journey for answers is what will give meaning to your life. If, at the end of it, you don't have the answers, that's okay because you will have spent a lifetime hunting, searching, exploring, and learning, just like Buttons did, and that's not a bad life at all."

His answer gave me comfort and I loved him for his honesty. Over the days that followed my sadness was replaced by something else. A new feeling, a hot feeling. It took up residence in the center of my chest and burned like when soda goes down the wrong way.

The way Buttons was murdered stuck in my mind like a splinter that I couldn't tweeze out.

The rock.

Could the murderer be the same one that tried to bring a rock down on my head?

I wanted to tell my dad everything, but I couldn't. Not until I was sure. The mom wouldn't like it.

Despite the trickle of fear that tiptoed down the middle of my back, I had to know, and I was going to find out even if it killed me. Be careful what you wish for.

4

MANOR BORN

"You're just chicken. *Bawk, bawk,*" John said.

"No, I'm not. I just don't wanna get in trouble," I said. "Besides, I don't wanna leave my bike out here, someone will steal it."

A chorus of "Chicken" with accompanying "*bawks*" and thumbs-in-armpit wing waving went up from the bike crew.

"Come on, guys, not cool," I said to the group of five assorted miscreants.

"Last one in is a chicken shit," John said as he led the charge through the opening, disappearing like a rooster into a coop.

Struggling to avoid the chicken-shit label, the rest of the neighborhood bike crew jostled for next in. One by one, they popped out of existence until the last set of dirty-soled Converse disappeared though the hole. Muffled calls of "*Chicken shit.*" "*Wow, it's dark,*" and "*Turn on the flashlight*" squeezed out through the centuries old wood.

I was officially ditched.

The imposing fieldstone walls of the three-story mansion loomed above me while I considered my options. I told myself that my hesitancy wasn't because I was afraid of the ghosts that all kids knew dwelled inside. I reasoned that my hesitancy had more to do with the criminal aspect. I was taught to respect property.

Somebody who obviously didn't respect property had cut a hole in one of the wood-shuttered windows of the two-hundred-and-fifty-five-year-old abandoned mansion. If the cops caught us, punishment was surely a solid ten years for just entering. I desperately wanted to join them. Who knew how long the hole would remain or what treasures and mysteries waited beyond it? This was a Hardy Boys worthy opportunity.

Bolton Mansion was kid famous. Along with having the best climbing trees, it was the bike ride meeting place in the spring and summer. In the weeks leading up to Halloween, kids would dare each other to walk up to its decaying porch and knock on the door. In the winter, the pitched grounds made for the best sledding. After fresh snow, the grounds would be covered with puffy-coated kids dragging their Radio Flyers.

If you said, "Meet me at the Mansion," every kid knew exactly what you meant. If they didn't know what you meant, they were a new kid and you had to immediately take them to the highlight of Levittown. It was common practice to tell new kids that the mansion was older than America, and it was also the most haunted place in America, because of all the murders and stuff. Nobody knew exactly how many kids were slaughtered within its walls throughout the centuries, but you would assure the new kid that it was in the hundreds at the very least. As you walked the new kid around the property, it was customary to ask them to close their eyes so they could hear the wind whistling though the old trees. When they did as requested, a scream directly in the new kid's face would send them running. It was a glorious tradition and made for days of recess recounting.

With the voices of my friends getting smaller, I decided that I hated being ditched more than I respected property or feared punishment. I walked my bike to the front of the house and pushed it into the overgrown shrubs, covering it from view from all but the most raven eyed.

Braced with courage gleaned from Frank and Joe Hardy, and with a final look around for any random witnesses to my crime, up over and in through the hole I went. I fell to the dirty wood floor with a slap.

I stood up and went still, adjusting to the darkness. The light coming from behind me lit a shaft across the dirt-and-leaf-littered, wood-slat floor, illuminating the worn wallpaper and a dark hole in front of me that may or may not have been a doorway straight to Satan's lair. The musty smell brought images of my grandmother's attic and how much I missed her. If I lived through this, I would call her and tell her I loved her.

Time to steel up. I smacked away the dust from my pants, igniting a storm of particles like living motes feeding in the light shaft. I sneezed uncontrollably.

Above my head came the clatter of size four shoes, the voices of the ditchers.

"Hey, guys, where are you?" I called, neck stretched northward.

"Up here, chicken shit," came a laughing response accented by the rubber slaps of Converse soles.

"How do I get up there?" I yelled toward the ceiling.

"The stairs, dummy."

"But where…" I started. "Never mind." I wouldn't get a straight answer.

The black hole in front of me resolved itself into an interior doorway. The light behind me was fading, soon to be gone. Demons, ghosts, or no, I committed to the darkness in front of me. It's what Joe Hardy would do.

Hands out in front of me, I said, "Guys? Guys, come on, where are the stairs? I can't see anything."

My outstretched fingertips found a wall. I followed it around to the left until I hit another wall. I followed that wall and came upon the doorway I had entered. I had to catch up with my crew before it was completely dark outside. John had the only flashlight.

This time I went right, fingers guiding the way. This must be what it was like to be blind. I wished for a cane or at least a long stick. My fingers bumped against the wood of a door surround. I walked my fingers, like little fleshy explorers, around and through to the other side, confirming the next room's existence.

I let out a "Yes!"

I moved through the opening into the next room. I stopped, ears reaching out for telltale sounds of the ditchers, or worse.

"Guys? Come on, guys. Say something."

The only sounds that came back were the scuffing sounds of my sneakers against the wood flooring as I shuffled nervously from foot to foot. Boy, oh boy, I missed Grandma.

I moved quicker through the blackness. Around the room I went, until my toe hit something. A few foot taps told me that I had found the stairs. My right hand found the banister.

I took the first step. It let out creaks like the sound my dad's car made when the engine cooled. I took the next step, slowly adding weight before adding the other foot. So far so good. How many steps could there be, anyway? Maybe ten, fifteen? I counted.

"Three."

"Four."

A concerning "*Crack*" went up from step five. What if the steps were rotten and I fell through and broke my leg?

Enough. I fast walked up the rest of the steps using the wall and banister as my guides. My feet ran out of steps at fourteen. My finger explorers told me there was an opening to the right and to the left.

"Shh, shh," and the sound of clothing rustling and a solitary giggle came from the left.

"Guys, come on. Where are you?"

I waited.

Silence.

I went left, fingers trailing on both sides of what I believed was a hallway. Another door surround stopped my fingers on the left. A giggle, a flash of light, and a slam came from that direction.

"Aha, found you guys." I rounded the door opening into another room.

Giggles from above me. Were there more stairs?

I felt my way around the room. Several windows, no staircase.

"Guys, come on, this isn't cool," I yelled at the ceiling.

A ripping creak came from directly overhead. The light from John's flashlight lit up the room from above and something hit my head, hard.

I went down. The blackness went blacker.

I returned to the living in time to hear the scattering of feet against wood combined with laughs fading away. In a blink, the sounds faded to gone.

"*Don'tLeaveMeHEREdon'tLeavePLEASEpleaseComeBACK!*" I yelled.

Bees armed with hammers were building a hive in my head as I lay on the floor. My fingers went to the throb. The impact site burned. It was slick, and my fingers came away wet. The spirits of the Hardy Boys faded. I was just one little boy.

Wetness slid down my forehead and met up with tears, and I missed my Nana more than ever and I shoulda called her more and why didn't I just stay outside like I knew I was supposed to? I was so stupid. Now I would join the hundreds of other kids that died here and gave up their spirits to the mansion. I didn't want to be a ghost. I had so much I wanted to do.

I was afraid to get up.

The words of my dad came to me like the voice from the burning bush in *The Ten Commandments.*

"What do we do when we fall down?" he asked.

Visions of me lying down on the sidewalk after falling from my newly de-training-wheeled bike swam in my pounding head. My father leaned over me, his grey eyes commanding my attention.

"Cam, what do we do when we fall down?"

"We get back up," I said aloud into the gloom.

I got up, hitting my shoulder on the extended attic ladder.

Wait until I get outta here and find the ditchers. Anger gave me new strength. Time to go. But which way? I was turned around, dizzy.

What was it Dad said?

"Breathe. Think. Then do."

I sucked in a breath.

Maybe I could retrace my steps.

"Now…DO."

I got up, found the doorway to the room, and went back through. My fingers found another door to the left, but were the stairs to the left, or right?

Choose, Cam, choose. My angry courage wouldn't hold out long and I was probably bleeding to death.

I pushed off to the left and walked into a face full of spiderweb. The web stuck to my wet face like a sweat-drenched summer sheet during a nightmare, thick, terrifying. I screamed, clawing at my face to toss off the head-sized spider I was certain was about to sink its inch-long fangs into my neck.

STOP. There is no Spider. Breathe. Calm. Think, Cam.

I wiped my face with the bottom of my T-shirt until I vanquished the feeling of a million spider babies. I was utterly turned around. My breath came faster and faster, filling the empty room with a sound like a bicycle pump.

Think, Cam, think.

"Always go left."

Yes! The corn maze last Halloween! The bearded man at the entrance! I remember. He whispered to me, "If you get stuck, just go left all the way out. Always go left."

Would that work in this hell house?

Left I went, tear covered, bloody fingers trailing the walls until another opening stilled my hand. Through, left, and around I went. I lost count of the rooms. Was it three? Four? Fifty? How many stupid rooms did the place have?

I banged my knee on something even knobbier. The stairs! My hands confirmed the rail. With new urgency, I worked around until I found the stair opening and made my way down. At the base of the stairs, I smelled the damp, early night air coming in from the exit room. It smelled like freedom.

I was almost out. It was going to be okay.

Sure, I was going to be in trouble for coming home after dark, but I survived the clenching, evil hand of Bolton Mansion. Ha ha! You didn't add me to the kid ghost gang. What a story it would be, and the first thing I was gonna do is call Nana and tell her all about it. And wait until I got ahold of John and the rest of the ditchers.

I went left around the room and into the next room I was sure held the exit. The temperature felt cooler and I heard outside noises. My stinging eyes couldn't make out detail, but I felt the outside air against the wetness on my face. The hole should be directly in front of me.

Except it wasn't.

A Slurpee brain freeze slid down my spine, landing in my groin.

There was something else in the room. A difference in room pressure between me and the exit.

Click.

My dilated pupils caught the blast of light. I stumbled back. I tripped over my own feet and went down on my backside.

A hissing laugh came from the figure.

"John?" I hoped. "Not cool, John, get that light outta my eyes."

I abandoned all the kid rules. "I'm gonna tell my mom and she's gonna tell your mom and you're going to be grounded forever. I almost died in here."

"Not John," the figure said, the light staying on my face.

I knew that voice.

Kaleb Jensen was between me and the opening.

"Look at you. Not so cool now, huh?"

Say something Cam. Say something fast.

"I...I don't think I'm cool. I just wanna get outta here. My dad will be here any second to pick me up."

"Liar!" he yelled, lowering the beam to shine on his free hand. Clenched tightly was a wood-handled steak knife. "You know what liars get? Liars get cut. Just you and me now."

"That's twice you scared me real good." I added a nervous laugh. "That's enough now, enough." I got to my feet.

"You think you're so cool, so smart. You and your stupid cat, so easy to catch." He twisted the knife back and forth, catching the beam of the flashlight, sending light beams around the room like a mirror ball. The light caught his face, and for a second I thought he was someone else. His head was unevenly shaven as if a dizzy chef had taken a dull potato peeler to his head, leaving tufts of hair and dried blood in its wake.

"Here, kitty, kitty," he said.

In that second, I knew. I knew that the missing pets, including my beloved Buttons, had died by Kaleb's hand.

"You shoulda heard it. Her head went, POP."

"Buttons was a he, you monster."

"Who cares."

My fear melted into a magma pool of hatred. The heat of my checks turned my tears to vapor and dried the blood to war paint. A scream ripped from my throat, and I launched at Kaleb. My forearms hit him in the chest and the flashlight went spinning like a police siren, hitting the floor with a pop where it lay, casting its yellow glow against the wall.

Kaleb went down in a pile, scrambled to a seated position, back against the wall.

"I'll cut you," he said, holding out the knife. "I'll cut you good."

I was rage. My thin frame seethed. I'd had quite enough of Kaleb Jensen. This ended here and now.

"I should take that knife from you and stick it in your heart for what you did."

I stood over him. Bloodied. Bruised. Brave.

"But I'm not you, so I'll give you a chance," I said. "Throw that knife away or I will take it from you and stick it in you."

Maybe it was the look on my blood and tear-streaked face. Maybe it was the rage in my voice. Maybe this was the first time someone had pushed back.

He tossed the knife away.

I was on him like a Doberman. I jammed my knees into his shoulders and rained down punches with everything I had.

"Stop... enough..." he pleaded.

"I decide..." I said from between clenched teeth, "when...it...is... enough."

I lifted off him and collected the flashlight and knife. I stood over him again and, for a second, I considered using the knife. Part of me wanted to, but I knew I wouldn't. I couldn't. I wasn't like him.

Kaleb was curled into a ball, sobbing. He was smaller than me. How hadn't I noticed that before? In my mind, Kaleb was a hundred feet tall and five hundred pounds of muscle.

The sight of him cooled my rage into something not quite pity. How had he become this? What had happened to him?

"Why?" I asked.

"Why what?"

"Why did you kill my cat, why the tree, why this?"

"I don't know. I'm…I'm…Just let me go."

"How could you do that?"

"I had to."

"No. You didn't."

"Just lemme go."

"Go."

He got slowly up and walked over to the window hole.

"No. Not that way."

"What way?"

"Into the house."

He did not move. "Now!"

The dark of Bolton Mansion swallowed him. I turned off the flashlight. I climbed out of the hole into the chilled air.

Back home, I told my father everything, starting with the attack under the tree and ending with Kaleb's admission to killing Buttons and the attempted stabbing. My father listened to everything I said with intensity, not once interrupting. He believed me. He hugged me gently for longer than usual.

"Call the police, Al," the mom said, handing me a damp washcloth.

I wiped blood and dirt from my face with the washcloth while my father examined the cut on my head.

"It's not bad, sport. The bleeding has stopped. A band-aid should do it, or I can have Mom sew it up on her sewing machine?" he said with that neutral face he used when he ribbed me.

"How about a stapler?" I said, echoing his expression.

"He's fine," Dad said to the mom, but mostly to himself. He went to the phone.

The conversation was short. My father slammed down the phone on the cradle, clenched his jaw, and shifted from foot to foot.

"What did they say?" the mom asked.

"They said I'm free to come down and fill out a report, but with no witnesses, there isn't much they can do. The sergeant said, 'Boys will be boys' and 'They can work it out between themselves with boxing gloves down at the Y,' and finished with, 'Keep your kid away from the mansion.'"

My dad shook his head as he pulled on his shoes. He collected his car keys, wallet, Kaleb's flashlight and pocketknife, and went to the hall closet. The clicking spin of the safe on the shelf above the coats worried me. That's where dad kept his gun.

"What are you going to do, Al?"

My dad kissed me on the head and left.

"What's happening?"

"It will be okay," she said, trying to convince us both. "Go take a bath, you're filthy."

Warmth and sleep wouldn't come. Tremors played my legs like a Spanish guitar. Hours passed before Dad came home. They argued in hushed voices. I made out some of the whispered words.

".... leave.... problem...worthless police...scare em..."

A louder "Enough!" from my father ended the conversation and silence took the house.

I called my Nana the next day. I didn't tell her what occurred; instead, I told her how much I missed and loved her, and that I couldn't wait to come visit her in Reading. I cried a little toward the end and she asked me what was wrong. I lied and said "Nothing." She promised me homemade shoo-fly pie and all the A-Treat soda I could drink when next I came to visit.

I never told anyone about "the mansion incident" as it came to be known in our house. When John made chicken noises at me in the school hallway, I didn't respond. I just looked at him. He must have sensed something in me because he stopped and never teased me again.

A "For Sale" sign went up in front of the Jensen house not long after that night. After Kaleb and his family moved away, rumors coated our section of Levittown like a contagious fungus. One of the stories was about a group of local men visiting the Jensen's house late one night and delivering an ultimatum.

When new owners moved into the Jensen house, more rumors went around. The conditions inside the house were near unlivable. The new owners put up a pool. In whispered voices, people talked about what they found in the backyard. Dozens of shallow graves containing the carcasses of small animals were uncovered.

Gradually, the missing pet signs disappeared from the poles in the neighborhood. My nightmares eventually stopped, but every so often, a creak of old wood, a musty smell, or a mote of dust dancing just right in the light brought it all back.

Some nights, I jolted awake and stiffened because I knew... Kaleb was still out there, somewhere.

5

THE DEATH OF HEROES

The sticky sweet smell of road tar permeated the air of my daily bike rides. Knowing what streets were recently resurfaced and avoiding both the tar and the sneaky, doughy asphalt-filled potholes was vital to the survival of bike tires. A few seconds of attention drift could mean hours with a screwdriver, prying out chunks of tar and fresh asphalt from the treads. A clean bike was next to godliness. Everyone knew that the cleaner the bike, the faster it went.

The road commission took over part of the park at the end of my street as a staging area for road work. Paving machines, steamrollers, pickups, and dump trucks were parked in a row alongside dozens of black 55-gallon drums of sealant tar lined up like ammo. On weekdays, it was a smelly hive of men in yellow vests and hardhats grabbing shovels and loading onto the backs of trucks to head out like bees. At 5:02 pm exactly, the bees reappeared at the staging area to be swallowed up by their cars and trucks for the ride home.

At 5:04 pm, the area swarmed with a different species of bee. The neighborhood kids rode their bikes to the staging area to inspect the machines. The bravest stood on the top of the big tires and jiggled the doors of the trucks, hoping to find one unlocked so they could sit behind the wheel.

Inevitably, someone's mom or dad driving home from work would see their kid and stop to yell, *"Getoffathatandgetyourasshome!"* This sent the swarm into a disorganized scatter. It was only a temporary effect, and after ten or so minutes, the kid bees started to buzz and hesitantly return, this time with antennas out, alert for parents.

I was told repeatedly to stay away from the hive, but it was tough. How could I, a young boy, head filled with all young boy things, not check out gigantic dump trucks? What kid didn't want to operate big machinery? The mere thought of moving mounds of dirt gave me a heart swell of power. If I didn't become an astronaut or a cowboy, I would certainly operate some sort of heavy machinery, at least part time.

I rode my bike in increasingly smaller circles around the activity, the mom's warnings playing in my brain, stopping me from getting off my bike. Some local kids, including a few of my biking crew, motioned to me to come closer. I stopped riding and watched them as they clambered and played. My heart divided between obeying the mom's stark warnings and the universe-sized gravitic pull of the action in front of me. If I was caught playing on or around that machinery, I would receive an epic beatdown, one I might not recover from. The chances were slim that the mom would catch me, because she was at home without any real reason to walk by the park. She didn't drive for some reason that was never shared with me, and dad was away working, so he wouldn't catch me. There was always the chance a neighbor would rat but get-home-from-work time was almost over.

Liking the odds, I slipped back onto the white banana seat of The Green Monster and peddled in. A few feet more couldn't hurt, I thought, as I moved closer to the action.

A group of three older kids, including a kid that I knew from my street named Mike, pushed one of the 55-gallon drums of tar over onto its side. After some rigorous discussion about what to do next, they rolled the drum away from the staging area. Mike and another boy kept the drum rolling and the other boy ran off at a furious speed. I kept at a distance, watching the drum be successfully repositioned about a hundred feet from the staging area. While another round of discussion took place, the other kid returned with a short-handled axe.

I rode a little closer.

"Gimme." Mike took the axe from the kid. "I'll show you how it's done."

Mike brought the axe down on the drum with a clang.

After several strikes, he repositioned himself, straddling the drum like Slim Pickens riding the nuke in *Dr. Strangelove.* The other kids tried to direct his energies to the sealed lid on the drum top, but Mike wasn't having any. He was intent on chopping into the drum's side.

After ten minutes of chopping action, a cheer came up from the group of three. Mike slipped off the drum like Slim Pickens dismounting a horse in the movie *Stagecoach*.

The crew conducted another animated discourse and rolled the drum again. This time they paused every two feet or so to let tar pour out of the hole, leaving behind puddles of the black liquid.

I rode in a little closer to get a better view. One of the kids took out matches. I moved in a few more feet.

The kid lit a match and tossed it onto one of the smaller puddles of tar. Disappointment was evident in his dirt-smudged face when nothing caught fire. He moved on to a larger puddle.

I moved closer.

He tossed a match into the larger puddle. The match burned a second and went out. Failure.

I edged closer.

Mike tore the matches from the would-be pyromaniac's hand and walked over to the drum.

Mike turned to me. "Hey, kid. You scared? You look scared."

"I'm not scared," I said.

He lit one of the matches and moved it toward the ragged chopped hole on the side of the drum.

"How about now?" He moved the match closer to the hole.

Yeah, now I'm scared, I thought as I scrambled to crab-crawl my bike backwards.

Too late.

My vision narrowed down to a four-inch square that contained the image of a hand holding a lit match between thumb and forefinger, releasing it into a black tar shiny opening like the maw of a hell beast. A freeze-frame of the match in mid-flight between his fingers and the vertical slit burned into my retina as my left arm instinctively flew up across my eyes. A roar like the pop your ears make when you hold your nose and blow into closed lips, only a million times stronger, closed off the world.

I flew back into a shiny, tar-soaked land where all was black and quiet.

First came distant sounds. Muffled, underwater plops and fizzles mixed with voices, like when you play Marco Polo and you're swimming under water to a new hiding spot.

Next came smells. Someone was making toasted hair. Wait, what? Why would someone toast hair? That makes no sense.

Then came the pain. Left arm. Forehead. Back of head. I screamed. I heard it Marco Polo-underwater-style in the center of my brain mush. I screamed some more.

Sight returned. Sort of. I lifted my head from the ground. The explosion had thrown me a good fifteen feet. Between me and a newly created hellscape of burning grass was my tar-covered bike. One of my sneakers was next to my head. My pants were smoldering and covered in splotches of tar. I was missing the other shoe and one sock. That's the problem with socks, I thought, always disappearing to the under-tree.

Pain knocked on my head and my arm, you know, just to say hello. I screamed and passed out.

Awake-ish, I sat up.

Voices? People? Were they close? Heading toward me? Away? So cold. Wait. Cold? That makes no sense. I was smoldering, how could I be cold? Shivers wracked my body. When did it become winter? Nothing made sense but I should go. Where? Dunno, go not here.

Stand up.

I'm up! I'm wobbly but I'm up. My poor bike. Get your bike. Don't leave it. Someone will steal it. I can't get it. It's too close to hell. Get the bike - then go. Legs moving. Shivers. My arm doesn't hurt that much now. My forehead hurts now. Hand up to touch my forehead. I feel tiny little pebbles of what? sand? over each eye where my eyebrows are? Were? Is that blood? Maybe, dunno. My bike! Get your bike. GO. NOW. Back of my head hurts so bad. SO WHAT. GO. HURRY. On the bike. Arm hurts. SO WHAT. RIDE. NOW. Where? Home? Yes HOME!

I made it half a block before I had to get off my bike and walk/drag my tar-covered green machine behind me.

A few hundred feet to my house and I had just enough energy to scream, "Mom. Help!" from a collapsed position on the sidewalk.

The screen door banged open and the mom screamed, "OhMyGodWho-DidThisToYou?"

"Mike did. I'm cold."

"Mike did this?"

"My head hurts."

"I knew that Mike was no good," the mom screamed.

Without another look at me, she grabbed me by my right arm and marched me to Mike's house. The shivers were getting worse, and I was getting tired. Maybe, if no one needs anything else, I could maybe take a nap? She dragged me to the front door of Mike's house.

She knocked and then slapped the door, all the while yelling, "Hello!"

Mrs. Mike's Mom opened the door and, looking at me, said, "Oh, dear. What happened?"

"Look what your son did to my son," the mom said. She pushed me closer to the door.

"My Mike? What? Is he hurt? I'm not sure what..." Mrs. Mike's Mom said, panic building.

"Your son did this to my son," the mom repeated, turning a lovely shade of red.

At this point I realized that the mom was so caught up in blame that she hadn't considered the obvious fact that I needed medical care. She seemed to see me for the first time. She dropped to her knees to assess my condition.

"I'm calling the police," Mrs. Mike's Mom said.

"Mom, I'm cold. Can we go home?"

"Your eyebrows are gone. What is this? Tar?" the mom said.

"Yes, tar. From the field. Can we go? My head hurts."

We started in the direction of home. Mrs. Mike's Mom followed us.

"Where is Mikey? Where were you? The police are coming," she said to our backs.

"At the field," I said.

"Don't talk to her," the mom scolded. She pulled on my arm to walk faster. It was the arm I had put up in front of my eyes to take the brunt of the fireball and the tar. I screamed.

The initial shock that dulled the pain faded. The shivers combined with the pain of my burns and head injury were hitting in waves.

My body said, *"That's enough."* I went down like a kite outta wind.

"Nac OYU Har tree?"

"Can UYo Hear Mreee?"

"Can you hair me?"

Oh, that one I almost understood. I mumbled a weak "Yes" to the nice EMT person.

"Wakey, wakey. No sleeping, alright?"

"Okay." I was on a gurney being loaded into an ambulance. The red flashing lights hurt my eyes.

The ride to the hospital was short but the severity of what happened sank into the mom with each mile that passed. The EMT gently wiped away tar and threw the tar laden paper towels on the floor. She picked out small rocks that were impacted into my skin.

"What hurts?" she asked.

"My head and my arm mostly."

"Okay, sweetie, stay still, we will get you fixed up. You'll be okay."

As the EMT did her checking and cleaning, the mom closed her eyes and put her head down. I could tell by the slight movement of her lips that she was praying. As the ambulance swayed and the sirens yelled, I thought, *Wouldn't a better use of her time be to talk to me to keep me calm and awake?*

The doctors at the hospital were surprised that I escaped with only second degree burns to my arm. The burns on my face and head were not as bad as they felt. The staff cleaned off most of the tar, cut off the burned hair, and dressed my arm, cheeks and forehead. They explained to the mom that they wanted me to be woken every two hours that evening, and if I showed any issues with waking, I was to be taken back to the hospital.

The police came by that night to ask questions. The officers said they were shocked that nobody died. They told me that I was lucky. The lid blew off the drum, releasing the pressure instead of the drum exploding and sending shards of metal into us. They found the lid more than fifty yards away from the blast site. The other kids had been burned as well.

That night, the mom woke me up every two hours. She didn't say a word when she did. She looked at me and left. In between the two-hour naps, I thought about what happened. Many things about the event bothered and confused me. How could you drag your smoldering son around the neighborhood to show off the damage? How did that take precedence over the pain I was experiencing? What part of her was so broken that her empathy took a backseat to her need to assign blame?

Part of me broke in those dark, still, moments of analysis. I saw the mom in a new light. It was obvious that her need to preserve herself or the image of herself was the top of her priority list. I was not at the top. If I was not the top, then where did I rank? Going forward, this was something I would watch. My survival instinct told me to file this somewhere safe and never forget.

The mom may not be reliable.

Dad must be the one.

6

AIXELSYD

"....and on Sunday, my dad let me help him cut the grass with the mawn lower."

The class erupted into laughter.

"He said mawn lower." Phillip pointed at me and doubled over in mocking laughter.

"Quiet down everyone," Mrs. Howse said with her best I-mean-business voice. "Go ahead, Cam, start over." She clasped her hands in front of her flowered skirt and nodded encouragement.

I looked down at my "What I Did Over the Weekend" homework. The words looked back, mocking me, clearly saying LAWN MOWER. Why couldn't I do this? There were a few chuckles and a whispered "Weirdo" as I started over.

"I rode my bike a lot and on Sunday my dad let me help him cut the grass with the..."

Another encouraging nod smile combo from Mrs. Howse. "Go ahead."

Why did the words look right but my tongue couldn't deliver? The letters and sounds played hopscotch in my head.

Deep breath in, "...cut the grass with the...with the..." Despite all mental effort it came out.

"Mawn lower."

Laughter and finger pointing was my reward. My face got hot. Why couldn't I read it out loud the right way? I can say lawn mower. What was wrong with me?

I'm stupid. I sat down and slumped into my stupid chair.

Mrs. Howse's I-mean-business voice boomed, "Class, that is enough. Thank you, Cam. How about Phillip read next since he laughed the hardest."

Phillip stood up and read his with no problem. No stumbles, no twisted words. His stupid voice droned on and on about his stupid sister and his stupid trip to his stupid cousin's stupid house with his stupid parents. He finished, looked at me, and smirked. Don't be cocky, I thought, I've seen you eat your own boogers.

I didn't know why, but words had been jumbling in my head for months. Not all words, just some. Numbers, too. I had to try my locker combination at least five times before getting it right.

The problems started soon after I got tarred and it was getting worse. I used to love reading and now, not so much. The school year prior, I was the first one with a hand up to answer every question. Now, the idea of raising my hand caused my stomach to do Olympic backflips. I no longer trusted my own stupid mouth. My stupid eyes. My stupid brain.

Being different in school is the kiss of death. The last thing you want to be labeled is "weirdo." I towered over the other kids, I was extremely thin, and I had a weird name. Add in the reading thing and I made the top of the bully target list.

The A-list predators in my classes smelled weakness. They tried to get me to jumble by making fun of me. I tried to stand up for myself, but my speech turned into a mix of stutters, pauses, and jumbles. Teachers told the bullies to stop, and they did for a period or two, but when the teacher left, they came back harder.

The worst attacks happened in the lunchroom. On two occasions, I physically went after my tormentor. Kids wouldn't talk to me or sit with me at lunch out of fear that they would be swept up in the line of bully fire. I sat at lunch, head lowered, eating as fast as I could.

They brought in the mom to discuss the fighting.

"Cam, this is the third time you've been in a fight. What is going on?" asked the guidance counselor.

"Dunno," I said.

"I'm sure it's just boys being boys," the mom said. "I'll take him to see the pastor on Sunday and we'll talk about how it's very un-Christian to fight. We will ask Jesus to help him with his anger. This won't happen again."

"We need to talk about your grades. They're not shaping up to be as good as last year," the counselor said. "Can you tell us how we can get you to stop getting into fights and apply yourself in class?"

I wanted to scream, "Tell the other kids to leave me the heck alone!"

A beating was already in store for me, and if I dared curse or talk back, the beating would be worse. If Dad wasn't home later, it would start with a pre-beating reading. Proverbs 23:13-14 was a favorite. "Do not withhold discipline from a child; if you strike him with a rod, he will not die. If you strike him with the rod, you will save his soul from Sheol."

To prove her love to God and Jesus above, the rod would not be spared.

The counselor said, "Cam, how about we get you some special help?"

The word "special" was not a good word in my world. Images of taking the "special bus" to the "special classes" ran through my head. That's all I needed. It would be life over if that happened.

The mom and I both responded with a simultaneous, "NO." But for different reasons.

The mom said, "We will trust in the Lord, not in men. He doesn't need any special anything. We will pray together for God to give him the will to change and be a good obedient child and student. I promise you this will be the last fight, and his grades will improve. Now, Cameron, apologize for your behavior and tell the counselor it will never happen again."

"I'm sorry. It won't," I said.

The mom did not spare the rod that night. To prove how much she loved me she broke two wooden spoons in his name, amen.

A few days later, as class broke for lunch, Mrs. Howse stopped me from leaving by placing a hand on my shoulder. She kept it there until the other kids left.

Mrs. Howse looked at me with her kind hazel eyes. She couldn't have been any older than thirty-five, but she radiated the same calming effect as my nana. Maybe it was the strands of premature grey running though her pulled-back hair. Maybe it was the way she was always the center of calm in a whirlwind of energetic kids. The thing I liked best about Mrs. Howse was the way she listened. When she listened, she went still, like she was listening with her entire body, opening all the listening pores to absorb the whole of you.

"Would you like to spend your lunch period with me in the classroom?" she asked.

"Am I in trouble?"

"Not at all, and you can say no if you would rather not."

It was difficult to say no to Mrs. Howse, and after my recent lunchroom altercations and subsequent isolation, I agreed.

"Thank you for eating lunch with me."

"You're welcome."

The room filled with the type of silence that gets heavier and heavier until the weight of it forces someone to say something. I broke it. "Why don't you eat with the other teachers?"

"I have to grade all the papers and invent new ways to torture my students with homework," she said, eyes a twinkle.

The dam of uncomfortable cracked.

"Do you like being a teacher?"

"I love being a teacher. It's all I ever wanted to do. When I was little, I would line up all my stuffed toys and give them lessons."

We both went back to eating.

The end-of-lunch bell rang.

"Thank you for having lunch with me," she said.

I gathered up my trash and stuffed it into the bag.

She gathered up her trash. "You can have lunch with me tomorrow if you would like."

I liked the peace of the classroom compared to the noise and pitfalls of the lunchroom.

"Okay."

Lunch with Mrs. Howse became a regular thing. For the most part, she kept the discussions light and airy. Word got out that I was eating lunch with her, so the "teacher's pet" and "the teacher is your girlfriend" insults became part of the bully abuse handbook. I didn't tell my parents about the lunch arrangement. It felt like something I should keep to myself.

One day, in between bites of a PB&J, Mrs. Howse asked, "Can you help me with something? I'm making a test, and it would be a big help if I could have you try it first."

"I guess."

"Great. First, I need you to name all the things on these flash cards."

She came out from behind her desk and sat in the desk next to me. I giggled seeing her squeezed into the kid-sized chair. She took out homemade flash cards and held one up. On it was an illustration of a car.

"That's easy, it's a car," I said.

"Correct."

Next card.

"Tree. Easy."

"They might get harder."

"House."

"Correct."

"Cake."

"Correct."

"Apple." Everyone would ace this test, I thought.

"Correct."

"Lawn mower."

"Correct."

"Boat."

"Yes, and here is the last one."

"Car again."

"Car is in the words. Try again."

I considered the picture again.

"Race car?"

"Excellent job. Now comes part two. On the back of the card, I have written the name of the object. This time, I want you to read the name out loud."

Panic stirred in my stomach.

"Ready?"

"I guess so."

"Excellent. Read the card whenever you're ready."

She held up a card with the word *car* written in block letters.

"Car."

"Correct."

"Tree."

"Correct."

"Hose."

"Close." She beamed me a smile and flipped the card over. It was the house card.

"Oh. House."

"Correct, you're doing great."

The next card was a jumble. My mouth went dry.

"No rush. Take all the time you need and remember; you can do anything you put your mind to."

"I'm not sure," I said.

Mrs. Howse flipped the card over, showing the image of a cake with candles.

"Cake," I said without hesitation.

"Close. What kind of cake?"

"Birthday cake?"

"Well done."

She flipped the card back over to the words, *birthday cake*.

"Can you do it again?"

"I know that one now. Can we do the next one?"

"Please just try reading this one more time."

I looked down to avoid the jumble of letters.

"Birthday cake"

"Did you read it or remember it?"

I didn't answer.

"Okay, next one."

The next word was *apple*. After twenty seconds of mental un-pretzeling, I managed to get it out.

"Apple."

"Correct."

The next word she held up was *Scsetsise*. That made no sense. I looked down at the desk; heat welled up in my face. I was STUPID. I looked up at the word again, mentally reviewing all the images and trying, by process of elimination, to decode the nonsense jumble.

STUPID seconds were hours and minutes were years. Time was ignoring the laws of physics, or perhaps inventing a new painful relativity to torture me. STUPID. My face was hot enough to fry an egg. STUPID. I wanted to leave. Time to go. This was all STUPID.

I lifted out of my chair.

"Thank you, Cam." She put down the card. Her words and a shoulder squeeze were enough to quell part of my panic. I took a breath and lowered back down into the chair.

"Are you alright?" she asked.

"Yeah."

"Of course, you are. Good job."

But I'm not alright, I thought. I'm STUPID. I know it, she knows it, and everyone else knows it. I wanted to leave. My teacher's gaze held me in place.

"I am sorry that I upset you. I did not mean to. I wanted to check something, and I thought this would be the easiest way."

"What were you checking?"

"Every boy and girl in the world are different. Some children are great at math, and some are great at English, and some excel in science. That's because every brain works differently. Some children might be great at everything else but have difficulty reading and writing certain words."

She let her words sink in.

"Do you know what I mean?"

"I guess," I replied.

"Is it okay for us to talk about it?"

"I guess so."

"Thank you. Can you tell me what happens when you read certain words?"

I told Mrs. Howse everything. I told her how some words were all jumbled up and made no sense, while other words were fine. I told her how angry it made me. I told her how much I hated being called on in class and how I would do anything to avoid reading in front of people, because the entire class made fun of me. I told her that it took me so long to read and write now that I got headaches and gave up. I told her that the worst part was how much I used to love reading, and I didn't want to anymore. I told her I was STUPID.

At some point during my purge, her hand regained its position on my shoulder. "Cam, please, don't ever call yourself stupid again. You're not stupid. You are one of the brightest students in my class. You are smart and funny and kind, and you can do and be anything you want."

"No, I can't. I can't even read the words *lawn mower*."

Her jaw tightened and her eyes narrowed. "I promise you that we can get you back to loving to read. It won't be easy, and it will take time, but we will do it. Before we start, I need you to promise me two things."

"What?"

"First, I need you to promise me that you will never again think that you're stupid. You're not."

"Okay."

"Second, I need you to give me your word that you won't quit, no matter how much you want to. In return, I promise I won't stop helping you until we have this licked."

Mrs. Howse took her hand from my shoulder and put it out for me to shake. "Do we have a deal?"

I desperately wanted what Mrs. Howse offered to be possible. I wanted to believe that she knew how to fix whatever was wrong with me.

I steeled myself with all the adult attitude I could find in myself, looked her in her listening eyes, and took her hand in mine.

"I promise. When do we start?"

Mrs. Howse shook my hand. "We already did."

Over the weeks that followed, Mrs. Howse made three lists. List one contained words I could read and write without any issues. List two were words I could read to myself but had trouble reading out loud or trouble spelling. List number three held the real problem children. These were words that were complete jumbles. Once we had the lists, she moved on to the next step.

She broke the toughest words down into the smallest sounds that made up the words and wrote each of the phonemes on a separate card. She would then take me on a tour of the word until it trained my brain to approach the complexity of a jumbled word as a chef learns a recipe.

Over the months that followed, the jumbled word list shrank. My reading and spelling improved, but some of the words were never fully resolved. Words that contained a "d" and a "b" continued to give me the most trouble. She wrote paragraphs that included the toughest words and assigned me the job of reading them ten times each. Some nights I asked my father to listen to me read them.

One of the most valuable concepts Mrs. Howse imparted was the idea that I could train my brain to do whatever I wanted it to do. She told me to imagine my brain as clay. My job was to sculpt it.

"Every book is a door," she said at the conclusion of a session.

"What do you mean?"

"I've never left the United States, but I've visited every part of the world."

"Huh?"

"Through books, I've seen the building of the pyramids in Egypt and the canals of Venice. I've sailed the sea with pirates and flown the fastest jets, all thanks to books. You don't need a time machine, a boat, or a plane. All you need is a book and through the door you go."

"My mother doesn't like that I read so much, unless it's the Bible."

"Well," she said, "the Bible is a fine book, but don't let anyone stop you from reading anything you want. Reading will give you freedom, strength, and courage. Most importantly, reading will expose you to new ideas. Things you never would have thought of unless you read it about it first."

I believed her.

As the school year came close to the end, Mrs. Howse suggested I pick out a book for the two of us to read. After school, I rode my bike to the Levittown Public Library. I had not visited in quite some time. It welcomed me back with its silence, its smells, and its secrets. I strolled the fiction aisles, reading the titles and running my fingers across the spines.

Glory Road by Robert Heinlein caught my eye. The author's last name was a jumble, but this time, instead of running away, I welcomed the challenge.

"Robert, I will read your book and I will not let your jumbly last name stop me. In fact, I will read your book BECAUSE of your last name."

In the final weeks of the school year, we read Heinlein's fantasy about facing insurmountable odds. We took turns reading chapters out loud. It was glorious, and I felt like an actor on the stage as I read the daring adventures of the lead character, Evelyn Cyril Gordon, in front of Mrs. Howse.

The reading exercises Mrs. Howse developed for me had an unexpected result. You know those stories about an average baseball pitcher who breaks their arm and after it's healed, they throw 100 mph fastball pitches? Yea, it was like that. After a summer of applying her method, I was able to burn through books in record time. I was back in love with reading and that summer, I read more than forty books.

Mrs. Howse was right. Books are doors, and I would never let anyone stop me from going through them. Good thing she helped me because I would need every word, every story, and every skill from every book I ever read.

7

INHERITANCE

"Dad?"

A slight shift of the daily newspaper to the side preceded his response. "Hey, champ."

"Can I move some of your stuff for my lab? Edison had a lab and it was cool, and he made things and sold them, like lightbulbs, and he was one of the smartest people in America and he was mostly deaf and liked to read and I want to be a scientist."

Another paper shuffle. "You don't say."

If I was going to be a world-renowned scientist, I needed a laboratory to conduct experiments. The shed would make a perfect lab if Dad allowed it. Obviously, I also needed a white lab coat. You simply cannot be a scientist and future captain of industry without these two things. And maybe goggles.

"Dad?"

"Yes, favored son?"

"I forgot I need one of your white shirts, the bigger the better, unless you have a white lab coat I can borrow because if you have a lab you need to wear a coat to protect your good clothes from acids and things, not that I will use acid, I won't because I'm just a kid."

Another shift of the newspapers. "Okay, champ."

"Thanks, Dad. Dad?"

The downward rush of the newspaper made it clear I was getting on his "last nerve."

"You're killing me, sport."

"Ha, ha, Dad, you're funny. I just forgot one more thing, but this last thing is pretty important and it can't wait until Christmas, okay?"

He brought his glasses lower on his nose. "Let's hear it."

"I need a chemistry set and a microscope."

"Oh, is that all?"

"And maybe goggles."

"That it? You sure?"

"Yes. That's it."

"No." Back up went the paper.

His one-word response stopped me cold. This was not the usual reply to a new "buy me a thing" request. Usually, there were more words. Where were the explanations as to why I couldn't have it or a restatement that he was indeed and, eternally, "not made of money?"

I needed a way back in, a foot in the door.

Hmm.

A plan bubbled up. A plan based on Dad's own words from just a few weeks prior.

Dad was under the hood of his car. After yelling a selection of curses at the "friggin thing," he called a break.

"Hey sport, please get us a couple apples from the fridge."

I grabbed two of the reddest of the bunch and a few napkins. He pulled up a lawn chair next to mine.

I lifted my apple to take a bite.

"Did you polish it?"

"Huh?" I lowered my apple.

"You should always polish your apple before you eat it."

"Why?"

"Because they spray stuff on them, and to make sure there are no worm holes. Never bite into an apple before looking and polishing. Polish it well. The harder you work, the sweeter the reward."

We sat side-by-side in our lawn chairs, polishing our apples with the napkins. A crack of a neighbor kid's cap gun accompanied by the cries of "I got you" and "Nuh uh, I got you first" came across the nearby lawns. The gunpowder smell wafted over and mixed into the grease and gasoline air of the carport.

I held my apple up for consideration.

"How's this?"

"Do you think it's enough?"

I went back to polishing. As I focused on the smooth, shiny, near-perfect red skin, I could almost taste it. The longer I rubbed and considered, the more I wanted it. The napkin ripped and pilled from the polishing. My mouth watered.

I held it up. "It's ready now."

My father held up his. "Mine too."

The apples gave up a satisfying *CRUNCH* under the attack of our teeth.

I've had quite a few apples in my day, going way back to my applesauce years. Surely this apple wasn't a regular old apple. It had to be a special apple from a special apple tree in a far-away land. The skin gave the perfect amount of resistance to my teeth, and when the skin broke, it gave up the sweetest juice I ever tasted. The juice ran down my chin.

"Wow," I muttered between chews. "That's...*chew*... really...*chew*... good."

"You know why?"

"Because I polished it?"

"Because you worked for it. You put in the time and you paid the dues. You kept your reward in front of you the entire time. Always remember, the harder you work in life, the sweeter the reward."

Now, about that chemistry set microscope lab coat and maybe goggles.

"Dad?"

"I said no."

"Yeah, I know, but I wanted to ask you something different."

He let out a sigh. "Okay, sport, what is it?"

"You know how you always say that you should work hard for your reward?"

I had him.

He gave up a corner smile. "Yes, I know what I say about working. Why?"

"I want to work for the reward of a chemistry set and microscope and maybe a lab coat and, oh yeah, maybe goggles, and I'm willing to work hard and play my dues."

"Pay your dues."

"What?"

"Never mind. I guess you have something in mind?"

Checkmate!

BIG BREATH —"I will clean my room and take out the trash and help you with the lawn and vacuum and remember to turn out the room lights and you won't even have to tell me or remind me cause I will just do it." —SMILE.

Dad pretended like he was still in charge, even though we both knew that I had him right where I wanted him.

"Maybe. We need to add a few things since these things are expensive and I'm—"

"Not made of money?" I finished.

If looks could kill, I'd be missing a leg. "Don't be a wiseacre."

He looked up at the sky and rubbed his chin in the classic fatherly thinker pose. "Hmmm, I think we'll add brushing your teeth after each meal and maybe some other things to the list."

"Okay."

"Are you sure? I haven't even said the other things."

"I don't care. I will do it." If I'd nodded my head any harder, it would have fallen off.

Dad wrote out an agreement for all the things I said I would do with an empty line for the things he would add later, and we both signed and dated it. He took it all a step further and made a chore chart and a tooth brushing chart. Each time I brushed my teeth after a meal or did a chore, I could draw an X through one of the hundred or so boxes. He explained the rules for box completion. I paid close attention. The future of science—no, the future of humanity itself depended on my success.

I drew the last X in the last box on a Friday and, true to his word, Dad and I went off to the local toy store the next morning. We arrived just as they were opening. A tired looking man with wrinkled pants waved a vague that-a-way to the educational toy section.

Sitting high up on the top shelf were the rewards for my strategic thinking and hard work. My father reached up and brought down the biggest, baddest, chemistry set I ever saw. He reached up again and came down with the matching microscope set. *Skillcraft* was emblazoned across the front of both metal boxes. Pictured on the front were two future genius scientists doing science-y things.

Oh boy, this was going to be great. My heart raced just imagining the stuff in those boxes and the things I would learn. The future was clear to me now. I shut my eyes, imagining the love and adoration I would receive after inventing all the amazing things I would invent. I bet they would name a university wing after me, or maybe even, dare I think it, an entire university. At a minimum, they would honor me with a yearly parade with ticker tape dropping from the windows and a commemorative stamp.

From that day on, my new home when not at school or the library was the shed laboratory. A few additional trips to the hobby store and hardware store for odds and ends, and I was ready to go. My father wrote my name on a strip of tape, placed it over the chest pocket of one of his white dress shirts, and I was ready to start my life of discovery.

I cracked open the instruction manual for the chemistry set and worked my way through all the experiments, learning the basics of chemistry along the way. I set up the microscope and got lost in examining everything I could get onto a slide. I spent a week dissecting a lightning bug and drawing its parts in a notebook. I yearned to understand the mechanism that allowed it to generate light. I poured over the poor thing for hours, attempting to decode its secrets. This led me to a book on entomology and eventually to a primer on biology.

If you want to know how they light up, please read the following paragraph. It's cool so don't skip it:

Fireflies control their glow by releasing a chemical into their abdomens to attract a mate. At night, along riverbanks in the Malaysian jungles, millions of fireflies synchronize their light emissions precisely and flash together in a synchronized display.

I know, amazing, right?

Many innocent bugs ended their days parted and magnified under my right eye in my never-ending pursuit of how things worked. I filled an entire notebook with drawings of insects and their parts.

A quick read of an advanced biology textbook taught me that every living thing on the planet had this amazing thing called DNA that held the secrets of life. Mind blown. Why hadn't anyone told me about this? Why wasn't this taught in science class? A burning curiosity about living things and how they were all connected drove my reading choices.

One fateful day, I checked out Darwin's book on evolution. His theories showed that not only was every living thing connected, but it was likely that we all had a common ancestor. Also, it said we inherit things from our parents via genes and such.

If Darwin was right, and evolution was true, what about Adam and Eve? What about God? What was I going to inherit from my parents? What would I become?

8

ON THE ORIGIN OF THE PROBLEM

It's a fact. Ties suck the life energy out of your head. It was crazy warm in the church. And boring. So boring. Watching-grandma-sleep in front of TV static boring. By my count, it was the sixth church we'd attended in the mom's seemingly never-ending quest to find one she liked.

The minister was five rows in front of us on a raised platform. Despite my tie, the hard seat, and the heat, I liked this latest church. It was the way the minister talked. Something about his sing-song speech cadence entertained me. His sermon was interactive. He asked the congregation questions and called on folks for answers. This particular Sunday, he was ministering on how good Christians should build a solid platform for their faith.

"Matthew teaches us that, like the wise man, we should build our houses on what?" the minister asked, looking at the congregation over his black-framed glasses.

I wanted to play. My hand went up.

The minister pointed at me. "This young man right here will give us the answer. Go ahead, son."

"Dirt," I yelled.

For some reason, the minister and the congregation thought my answer was funny and let out a collective chuckle.

"No, son. The Bible teaches us to build our houses of faith on rock."

Agreement noises and positive head nods spread across the rows like a wave.

Laugh at me will ya? I think not. My hand popped back up. I didn't wait to be called on.

"Our house is built on dirt and so is this church."

Gasps and "Oh my's" did the wave through the pews. The mom put her hand tight across my mouth to stop whatever else I was priming for release.

"We have a little one in need of Sunday school, right, Mom and Dad?" the minister said, nodding in the affirmative. "Perhaps next Sunday? Perhaps vacation Bible school in the summer?"

Cue a replay of the agreement noises, positive head nods, and a lone *"Ha!"* from the elderly lady next to me. She smacked me on the knee with her rolled up program for emphasis.

Whatever I thought of the church, you couldn't say the congregation wasn't well trained. The mom gave me the look I came to know as the "there will be very real pain in your future" look. I banked on a beating, when she could get away with it, to remove any and all signs of demonic influence. The mom removed her hand from my mouth and transferred it to a vise grip on the back of my neck. It was a very long service.

Here is a list of highlights from the mom's after dinner speech.

1. When bad things happen — demons.
2. Demons are in the employ of the devil and they rule the Earth.
3. Yes, they were real. Don't be ridiculous. Why would you ask that? That must be a demon speaking through you.
4. They can possess people and animals.
5. They can get into your house by possessing objects like that chair you bought at the yard sale.
6. In the event of a suspected demon event, you can retaliate by throwing away newly acquired, possibly demon-filled objects or calling out to God and praying.

In my case, I had to have the demons beaten out of me. You can never be too careful when cleansing your children of demons. Everyone knows that demons are tricky. Heck, the Puritan's drowned the demons out. This had the unfortunate side effect of killing the person but, oh well, you got rid of those pesky demons.

This recent bad thing I did at church was obviously caused by a demon. I mean, come on! Yelling out and back-talking a minister was an A#1 "Are you kidding me!?" kind of an obvious demon-y thing.

Post lecture, it was time for a demon removal session.

How to survive a demon removal process:

1. Head down and agree with everything with verbal *yeses* and head nods.
2. Ignore the pain as best you can and think about something, anything else.
3. Don't dare object or the strikes moved from the body to your face and head.
4. Never tell Dad. If you do, the mom might get hit and then you're back to number one.

The mom's childhood was hell. When and where she was raised, children were often seen more as free labor or a possession than something to be loved and cherished. My grandmother was a real fire-and-brimstone type of Christian who spoke of Hell and damnation on a loop. Every small offense was another step closer to eternal torment in a lake of fire.

The mom's parents divorced when she was young, and my grandmother remarried an abuser, putting her in a combined family of seven children. Verbal and physical abuse began right after the "I dos." When it reached a crescendo, the mom ran away to her birth father's home. Waiting for her there was more abuse from a stepmother who wanted no part of her new husband's children. Verbal abuse progressed to physical abuse, and soon both rained down on her nonstop.

One evening after dinner, her new stepmother threw her down a flight of stairs because she failed to clean a plate to the stepmother's liking. She fled the home and soon found herself pregnant and married at seventeen to an abusive alcoholic. After the baby was born, she was given a choice: stay in the abusive situation or leave without the baby. She left and ended up in my father's arms. Her fear of a punishing God, hellfire, demons, and the devil went deep, thanks to her upbringing and lack of education.

My "dirt" outburst at church was not only rewarded with a lecture and beat down, but also won me the privilege of attending Sunday school. Our teacher did his best to be a hip Jesus type. His hair was parted in the middle and longish, his clothes were casual, and he spoke in that way some adults speak when trying to sound "in touch" with kids, but which ends up sounding ridiculous.

"Let's welcome little Cameron to our group, amen. You can call me Brother Jim."

I guess he thought calling me little was funny. I towered over kids my age. His false enthusiasm itched my ears like poison ivy between your toes.

"Today, we will be learning about Jonah and the whale, amen."

He took a stance at the head of the room. Puffing up his razor-thin chest, he began.

"God told Jonah to go tell the people of Nineveh to stop sinning. Amen! Jonah feared to go because the people in Nineveh were scary and bad, so Jonah found a ship to run away from what God commanded him to do. Amen! Maybe Jonah thought God would forget about him and get someone else to do it, but we know God sees and knows everything. Amen!"

Brother Jim passed out paper.

"Wouldn't you know it," Jim continued. "Jonah went out on the boat and the winds started getting so bad and the seas so rough that the ship started to sink. The captain of the boat tried to lighten the load by throwing cargo overboard, but it didn't help. Amen! Jonah told the men on the ship that the trouble was because Jonah disobeyed God and God was mad. Jonah told the captain that they best get to throwing him into the sea. They did as he asked, and as soon as they did, the sea calmed down. Amen, amen!"

Brother Jim passed out broken crayons.

My hand went up. "Brother Jim?"

"Yes, little Brother Cam?"

"Why didn't God just stop the boat from leaving instead of almost killing the captain and his men and letting them toss Jonah in the sea?"

"We do not question the ways of God. AMEN!"

"Why?"

Brother Jim's face clenched, and his left eye twitched. He did his best to avoid looking directly at me.

"Because he is God, AMEN, and he made us. We must listen and obey and not question him. AMEN!"

"How did he make us?"

"Why, surely you know about Adam and Eve. He made Adam from the dirt of the earth and Eve from one of Adam's ribs, and that's why boys have one less rib than girls. Amen!"

Little hands were counting ribs.

"But, but, in the book *The Origin of Species,* Charles Darwin says we evolved. We weren't made from dirt and, oh, by the way, boys and girls have the same number of ribs."

"What did you say?" Brother Jim blurted, his face reddening, pulling the attention of every rib-rubbing kid. His voice dropped to a hissing whisper. "Where did you see that book?"

"The library. I'm nearly done reading it. Some of it is tough to understand but—"

"That's enough, little Brother Cam. Little brothers and sisters, take your crayons and draw a whale. I will be right back."

Brother Jim grabbed me by the wrist and pulled me out of the room, levitating me down the hall to an office waiting area.

"Charles Darwin indeed. Take a seat, little Brother Cameron," he said as he knocked on the minister's office door and went in. I heard murmurs and wondered what I did wrong and what punishments were headed my way.

Brother Jim came out of the office, game face rebuilt and sat down next to me.

"The minister is too busy to talk with us now. Maybe it's best we wait until Mom and Dad come to pick you up. I must get back to the other little brothers and sisters now. Wait here."

Without another word, Brother Jim left, leaving me alone in the waiting area. My father, looking confused, showed up an hour later. The minister had a short, punctuated, conversation with my dad before we left, and we didn't go to church services that day.

I overheard part of a heated conversation at home that Sunday evening.

"...yes, of course, but he needs to learn about God, and he needs to stop questioning the word of God. Why won't he listen and be obedient to God's will?" the mom said.

"He isn't interested in that. He loves science and reading. We should encourage him. Who knows what he can become? Just leave him be," Dad said.

"That book is going back to the library tomorrow. It's demonized."

"Not this again. You see demons in everything. That's crazy talk. Enough."

"It's not crazy talk. In the Bible, Jesus cast the demons out of people and into pigs and—"

"*Enough!* I'm done. No more. I don't want you dragging Cam to anymore churches. And no more Sunday school. And no more demon talk. That's it."

The fights were long and loud that week. They only stopped because my father left for a job in New York City. After he left, the mom spent some quality time purging my demons with a thick leather belt.

The mom's demons were tougher and went much deeper. A belt would never purge hers.

They were about to get louder.

9

CRAYON YELLOW SUN

On the day my baby brother came home, the mom whispered to me as I held him for the first time, "You know, I had four miscarriages trying to make you a brother."

"What is a miscarriage?" I asked.

"It's when the baby dies in your belly before it's born."

It felt and tasted like blame. Horror and shame filled me. My joy at meeting my baby brother sloughed away like burned skin.

Despite creating new life together, my parent's rift was still ever present. The screaming, door slamming, wall-punching fights morphed into soundless tension. I was lost somewhere in the middle, free to bury myself in my reading and writing, unfettered by most of the mom's constant criticism and judgment. Dad was still my reliable shield, but a short-fused storm simmered under his surface. He had a terrible temper that he mostly kept in check, only allowing the tip of it to be seen during fights with the mom. But like the iceberg that sank the Titanic, there was a mountain underneath that tip. I had seen his full-on temper on a few occasions, and its intensity terrified me. It appeared when he felt he was not being treated fairly, or if he felt someone in his orbit was being disrespected. His temper was most of the reason why I didn't tell him about the way the mom punished me.

I never understood how a man so loving, sensitive, and full of compassion could have such a hard-edged temper. It was a mystery to me, as was most of his past. I knew a few things about his childhood, but not enough to have a clear picture in my mind of what it was like. I knew his mother wasn't very loving and his father was strict. When I asked him for more details, he'd change the subject.

Soon after my brother's birth, the mom's new baby shine went away. Her smiles for baby brother were still there, but when he looked away from her, a neutral gaze fell like a curtain across her face. The mom, always an impeccable dresser, always concerned about how her hair and makeup looked, lost her vanity.

Dad and I noticed and pretended it would be okay. Until pretending was no longer possible.

It was early evening, just past dinner, and I sat on the living room floor. On the TV, Captain Kirk put the final beatdown on the evil, lizard skinned Gorn. In my hands were my Major Matt Mason spacemen. The mom dragged a dining room chair into the room, leaving carved marks in the thick carpet like ski tracks in green snow. On her lap was my gurgling baby brother. He smiled at me, or maybe it was gas, hard to know. I smiled back. Across from them, sitting on the low-slung sofa, was my father.

"Al?" the mom said.

Dad held a newspaper in both hands, reading the daily news, as usual. He was intent on his reading, his black-rimmed glasses low on his nose, the black of the frames a stark contrast against his crew cut. As the mom moved to say more, he intensified his focus on the paper, giving it a quick angry shuffle that said, *"Not now, I'm reading, can't you see?"*

"Al, I need to tell you something. Something important."

He looked up.

"I have rabies," she said.

It would seem, to someone less familiar, that he saw the tableau for the first time, but I knew better. He was keenly aware of everything and all of us. Always was.

"I know it's the rabies because of the dripping in my head. You and the boys have it, too," she said, her urgency rising. "I've been smelling those awful smells again. It's the demons. These are warnings from God that he will destroy the world any second. We aren't ready, Al. We really aren't ready and I'm afraid for the boys."

For periods in my life, I've lost this memory, but it comes back and visits me at the oddest times. A smell, a color, something unnamed will bring it back, unbeckoned from a storage room somewhere in my mind. The kind of room where you keep stuff you haven't used in a long, long time, but which you can't throw away, because the moment you do, you'll need all the stuff. The memory is accompanied by waves of a feeling akin to déjà vu. Each wave reinforces the memory, reminding me that this thing happened. *Don't forget. Here. It's yours.*

For a second, my father's mask of bravado slipped, and he saw it. It's not what he thought it was. A corner had been turned. Every inch of his body tensed, like the leg of a lion I'd seen at the zoo before it pounced. The newspaper in his hands was forgotten, frozen, like it had been transmuted into sheet metal by an invisible alchemist. Dad took out each of his words and weighed them carefully. When he spoke, his voice contained a falseness that he hoped would go unnoticed. Almost, Dad. Almost.

"I'm sure they're both okay, hun. How about I hold Sean?" He reached out his arms to take my brother.

The forgotten newspaper dropped, returned to its natural molecular state, and ruffled to the ground, sounding like a wounded dove. A partial headline, "Dead in Overnight…" flashed in view before it flattened onto the carpet.

The mom pulled my baby brother tighter to her chest. She looked to me, to my father, then back to my brother, shaking her head. "No, Al, it's no use. We are dying."

"Please. Give. Him. To. Me."

"But…"

"Now. Please."

Soundless tears flowed, dragging a black line of mascara down her left cheek. She soundlessly handed my brother over and walked to the bedroom. The door shut behind her with a soft click.

Dad slid the squirming baby into my hands. "Hold your brother."

My father went to the kitchen, lifted the olive-green receiver, and dialed a number. He nodded his head as he whispered and listened. His hand fiddled with the magnets on the refrigerator door. Dislodged, my crayon drawing of our house with four stick figures standing in front under rays of a yellow sun fell to the floor. He hung up the phone gently, as if the receiver were made of glass and might shatter it into a million pieces from the transferred tension. He went to the bedroom door, opening it just enough to let him enter, but no more. The house was quiet. It too waited—tensing, tightening.

Like a Bernini sculpture, my brother and I were locked together, his cheek pressed up against mine. I smelled his strawberry milk breath. A *"Caa"* from my brother's tiny lips broke the silence. His little fingers found their way to my mouth and grasped my lower lip. His nails were sharp, but I didn't react. I willed him to be quiet so I could hear. A stab in my chest reminded me to breathe. I took in air. I held it.

Still. Be still.

"Caa..."

"Shh."

"Caabluur."

"SHHH, be quiet."

No sound came from the bedroom. The silence was so complete that it had its own presence, which was almost a color. A dog down the street barked once. A knock on the door caused us both to jump.

The bedroom door opened and closed. My father moved to the front door with precision, then opened it to admit a man in all black. The minister. Words were shared. Some were highlighted in the air as if with a yellow marker and some words punched through like cotton-wrapped bullets. "...sick…hurt…demons…danger…self…hospital…help...baby…"

The minister and my father moved into the bedroom. They came out fifteen minutes later. There was a quorum. A decision made.

My father knelt before us and took my baby brother out of my arms.

"Everything is okay."

"No. It isn't."

He looked me in the eyes. His eyes were grey. Grey like steel. They were strong and reassuring. There was strength in them. Just not enough for the moment.

"Now, now, everything will be alright."

He drew me in with his free arm and held us tight.

Over his shoulder, through the open bedroom door, I saw the side silhouette of the mom sitting on the edge of their bed, her arms resting on her knees, palms up, head down. There is a tissue in her left hand. She drops it. Time slows, and it falls like the forgotten feather of a mourning dove. A single needle of ice, thinner than an eyelash, penetrates my heart as the tissue hits the ground.

No, everything will not be okay. Not now.

I heard a siren far off, then closer. Louder. A dog barked twice. The siren, closer. Two dogs barked. A car horn sounded. Two beeps. The siren was out front, then off, leaving red light sprayed against the front curtains. Hard knocks on the door. Two men were let in.

They took my mother.

"Your father has to leave for a bit. I will stay with you," the minister said as he took my brother from my father.

My father hugged me and left.

I tried to stay awake, but the shadow side won. When I woke up, it was early morning. My grandmother, my father's mother, was standing over me with Sean in her arms, his little feet kicking her side. She mumbled something and left for the kitchen. *Mumbles* was my nickname for her. She barely spoke, and she hadn't ever spoken directly to me that I could recall.

I headed to the kitchen.

"Where's Dad?"

"*Bcks oon mns.*"

"What?"

"*Bask son.*"

"Back soon?"

She nodded a yes.

A baby bottle warmed in a pot on the stove. She held up a box of Cheerios and nodded at me for affirmation.

"Yes, please."

She poured me a bowl of Cheerios. I thought about asking more questions, but I didn't have the energy or a mumbles-to-English dictionary. I ate my Cheerios and went to my room. I tried to read, but I couldn't focus. Instead, I prayed. I prayed that the mom would be okay. I prayed that my father would fix all of whatever this was. I prayed that my little brother wouldn't remember any of it.

The sounds of my father arriving home interrupted my prayers and I ran out to him and into his arms.

"Hey, hey, now. It's okay."

"Where's Mom?"

"Your mom..." he started, "Your mom has been feeling sick for a while. She's not getting better so the doctor thought it might be best if she stayed at the hospital for a few...some time."

"Why? How long?"

"Sometimes moms get tired from all the hard work they do, and they need a rest."

"For how long, though?"

"A few days and then we'll see how she feels."

"Does she have rabies?"

"Nobody has rabies."

"Do I have rabies?"

"No, you don't have rabies. Everyone is good. No rabies. Promise."

"Okay."

"Grandma will be taking care of you both when I can't be here. I need you to help her every way you can. I need you to be the man of the house and help with your brother. Okay?"

A few days without the mom turned into three and then five. The wear showed on my father's face, and his usual quick, confident pace was replaced with a forward stooped shuffle. He spent a lot of time talking on the phone in hushed tones. I repeatedly asked when she would be home. "Soon," he would say. "Soon." He didn't sound certain.

I sat on the living room floor, drawing with my crayons. Without warning, the mom came in the front door with my father behind. She took my brother from my grandmother. His chubby face lit up like a firefly. She kissed me on the head as she walked past to sit on the sofa. Her hand left a square of warmth on my shoulder. I wanted to hug her, but I didn't know if it was allowed.

"I'm glad you're home. Why were you gone for so long?" I asked.

At the recommendation of the mom's doctor and the minister, my father had committed her to The Philadelphia State Hospital at Byberry.

"The screams went on all day and night. I couldn't sleep," she said.

My father whispered something in her ear. She pushed his face away.

"They gave me drugs and they turned me into a zombie."

My father put his hand on her knee. "Maybe now isn't the time for all that."

"That place," she said, disgust dripping in the words, "is full of demons and demon-infected people."

"Enough, Pat, enough."

She sighed.

While she was there, the minister visited her exactly one time. She told him about the demons and the visions. She told him how it was all spoken of in Revelation. The extent of his help was to tell her to read Mathew, Mark, and Luke instead of Revelation.

"The important part is that Mom is home." My father's hand squeezed her leg.

She nodded a yes and smiled.

My father's jaw relaxed, but his brows didn't. He was watching and, going forward, he always would.

I handed the mom the new crayon drawing I made, the four of us in front of the house, green grass below and a sun above.

"Welcome home, Mom."

She looked down at the drawing.

A single tear fell from her eye, landing on the yellow sun, leaving a dark spot.

"Everything is okay now," she said.

No one believed it.

10

TRUTH OR CONSEQUENCES

The mom found what she was looking for at the chiropractor's office.

"Of course, demons are real," the receptionist said. "By studying the Bible and becoming one of Jehovah's Witnesses, you can learn how to protect yourself from Satan and live forever in a paradise Earth. We're living in the end times and Armageddon will be here any moment."

The mom's face radiated like she'd used uranium face cream. Finally, after a lifetime of searching, she found her people in a shabby chiropractor's office amid the dog-eared Woman's Day magazines, worn brown carpet, and cheap folding chairs.

"There are millions of us, and more are getting baptized every day," the receptionist said, handing her a blue book. Across the front, gold lettering read, *The Truth that leads to Eternal Life*.

Not long after the office encounter, the mom started a Bible study with one of the Jehovah's Witnesses. In Jehovah's Witness groups, you weren't allowed to study the Bible without guidance. Jehovah's Witnesses were forced to use approved books and magazines as study guides. These publications were written by a group of men known as the "Governing Body." They lived and worked at the JW headquarters in New York known as *Bethel*. What the group of elderly men said was considered God-inspired law. Until they changed their minds, issued new rules, and punished anyone who followed the old rules. This happened regularly. Fun stuff.

The mom was particularly animated after one of her Bible studies. She cornered my brother and me out of Dad's earshot.

"We will be going to meetings at the Kingdom Hall three times a week. We need to obey Jehovah. God's judgment will be upon us at any second, like a thief in the night."

"Church three times a week?" I asked.

"Not church, the Kingdom Hall. We want to survive Jehovah's judgement. You don't want to be bird food, do you?"

"Why would I be bird food?"

"If you don't obey, you will die at Armageddon, probably by fire. After, the birds will feast on your flesh."

This was a new level of crazy. "Do you believe this?"

"This is what we all must believe. If you obey Jehovah's rules, you will live forever in a paradise Earth, and we even get to pick out a big new house to live in. Isn't that good news?"

"What new house? Are we moving?"

"Sister Madison, my teacher, has one all picked out. It's in New Hope on the river. Maybe we can live next door to her. She has kids your age."

"When will this happen?"

"Soon, very soon." She leaned in closer and adopted a whisper. "The brothers and Elders are saying everything points to October 1975. Isn't that wonderful?"

I ruminated about what she said. The mom and her new friends thought it was good news that billions of people would be slaughtered so they could upgrade their real estate.

"Some of the brothers and sisters are selling their homes and property to spend the last days in this old system in the pioneer service. Wouldn't that be great if we could sell our house and give the money to the society?"

Sell the house? Where would we live? Where would I go to school? I hoped Dad would have something to say about this.

"But I want to go to college and become a scientist. I won't have any place to live if you sell the house."

"You don't need to go to college. The end will be here before you get a chance. We won't need scientists in the new system of things. We will need builders and cleaners and boys that know how to use their hands to clear away all of the destruction."

I was speechless.

The mom discovered a religion that agreed with everything she believed.

Demons? *CHECK.*

Possessions by the devil? *CHECK.*

End of the World? *CHECK.*

Beating your children into submission with the creator's approval? *CHECK.*

A new group of friendly people that accepted her? *HEAVEN ON EARTH.*

Jehovah's Witnesses believe that the devil and his demons are real and up to all kinds of shenanigans. They believe that demons can inhabit people and things. They also believe that demons love it when you talk about them, so when the Witnesses speak about demons, they do so in hushed tones. I guess demons can't hear whispers. Perhaps there's a market for demon sized hearing aids?

The mom took us to our first meeting on a Sunday. Dad stayed home to conduct his yard ritual. Sean and I were freshly bathed and wearing our best clothing. I even shined my shoes. The meeting was boring, until the beatings started. Then it was terrifying.

Jehovah's Witnesses believe you should beat children when they're misbehaving, even small children and babies. According to what they believe, withholding physical punishment means you do not love them. In fact, it means you hate them. "If you spare the rod, you will ruin the child" was a parental mantra in the JW world we now inhabited. Children were expected to sit at full attention for hours during three weekly meetings. Fidgeting, squirming, or talking resulted in a trip to one of several small rooms in the back of the meeting hall. They called them meeting rooms. We called them beating rooms.

Every meeting, small children, including my brother, were dragged to these rooms, sometimes by their hair or a nearly dislocated arm. Muffled screams of terrorized children punched through the drone of the speaker on stage. Congregation members laughed at the wails and the sad, pleading, little voices that escaped the beating rooms. After a beating was delivered, a sobbing child would be marched back to their seat in front of the entire congregation. Members were praised for doing this to their children. Beating methods and items used were shared between parents. It was openly said that children needed to have their rebellious spirits beaten out of them, and every meeting they tried. Boy, oh boy, did they try.

The mom accepted all of it and believed it with fervor. Through the weekly meetings and the receptionist at the chiropractor's office, she was introduced to more JWs. They all welcomed the new convert with open arms. Since they would be neighbors in the "new world" (after cleaning up the bodies, of course) it made sense that everyone get to know each other. At first, there was no judgement from the members, just loving acceptance.

With her new friends, the mom had receptive ears willing to listen to her demon-flavored rants. This shift gave my father's ears a break. This made things smoother between them, but worse for me. She treated me as her confidant. She cornered me regularly with her Armageddon talk. I was afraid to push back, and I didn't know how, so I politely listened.

Sean and I were dragged to meetings three times a week to hear cheap-suited, middle-aged men drone on and on about how "we're in the end times" and "the time is now to spread the word," and how "only Jehovah's Witnesses have the TRUTH, and the rest of the world is controlled by Satan."

It was easy to see the set-up of the group if you were paying attention. In their world, everything the JW's believed was truth. Everything else was suspect because everything except the JWs was controlled by the devil. This created a bubble of belief that was, in every way, sealed and protected from criticism. If you criticized their beliefs and teachings, you would quickly find yourself thrown out of the group and shunned via a process called *dis-fellowshipping*. Even children could be dis-fellowshipped, sometimes for something as simple as objecting to a belief that the Governing Body members in New York ended up changing anyway.

The mom's favorite time to corner me was late in the evenings after the meetings. The main themes were the four Ds. Death, destruction, the devil, and demons. She went on and on about Armageddon and the destruction of most of the world's population, while waving the Bible opened to the Book of Revelation. The four horsemen, predictions of the beast, and 1975 were her favorite rants. The most chilling part was watching her say it all with a smile.

These sessions were a waking nightmare for me, and I had to smile and nod my agreement all the way through. I would go to bed and shake under the covers for hours, unable to sleep, thinking about the horror of God destroying all my friends and family members. Before her barrage of fear talk, I was on my way to becoming a skeptical, critical thinker, but I was still a child, and she was my parent. The regular rain of horror took a toll on me.

I was introduced to JW kids at the weekly meetings. I ached for friendship and acceptance, but I had nothing in common with them. They were little walking, talking versions of old fire-and-brimstone preachers with cheap lawyer degrees. They talked about the end of the world like it was Christmas.

"You know, when Armageddon comes, we'll be able to have a pet lion," JW kid #1 said.

"After Armageddon, we'll live forever and we won't have to deal with all these worldly people because Jehovah will kill them," JW kid #2 said.

"What if it's your best friend at school, or your grandma?" I asked.

"Oh, well. It's their fault. They were offered a Bible study and they stubbornly refused to listen to THE TRUTH," JW kid #1 said.

There was a culture of anti-intellectualism among the JW parents and children. No surprise, since not much reading was taking place other than JW-sanctioned books and magazines. They looked at me like I was crazy if I talked about my interests in science or art. They told me I sounded "worldly." This is a catch-all expression for anything deemed not in the approved JW bubble. The most pious among them were mini narcs, and they reported everything you said to their parents. If they believed you were even thinking about breaking one of their hundreds of rules, they reported you to an Elder. It was like being asked to become friends with the *Children of the Corn.* I hated being around them.

Except for Sid.

I met Sid at a forced sleepover at the chiropractor's receptionist's family's home. The family had three kids—two boys and an adopted girl. Sid was friends with the kids. The mom wanted me to become friends with them because they were a "very Christian family that can help you understand Witness values."

Their house was in the middle of a field of dirt in the middle of nowhere. Driving up to the house, I was sure I would never be seen again. The house had few windows, and the basement, where the kids slept, had none. When the lights were turned off in the basement, it was pitch black. It was scary, and so was their father. There was something off about him. He gave me the creeps, and I gave him a wide berth. Something about the way he looked at his adopted daughter made me cringe.

Sid and I couldn't have been more different on the outside. I was well on my way to my eventual height of six feet, four inches tall, and Sid was five feet at best. He was dark brown, and I was Viking white. He was the first black kid I'd ever met. Sid was only a few years older than me, but he had wisdom and life experience beyond his age. He listened to music I didn't know, used slang I didn't understand, and he had a carefree attitude that I envied.

"I'm Cam."

"Hey, Brother Cam. Where you from?"

"Across the bridge in Levittown."

"Cool. What hall?"

"The Levittown hall, I think?"

"Cool. Are you born in?"

"Am I what?"

"Were you always a JW or did you become a JW later on?"

"Oh. My mom is becoming one."

"Is your dad becoming one?"

"No, he doesn't like it."

"Just like my dad. He doesn't want anything to do with it. I still get presents, though."

"What do you mean?"

"For my birthday and Christmas. My mom doesn't like it, but he still gives em to me."

"Why doesn't your mom like it?"

"Because JWs don't celebrate birthdays or Christmas. They're pagan holidays. You don't know?"

"Wait...What?"

"Oh, man," Sid laughed. "They didn't tell you all the stuff yet, did they? Ain't no Christmas or birthdays in the JWs. You can't celebrate any holidays, not even Easter. No saluting the flag or playing sports at school, either. And you're not allowed to hang out with worldly people. How long have you been going to meetings, anyway?"

"Not that long."

"They make you go door to door yet?"

"No, what's that?"

"Come on, Buck. Let's head outta here away from these dubs and I'll tell you what's up."

"Buck?"

"Yeah, you're a young buck that needs to know some stuff. You're not gonna like it, but I'ma take care of you."

And, just like that, I earned a nickname and gained a life-long friend.

Since that day, I've often wondered. If we could have seen the future, would we have run in opposite directions?

11

BLUE SKY

Our family fell into a new rhythm. The mom spent most of her time with her new JW friends. I was dragged along to the three meetings per week and forced to read the sanctioned magazines and books to prepare for the meetings. Then there was "field service." This is the spreading of the "good news" of Armageddon and the death of billions by knocking on stranger's doors to sell them a Watchtower or Awake magazine and get them to agree to a weekly Bible study. Mostly, it was getting into arguments with pajama-clad strangers enjoying their first cup of coffee and then the treat of a door slammed in your face. I hated every awful minute of it.

Since the mom didn't have time for my father, the divide between them grew to a chasm. What was once a screaming match of a relationship was replaced by a cold war of avoidance.

The JW rules crept into our life. It started with the mom throwing away anything she deemed "full of demons" or "worldly" or "immodest." She went through her records and threw away anything that was remotely sensual in nature. The hems of her dresses were apparently too high, so she threw away half her clothes, keeping the "conservative, appropriate clothing that a good God-fearing Christian would wear."

Lots of things disappeared from the house. When asked about something that had vanished, the mom would reply, "It's not something we as followers of Jehovah should own."

Halloween costumes ended up in the trash. My comics and records followed. Before she had a chance to purge my books, I hid them in the shed.

The most impactful rule was "no more holidays." In advance of Jesus's upcoming birthday, the screaming matches returned.

"Why? Why in hell would celebrating the birthday of Jesus be against God?" Dad said.

"Please don't curse," the mom said, hands on hips and ready to dance. "It's not his actual birthday, and Christmas is rooted in the worship of other gods."

"That's ridiculous. What other gods? That makes no sense!"

"I can no longer celebrate Christmas. It's pagan."

It went around and around this way for the entire second half of November. Just before Christmas, my father sat me down.

"Are you okay with this no holiday business? Your mother said that you don't mind not having Christmas."

Oh, great. I was now a pawn in the argument. I had no idea what to say. Of course, I wanted Christmas. I loved presents. Who didn't? I loved all the trimmings. I loved the trip to the tree farm to buy a tree and decorate it. I loved wrapping presents for everyone. I delighted in the anticipation and sleep deprivation of Christmas Eve. Most of all, I liked the feeling of family and comfort on Christmas Day as we lounged together amid the ripped wrapping paper, the shiny presents, and the glow of the fireplace.

If I admitted that I wanted Christmas, the arguments would never end.

"I guess I don't mind."

"We can still have Christmas—you, Sean, and me."

"No, it wouldn't be the same without Mom. It's okay."

As Christmas neared and the neighborhood kids were winding up for the big day, I did my best to act like I didn't care. I did my best to ignore all the lights, the decorations, the Christmas-themed everything. I could maybe fool a few kids, but I couldn't fool myself. I went to bed that Christmas Eve sad and resentful. It wasn't fair. No visions of sugar plums for me. Instead, I cried myself to sleep.

Christmas morning came, and I headed into the living room for some cartoons. On the table next to the sofa was a single two-foot by two-foot box. It was wrapped in plain brown wrapping paper. I tore off the paper to find a Cox model airplane. I had wanted one of these desperately. They had real miniature gas engines and you flew them in a circle, guiding them with a control cable. A card was taped to the gift.

This is not a Christmas present. It is a just because present. Just because I love you. –Dad

---

After that Christmas, Dad decided it was time to spend less time in the orbit of the mom and chase down a few of his own dreams. There was a small airfield not far from where we lived. My father drove us over to watch the planes take off and land. After a few hours of watching the private planes do their sky dancing, we wandered over to a red hanger. A hand-painted sign hung over the hanger doors. In big happy letters, it read, "Horton Aviation — Learn to FLY today!"

A man in a navy-blue jumpsuit covered in grease smudges greeted us.

"Hello there. What can I do for you two men?"

My father went right to it.

"I've always wanted to learn to fly, and I'm here to do just that. My son and I are here to take an introduction flight."

Two men were seated at a long table looking over maps and charts. One of them stood up and walked over.

"Welcome to Horton Aviation. I'm Bob." He reached out a hand to my father. "Give me ten minutes to fuel up and we'll get you up in the air."

They shook hands.

"I'm Al and this is my son, Cam."

Bob gave me a quick salute and wink, then disappeared out a side door. My father smiled at me and nodded. His smile said, "That's how you start working on a dream."

There was something about the can-do, will-do attitude these old-school men shared that I admired. It was simple. Straightforward. They didn't talk it to death. There were no wasted words or movements. No bravado. My father had decided to fulfill a dream. He went to the place where that dream could be made real. They recognized his seriousness and got to it.

True to his word, Bob came back to the office ten minutes later, decked out in sharply pressed khaki slacks and an olive-green flight jacket. He looked like a vintage airman from a World War II movie, ready to take to the sky and shoot enemy planes out from under lesser, weaker men. A few signatures later and we were ready.

"Let's fly," Bob said.

He walked us out to the taxiway, where a small blue and white, four-seater airplane sat ready for us. I got into the back seat and my father hopped into the front seat to Bob's right. We all donned headsets with microphones so we could talk over the engine noise.

Bob tapped the face of some instruments and made marks on a clipboard. His voice was inside my head. He sounded like how I always imagined a flying ace would sound. No nonsense, confident, reassuring with a hint of whimsy.

"Alright, men. Before we take off, here is your pre-flight briefing. Make sure your seatbelt is secured. If you feel like you might get sick, there are sick bags here and here. We will be flying for approximately forty-five minutes, so if there is even a slight chance you will need to go to the bathroom during that window of time, do it now before I close the lid. Once the lid is on, you will have to hold it. Al, while we're up in the blue, I will give you a chance to take the wheel. Everything Alpha, Oscar, Kilo?"

What's that? I thought. Oh, I know! "A-Okay?" I said pulling the microphone close to my mouth.

Bob nodded a yes and turned to my father. "He's a smart one, isn't he?"

Bob started up the engine and the propeller began spinning.

"You have no idea," Dad said.

My heart brimmed. We took off into the bright blue sky.

Very little compares with flying in a small plane for the first time. It was my first time in a plane of any kind, and I loved every second of it. The transition from the bumpy runway into the sky gave me a roller coaster belly drop. Despite some initial turbulence, I had no fear. I knew from the instant we took off that flying was something I wanted to do over and over again. My father looked back at me, and his smile told me everything I needed to know.

After reaching altitude, Bob gave my father the okay to take hold of the duplicate set of controls in front of him. Bob guided him through some simple turns, climbs, and descents. Aching to take those controls in my hands, I mimicked his hand movements with my own.

Bob's voice came over my headset. "Great job, Al. You're a natural."

And indeed, he was. From the first turn, it was obvious. My father was a natural. He executed Bob's instructions with smooth precision. Bob's hands eventually left his controls to give my father complete control over our destiny. Factories and processing plants, houses and schools passed below our feet. We flew over excavation sites and dumping grounds as we flew toward the Delaware River.

The water glittered like it was covered with floating diamonds. Small boats bobbed up and down on the river like toys in a giant, grey-blue bathtub. A flock of white birds flew below us toward a big green suspension bridge with white letters across its span that read, "What Trenton Makes the World Takes." What did Trenton make, I wondered? Why did the world take it? Where did that bridge go?

I was so small, and the world, so big.

Big it may be, but you just wait, I thought. I would see it all, and nothing would stop me.

I closed my eyes. I let the sensations take me.

It wasn't a plane. It was a spaceship, and I was the brave pilot, pulling back the controls into a steep climb, higher and higher, closer and closer to the edge of space itself. Higher and higher my ship went, bravely fighting gravity to free me and my crew from our tiny lives lived on boring old dirt. Up here, we could do anything. Be anything. See everything. Next stop, the Moon, and wherever else my rocket and guts would take me!

Bob's voice in my headset brought me back from space. He was pointing out a landmark and asking my father to head toward it. My father flew us to the landmark, executed a perfect turn, and headed back in the direction of the airport. Bob took over the controls and landed us, light as a feather, onto the runway. We taxied back to the hanger and stopped. Bob turned off the engine. The world was still, small, and quiet once again.

Something in me was changed. I was not the same boy that took off. The unwritten list of my life's possibilities had increased exponentially. If a simple test flight in a small plane could make me feel like this, what else was out there in the world? What adventures awaited me? What could I do? What should I do? Maybe I could become an astronaut, a pilot, or an explorer. Infinite possibilities roared through my cells and sparked my soul.

"What do you think, Al?"

"When can we start?"

Bob smiled. "We just did." They shook hands.

My father committed to his dream. They hopped out of the plane. My father motioned with his hand for me to follow him out.

"Come on, ace."

I didn't move. I willed my body to become part of the plane so I could spend the rest of my life with this feeling of adventure and hope.

"Can we do it again?"

"We can, and we will. But not today. Come on." He laughed.

"You promise?"

"I promise."

Dad kept the promise.

Over the next eighteen months, my father attended ground school and logged many hours in the air. He brought me with him as often as he could. One bright Saturday afternoon, one of his new flying buddies, Ted, invited us to take a flight.

I got into the back seat.

"Hang on, ace," Dad said.

"What's wrong?"

"Nothing's wrong. I'm in the back today."

"Huh?"

"Today, you are the co-pilot."

I climbed into the front seat next to Ted.

Once at altitude, Ted asked me, "Ready to take the stick?"

"Really?"

"Yes, really," Ted said.

My mouth no longer worked, but my hands did. I eased my hands around the controls like I'd seen my father do many times. My father's hand came from the back seat and squeezed my shoulder.

"Are you ready, Cam?" my father asked.

I mustered my most adult sounding voice.

"I'm ready, sir."

I tightened my grip on the controls.

Ted removed his hands from his controls.

"You have the controls. Fly this bird," Ted said.

I was flying a plane.

The sky was mine.

Anything is possible. And nothing could stop my dad and me. Well, almost nothing.

A few flights short of the required hours to receive his private pilot's license, my father was forced to stop his lessons.

At forty-five years of age, my father, my protector, was diagnosed with stage-four lung cancer.

EXODUS

12

BEREFT

"Al, is there any way you can change out of your clothes at work?" the mom shouted from the laundry room. "This stuff gets everywhere."

"No."

"Can you maybe change in the backyard, or at least leave your boots and socks outside?"

"Sure."

"What is this stuff all over your clothes?"

"We're changing out the pipes at a roof shingle factory in Ambler. That crap is everywhere."

"What is it? It's itchy."

"Asbestos."

My father worked at the asbestos plant for several months. They had him crawling around in the walls and ceiling, installing new piping five days a week. Like the rest of the work crew, he worked unmasked. No safety gear was required or provided, other than a helmet. Combine the asbestos exposure and his pack-a-day Camel habit, and the cancer fuse was lit.

A year after the asbestos factory job, my father started experiencing problems breathing. He had a chest-racking cough that left him red and breathless. He attributed it to smoking too much and tried to quit. As he often joked, he was a good quitter, since he quit all the time.

My father ignored his symptoms as the man code of the day required. By the time his symptoms forced him to the doctor, his cancer was advanced. The mom doubled down on prayer and meetings. The cancer didn't care. I went to the library to learn what I could about cancer. I was determined to understand the causes and treatments for what was eating my father's lungs. I thought that if I only had enough knowledge, I could save my father. Perhaps somewhere there was an experimental treatment or some unknown research that could help. There wasn't any useful information at the public library or my school library.

I approached my science teacher and asked him where I could find information on cancer research.

"Why do you want to read about that stuff?"

I didn't want to let anyone know about my father's illness. "I want to be an oncologist."

I got a blank look. "What's an oncologist?"

"Never mind. You're useless."

He was surprised by my rudeness, but I was on a mission. *Either help me or get outta my way.* I didn't have time to waste.

I desperately wanted to talk with my father's doctors about his cancer and treatment, so I asked to speak with his oncologist. The mom didn't think it was a good idea and my request was denied. The doctors started my father on a round of chemotherapy.

Word about my father's cancer spread at the Kingdom Hall. The outpouring of love and empathy from the other members was touching. There were advantages to being in the bubble. I overheard them tell the mom that if he died, she should be comforted by the knowledge that he would be resurrected after Armageddon. This made me furious. They were talking as if his death was inevitable. It was not. He couldn't die. He had way too much to do. Science would save him. He would live to see me grow up and do amazing things!

Some of the members asked the mom if they could visit my father to share the "good news" of the resurrection with him. He was home recovering from the chemo and having a rough time of it. My father and I were sitting on lawn chairs in the back yard enjoying some sunshine when one of the congregation members dropped by for an unannounced visit. The mom led him to us.

"Al, this is Frank. He was passing by and wanted to say hello. I hope you don't mind."

Of course, my father minded. Who wants to meet a stranger when you're coughing and vomiting? He mustered up as much politeness as he could.

"Hi, Frank." A half smile made it to my father's strained face. "Have a seat."

Frank sat down next to us. He wasted no time on small talk.

"I'm sorry to hear about your cancer. How's it going?"

"It's going. Not sure where yet, but I'm sure it will all work out."

That last bit was said for my benefit, and I knew it.

Frank repositioned on the aluminum lawn chair. He pulled a brown paper lunch bag from his back pocket. He removed a handful of what looked like dried seeds from the wrinkled bag and held them out. "Have you heard about Laetrile? It's found in peach pits."

"I haven't heard of laya-whatever," he said, "but I have a peach tree right over there, not that it gives many peaches anymore." He tried to laugh but it turned into a cough.

When the coughing subsided, Frank resumed. "There is something inside peach and apricot pits that can cure cancer. They are curing cancer with it every day down in Mexico."

My father drew a long pause and examined Frank's face for an uncomfortable amount of time.

"And how do you know that, Frank?"

"The government doesn't want anyone to know about it, but it works. They won't make any money off it because you can grow it yourself. All you have to do is grind down the pits and eat it. It's completely natural."

A longer pause hung in the air between them. My father was fidgety, his knee bouncing up and down.

"Who won't make money?"

"You know. The doctors and hospitals and the chemo makers. It will put them all outta business."

"So, my doctor knows that eating those seeds will cure my cancer, but he won't tell me?"

"I don't know about all doctors. Maybe your doctor doesn't know what they're doing down in Mexico. It's a miracle."

"How does it work?"

"You grind the peach pits in a blender, then you mix them into a drink."

"How many do you need to take?"

"Word is, five or so a day will do it."

"That's a lot of peaches."

"You can use apricots, too. I can bring you peach pits every day. My family loves peach pie, so it's no problem."

My father's expression softened as a realization took hold. Here was this total stranger, that he'd met only moments before, offering to bring him peach pits every day.

Frank put the peach pits back into the wrinkled lunch bag and rolled it closed. He held it out to my father. My father accepted the bag tenderly as if it was a living thing. My father offered his hand to Frank. They shook. Their hands were identical. They were working man's hands. Calloused and worn, they had the kind of fingernails that never got completely clean, no matter how many times they were scrubbed. They sang of the hard work they had proudly done. They had lifted and carried, hammered and pried. They had gently guided a child, caressed a cheek or two, and, at some point, been forced to turn to steel and settle a score, right a wrong. On the occasional weekend morning, those hands had held a toasty thermos of coffee in one hand and a fishing rod or a rifle in the other, waiting, still and silent, in the fall chill. Neither of these men needed work gloves. They had them on at all times.

"Would you pray with me, Al?"

"I would, Frank, I would."

They both folded their hands in prayer. I folded my small, fresh-skinned hands with them. We prayed.

My father asked his oncologists about the peach pit cancer cure. The doctor told him that there was no evidence to suggest it provided any benefit in the fight against cancer. He also warned him that the body turns the Laetrile found in the seeds and pits into cyanide. You could die from cyanide poisoning if you ingested enough. He told my dad that it was tried as a cure but it turned out to be more poisonous than chemotherapy. That was enough for my father. He never took it.

Frank visited a few times a week, and true to his word, he always brought a paper lunch bag of peach and apricot pits with him. He also brought us some delicious peach pies. Despite knowing that Frank's "cure" was anything but, my father graciously accepted the gifts. At some point, he told Frank that our peach tree was fruiting, and we were set for pits, so he didn't need to go to the fuss. Frank still visited. They ate pie and talked for hours about God, the Bible, and the Philadelphia Eagles, although not necessarily in that order. Frank would occasionally hear about a new cancer "cure" and bring it up during their conversations. My father would smile and be gracious.

The year progressed. So did the cancer. It went to his brain. The doctors recommended radiation to slow the growth. My brother and I were allowed to visit my father once while he was in the Thomas Jefferson Hospital in Philadelphia for the procedure. He'd lost so much weight; I couldn't make out his body amidst the blankets on the hospital bed. He looked like a head floating on a river of wool. They had shaved the little hair my father had left post chemo. He had dark blue lines at regular intervals inked on the front of his head like a fleshy clock face.

"What are those lines on your head, Dad?"

"Those are my new tattoos. Like them?" His smile exaggerated the thinness of his cheeks.

"What are they for?"

"The doctors use the lines to make sure they're shooting the radiation beams into the right spot."

I was intrigued and horrified at the same time. But I knew this would save him. After he came home, we would fatten him up with pie and all the other foods he loved. Then everything would be good, and we would go flying, go to the movies, go see the Eagles play, and do all the things he loved to do.

It had to work. If anything happened to my dad, there would be nobody left to shield me from the mom.

13

A NEW HOPE

I first saw the movie, *2001 A Space Odyssey*, in 1968, five years before my dad's cancer diagnosis. I was seven years old. I watched from the backseat of our family car at the drive-in. The dawn of man scenes in the beginning, where primates fought over food, were violent and scary. I watched from behind my fingers until the movie time hopped into the future and launched into space. From that point on I watched with every vibrating cell of my body.

During the drive home, my father did not stop talking about the movie. The movie captured him as well. We stayed up late that night talking about every scene, the space race, the possibility of alien life, and the upcoming NASA missions. When I say talking, it was mostly him talking and me nodding.

After that night, I was obsessed with the Moon, space exploration, astronauts, and all things science. *2001* woke up a feeling that there was something bigger out there in the universe, that humankind was on the brink of discovery and maybe, just maybe, I could be a part of it.

2001 became our thing. The film stayed in theaters for a long time, and over the following six months, he took me to see it eight times. We spent four straight hours together every time we went to see it. I was so thrilled to have this time with my father that was just for us. Each time we watched it, we would find some new detail to discuss, some new theory about what the movie meant. Most of it went over my head, but I didn't care. What wasn't over my head was the sheer beauty of the film. I was fascinated with how every scene was framed like a piece of art. The special effects were flawless, and the spaceships and Moon vehicles looked real. *2001* taught me that a movie could be more than just a few hours of mindless entertainment. It could be a launch pad to considering our place in the universe. It could provide brain fodder for hours and hours of discussions. It could be the star that guided the voyage of a man and his son into friendship.

I have never been as content as when my father and I were sitting in that dark, cool movie theatre, eating popcorn and watching *2001*, the colors from the screen playing across his face, amazement shining back at the screen from his eyes like incandescent projections of his soul. Even then, I knew they were the best moments, the important moments, and during those moments I wanted the movie to go on forever.

But they never do. The end credits always roll.

My father, Alexander Ronald Gilchrist, died a few weeks before Christmas, 1974.

My shield, my protector, was gone. I was twelve.

The last time I saw my father alive was when the ambulance came to pick him up at our home and take him to the hospital. In his final days our living room had become hospice care, with a hospital bed and oxygen. The mom was by his side tending to him in his last months. There was nothing more to be done, aside from making him as comfortable as possible.

After school, I would stand by the bed and hold his hand, willing the life force to flow from me to him. If the soul was transferable, I would gladly have given him all I had. My gaze would move from the TV screen to my father's face, waiting for him to be awake enough to acknowledge me. My hyper-vigilance wore me out, and I would go to bed exhausted. Just a little more time is all we need, I thought. Then he'll start to get better.

When the ambulance took him for the last time, I lay in my bed praying for hours, asking God to save him. The next day, the mom told me he was gone.

My father was cremated. I didn't get a chance to see his body or say goodbye. Maybe that was for the best. There wasn't much left of him at the end. There was a service at the Kingdom Hall. The Elder that spoke during the ceremony didn't know my father or anything about him. He mentioned my dad exactly one time and spent the rest of the service talking about Armageddon and how death is not final.

I was furious. Couldn't he have learned something about my father? Couldn't he have mentioned something, anything, that brought him to life in the minds of the attendees? After the talk, I wore my frustration and anger so prominently that everyone was afraid to approach me. That was perfectly fine by me.

Frank found me alone in the back of the room by the exit door.

"How are you holding up?"

"I'm fine."

"It's okay if you're not."

"I'm fine," I said with a little more force.

"I'm sorry. I didn't mean to push. Do you want to be alone?"

I didn't answer.

"You know, after Armageddon—"

"Stop!" I yelled.

The heads of the attendees all swiveled toward us.

"How about we get some air?" Frank opened the rear door. We stepped outside.

"Your father loved you and your brother and mother very much."

I nodded.

"He told me how proud he was of you," he said. "He told me how smart you are, and how you should be a doctor or something smart like that. I want you to...I need you to know what he asked me to do."

Let's get this over with, I thought. "What?"

"Your father asked me to look out for you and your brother and your mom. He knew it would be tough for all of you. I need you to know that I am here for you. If you need anything, just ask me. Anything at all."

After the funeral, I withdrew completely. I lost touch with Sid and the few friends I had. I didn't want to talk to anyone and seldom did. We had no income and no savings left after the medical bills, and the mom was in no condition to work. We lost our house to the bank. We moved from our family home to a one-bedroom, low-income apartment.

The move put me into a new school district and a thirty-minute bike ride to the library. Going to a new school mid-year with a new group of kids would be tough for anyone. Add the fact that I was depressed and I had to abide by the mom's religious restrictions and countless rules without my father around to provide balance. It was not tough, it was hell.

The only thing worse than being ignored by the other kids at school was catching attention for being different. I broke the record for weirdness on the kid scale. As if I wasn't already ostracized enough, I was not allowed to play school sports, engage in most after-school activities, or be friends with anyone who was not a JW. This also included family. None of my cousins or other family spoke to us anymore because of the mom's incessant preaching. According to the mom, they were "worldly" and "controlled by demons."

The mom retreated completely into her Bible studies and field preaching. When she wasn't doing that, she monitored my every word and action, giving me instant criticism. If I listened to music, she monitored every song, asking me to repeat the lyrics to see if they were okay to listen to. It was like living with a full-time censor. It was soul sucking.

"Mom, can I please just watch TV without all of the talking?"

"I'm just looking out for your eternal life in Jehovah's new system after Armageddon."

"Can you do it quieter? I can't hear any of *Charlie's Angels*."

"This show is worldly. You shouldn't be watching it. Look at the hem on that skirt she's wearing. It's disgusting."

"Mom, it's just a dress!"

"Jehovah doesn't think it's just a dress. We should dress modestly like it says in first Timothy, two, verse nine—"

"I wish I was dead like Dad so I wouldn't have to hear your constant judging."

I instantly regretted saying that.

"Do you want to kill yourself?"

I didn't answer.

The next week I found myself in front of the Elders at the Kingdom Hall. I wouldn't speak with them, and I soon found myself in front of a therapist. After a few words of introduction, the therapist handed me a questionnaire. On the two pages were questions related to self-harm. I thought about checking "Yes" on the question, "Over the last week, have you considered harming yourself?" I checked "No." I handed over the questionnaire and that concluded the extent of my professional help. At least she didn't take me to an exorcist. Instead, she took us to Bermuda.

The mom received a payout from my father's life insurance. It wasn't life-changing money, but it could have been enough to give us a head start.

Instead of banking that money for our education or using it to buy me some pants that fit, she gave most of it to the Jehovah's Witnesses to help them pay for some building remodel costs. She was so happy after she handed over our only money. She beamed with pride as the Elders at the Kingdom Hall took almost everything we had in the world.

According to the mom and everyone she now considered a friend, the world was going to end soon, so who cared about money? She used the thousand or so dollars that was left over to take the three of us on a trip to Bermuda. It was my first time out of the country, and while it was beautiful, I mainly sat on a pool chair by myself while she befriended the local JWs.

When we returned from the vacation, I retreated back into isolation with the only other friends that never judged or abandoned me. Books. I was a reading automaton. The library was now my first home, not my second. I mainly read science fiction and books on the hard sciences. I escaped from my life and into the arms of Robert Heinlein, Isaac Asimov, Ray Bradbury, and Carl Sagan. Their words took me to better worlds, where death was defeated, science won over all adversity, and bravery was enough. They took me to places where you could become more than what you were destined to be.

In those books, it didn't matter what piece of back-alley dirt you were born to, you could secretly be a prince of the royal-born ruler of the known planets, and when you completed your quest, you ascended to your rightly throne. There you would have all the friends and love you could ever possibly need and live happily ever after.

Meanwhile, in the real world, helplessness and depression overwhelmed me. I stopped speaking, except when absolutely necessary. The mom's criticism and judgment never stopped, no matter how I responded, so I stopped responding.

School was a nightmare. The boredom was the worst part. I was light years ahead of the lessons, especially in the sciences and literature. My new teachers didn't treat me any better than my fellow students. I was the weird kid who did not celebrate Christmas, Halloween, or birthdays, wouldn't stand for the Pledge of Allegiance, and didn't speak. I was taller than everyone, and my clothes were old and didn't fit. If you tried to design an outcast from scratch, you couldn't do better than the reality of me. At some point, I just stopped going. I stayed in bed when the mom told me to get up for school. I told her my back hurt so bad that I couldn't sit at a desk all day. It wasn't a complete lie. I was in pain at school, just not from my back.

Frank stopped by the house in an effort to help pull me out of my depression. Despite his kindness, I only pretended to listen to appease him. I turned down his repeated offers to join him and his family for dinner, or bowling, or a trip to the park. I felt guilty turning down his kindness.

One day, Frank called to invite me to see a science fiction movie. I missed movies. We didn't have movie money. We needed every dollar for luxuries like rent and food. I said yes.

The line in front of the Fairless Hill's movie theater wrapped around the building. I hadn't asked what movie we were going to see, but as we got closer, I read *Star Wars* on the movie marquee. As we moved closer to the door, the lobby posters with scenes from the movie came into view. From the pictures, it didn't look very science fictiony. Everything looked old and dirty in the pictures. This looked nothing like *2001*. It will probably suck, I thought.

The movie theater smelled like popcorn and that musty smell older theaters have. The smell took me back to the happy hours of watching *2001* with my father. A pang of pain from the memory found me. The theater was full and there was a buzz of excitement. The lights dimmed and the crowd noise disappeared as if by telepathic agreement. I felt that pre-movie jittery anticipation. I realized how much I missed that feeling.

The rolling of drums and horns accompanied the "Twentieth Century Fox" logo. "A Lucasfilm Limited Production" faded in and out. Against the blackness of the dark screen, a blue, glowing sentence appeared.

A long time ago in a galaxy far, far away...

A cheer went up from the audience, startling me. Cheering before the film? Had everyone already seen this movie? What did they know that I didn't?

For the next 121 minutes, I sat transfixed. *Star Wars* was the most amazing adventure-filled movie I had seen since *2001* and I loved it. Unlike the clean aesthetics of *2001*, *Star Wars* was gritty, dirty and lived in. Where *2001* was populated by scientists and astronauts, the *Star Wars* universe was populated by heroes, villains, and scoundrels. Where *2001* challenged me intellectually, *Star Wars* got me in the heart. It wasn't until halfway through the movie that I remembered the popcorn in my lap. By the end of the movie, I knew why they had cheered at the beginning, and I joined with my new *Star Wars* brothers and sisters and cheered and clapped and yelled as the end credits rolled.

If you haven't seen *Star Wars* (is that possible?), it's the story of an adopted farm boy, whisked away into an adventure of galaxy-impacting importance. *Star Wars* is also about family and the loss thereof. It's about finding family, even if it's one we construct out of the people we meet along our journey.

Sitting in the cool darkness, watching the credits roll, tears slid down my face. I wiped them away before anyone could see. My tears were a mix of sadness and joy and popcorn butter. Sadness because my father was not around to see the movie. He would have loved it.

Leaving the theater, I was buoyant. For the first time since my father died, I felt hope. The rays of story-filled light travelled from the projector to the screen and bounced back to me at light-speed to crack the shield I'd put up around my own Death Star. Through the crack came a whisper.

You can be more.

14

RESOLUTION OF HAPPINESS

Since my father's death, I'd accepted the way I felt as my new normal, but the sadness was exhausting. I wanted to be happy, but I didn't know how to get there. If I went to the mom, she would either take me to the Elders or tell me to study the Bible and pray. I didn't need to be judged by some old men in a basement of a church. I needed something else. I needed an onramp to the old me.

"Hey, Mom, isn't that the book Nana gave me?"

"Which one?"

"This one." I pulled a book out of the box on the kitchen counter.

"That book and all the rest are going straight into the trash. Especially that one." She turned back to washing the dishes.

The mom was doing another demonized, worldly item purge. Somehow, a box of books had avoided her earlier clean-outs.

A few years prior, my grandmother, on hearing about my interest in flying, sent me the book, *Jonathan Livingston Seagull*. She thought it was a children's story about a seagull that learns to fly and thought I might enjoy it. She mailed it to me with a $2 bill inside for my birthday. I hadn't read it, and it ended up forgotten in a box. Now it was destined for the righteous, demon-killing, cleansing fire of the Levittown trash dump.

"Please don't throw it away. Nana gave it to me."

"Sister Vera told me that book is demon-inspired. It's about Buddhism. It's pagan."

"But it's just a story about a seagull. I mean sure, seagulls are annoying, especially at the beach but—"

"Don't argue with me. It's going into the trash. I won't have pagan, worldly books in this house. That's how the demons get in. Why are you so disobedient?" she said, waving a wet wooden spoon at me.

"Fine. Whatever. Throw my things away. I can read that book anytime I want."

"You won't read this copy."

She ripped the book out of my hands, her wet hands ruining the dust cover.

She slammed the book back into the box. "And don't talk back to me. When will you learn that Jehovah God wants you to be obedient? You are so willful and headstrong that one day…" was the last thing I heard as I jetted out of the apartment.

I'd show her. I hopped on my bike, rode to the library, and cracked open their copy of *Jonathan Livingston Seagull.*

Jonathan Livingston Seagull was a regular seagull that got tired of squabbling and fighting over scraps of food. Instead of squabbling with his fellow seagulls, he tested his own flying ability by flying faster and higher than the other seagulls, flying for the glory and joy of it. This was un-seagull like behavior, and it caught the notice of the other seagulls, who cast him out of the group. As the story progresses, a wise mentor seagull, Chiang, guides him on a journey of self-realization. He teaches Jonathan how to move instantaneously to anywhere in the universe. The secret, Chiang tells Jonathan, is to begin by knowing you have already arrived. You must stop seeing yourself as trapped.

A light went on in my heart as I read Chiang's teaching.

Hmm…according to a wise seagull, to change you must first see yourself as changed. What a new and intriguing concept. There was a time when I believed that I could be and do anything. That belief disappeared with my father. What I wanted most was to recapture my former spirit.

Could I believe myself back into the hope-filled version me?

Could it be that simple?

How?

I was depressed. I was sad. I was hopeless. How could I see myself as not those things if I truly believed that I was those things? This circular reasoning was frustrating but something about it was appealing.

Could I fool my own mind into a permanent change?

I finished *Johnathan Livingston Seagull.* There were no "how" answers in its pages. I got up and paced. Movement helped my brain work. I strolled the beloved aisles of my holy fortress of knowledge. Perhaps a book would leap off the shelves with more answers.

I stalked the small philosophy section, letting my fingers run against the book covers. I meandered down the aisles, hoping that something, a tingle perhaps, like a static shock, would alert me to an answer hiding deep in a tome. Perhaps I could take out a book and let it randomly fall open. The words would alight in a golden glow and, like magic, there would be a way.

To the searcher comes the knowledge. Doesn't it? Nope. Nothing. Nada. Zilch. The book gods were quiet. Not a page ruffle. Not a whiff of paper or ink jumped from the shelves. More finger gliding on spines led me back to my favorite table.

I hate feeling like this.

I know.

Of course, you know. You are me.

Yup, and I'm sick of me.

I know.

Maybe we don't need to acknowledge that we know EVERY time.

Fine.

I'm sick of being sick and tired.

I know.

Really?

Sorry, I'll stop.

No one is going to help us. Not that they don't want to. They just can't.

Agreed. We must do this by ourselves.

But how?

Maybe the bird is right.

How so?

Maybe we just decide not to be trapped. Maybe we decide to, just…be… different?

It can't be that simple.

Probably not. But it might be worth a try.

What's the worst that could happen?

Can't be much worse cause this is no fun.

The journey of a thousand miles begins with a single step.

That sounds like a Hallmark card.

Nope. Fortune cookie from last week.

Some truth to that.

Yup.

So.

So.

What's the first step then?

How about we fake it?

Let's try it.

My analytical brain was having a hard time accepting a "fake it until you make it" strategy. Besides, this was just a concept from a book about a seagull. I pushed the doubting voice aside.

"Starting right now, you have permission to be happy. In fact, you are happy," I said aloud.

The forced words left a briny taste in my mouth.

Could it work? I could call myself a firetruck, but if I didn't have four wheels and a siren, it didn't matter how many fires I peed on, I would not be a firetruck. I'd be delusional.

Maybe delusional was better than depressed?

It was a start. At least I could try something. Perhaps there were other books like *Johnathan Livingston Seagull* that could help. The mom said the book was about Buddhism. I didn't know what that was. Maybe there were other Buddhism books that would help me with my journey back to me.

"Excuse me. Do you have books like this one?" I asked the librarian.

"Books about seagulls?"

"No," I laughed. "Books about Buddhism."

"Buddhism? You always surprise me. Did you try the card files?"

We did this dance every time. She knew I didn't use the card file because of the way my brain worked. I explained my challenge to her many times, but she still asked every time. Honestly, I loved that fact that she always asked. It was expected, and somehow comforting.

"No."

"Hmm." She went to the card box. Under her deft fingers, the snap of the index cards sounded like a paper machine gun, snapping book rounds into the room. "Do you want a book about the history of Buddhism?"

"I was thinking something more like a story like this one that helps you with changing things."

Wow, Cam, way to be precise.

More card snapping.

"Hmm." She took off her glasses and chewed on the end of the frame with one hand, the other hand smoothly maintaining the rifled card search. I loved seeing someone perfectly suited for a task effortlessly perform it.

"Have you read *Zen and the Art of Motorcycle Maintenance*?"

"No, I'm too young to have a motorcycle. I like them, though. What do motorcycles have to do with Buddhism?"

"What indeed! The book isn't about fixing motorcycles. Well, it is, but, I mean, if you're interested in Buddhism you might want to read it."

"Have you read it? Is it good?"

"I have. It is." She put her glasses back on. "You should."

I did. It's not about motorcycles. Well, it is, and it isn't. Sort of.

Zen and the Art of Motorcycle Maintenance is the story about a father and son that take a road trip on motorcycles. During the trip they discuss philosophy and big life questions. The book lost me about mid-point in the story, but not before it sparked my interest in finding out more about the subject of philosophy.

My favorite chair at my favorite table was taking on a permanent imprint of my thin ass as I took a tour of the best-known philosophers' heads. I started with "A" and worked my way through the biggies. Most of the books I found were heavy, long, and complicated, and not written for the average person, let alone a child, but I burned through them as best I could to distill their respective philosophies.

Your philosophical mileage may vary but here is what I took away.

- **Aristotle** - Observe, make claims, use logic.
- **Buddha** - Existence is suffering. Suffering is caused by attachment. The self is an illusion.
- **Descartes** - Throw away all beliefs that are not certain. Start from there.
- **Foucault** - First, study history. If you are subjugated, rise up.
- **Hume** - Nothing is morally absolute. We can never truly understand ourselves.
- **Kant** - There are moral absolutes. Suck it, **Hume**.
- **Kierkegaard** - Religion is subjective and should be kept far away from government.
- **Mills** - Speak your mind. Keep a close eye on the folks in charge.
- **Nietzsche** - Nothing has meaning except what you give it. Live your truth.
- **Plato** - The world doesn't revolve around you. You better justify!

- **Sartre** – You're going to die. The universe doesn't care. Own it.
- **Socrates** - We know nothing.

After my self-directed crash course in philosophy, the only concept I could completely agree with was Socrates. He was right, I knew nothing. That's not entirely true. I knew a few things. There was one nugget that was growing bigger in me by the day. I was coming to understand that no one has "THE TRUTH." Anyone that claims to have one universal answer is trying to sell you something or steal something from you.

From the day the mom ripped a book about a Buddhist seagull out of my hands, I began most days by giving myself permission to be who and what I wanted to be. Most days, I wasn't sure exactly what I wanted to be, besides happy, but that was okay. I would get to happy first and figure out the rest later.

I didn't have the term for it at the time, but my daily affirmation was the zero point for easing myself out of my depression. It gave me strength. It helped reinforce my individuality against the storm of conformity. The wind wore down my outer shell, but my inner core grew stronger, firmer.

After my deep dive into philosophical concepts, I chose what I liked most from each philosopher and tried to integrate their teachings into my life.

I wrote down a list of rules for my life in an old, dog-eared notebook.

1. I know almost nothing and I'm not the center of the universe.
2. I'm going to die, so I better get to living. Time does not wait.
3. I will learn from history and from those who have journeyed before me. Their stories will help light my path.
4. I will never let anyone silence me or tell me what to believe or say.
5. I will use logic and observation to understand the world and build my truth on that foundation.
6. With the help of books, mentors, and friends, I will find my place in the world.
7. I will find love. I will find joy. I will find meaning.
8. I will never stop searching until the day I die.

Losing a parent at a young age is devastating. It rewrites you. It leaves your fantasy of immortality shattered like a dropped vase of flowers. It runs over you like a million-pound steamroller, setting you adrift on a black lake of despair.

Recovery was slow. I had highs and lows, but I kept focus on my rules. When the memories and pain of losing my father got unbearable as it sometimes did, and I abandoned my hope, I would find a place with a view of the stars. Looking up, I would consider the vastness of the universe. As the astronomers discovered and Carl Sagan told us, I was on one out of billions of rocks, spinning around one of the billions and billions of stars. As I considered the glittering vastness above me, I shrank smaller and smaller, regressing to a mere mote of matter. Compared to the infinite, my feelings, my pain, and every single thing on Earth revealed itself to be insignificant. Everything I was faded to nothing in the shadow of the universe. This calmed me. Soothed me.

There is more unknown than known. Who knows, maybe my father exists in some form in the universe. Maybe the essence of who and what he was is eternal. Maybe not. Maybe all he was is a part of some bigger thing. Maybe he is only atoms, star stuff drifting in the void. I may find out one day, or I may not. In those moments, when I was small, and still, and at peace, my father spoke to me.

Go live your small, insignificant, important, wonderful, painful, amazing, boring, joyful, life for all it's worth.

"I will, Dad. I will complete school. I will go to college. I will become everything I want to be. I will become more."

I know you will. Get to it, ace.

15

THE KING OF WISHFUL THINKING

"You should drop out."

We weren't in his office for more than six minutes when the school counselor delivered his "guidance" in a rushed tone from behind a beat-up desk that looked like the last thing you would see before the Soviet politico officer sent you to Siberia for a life of hard labor.

"It's really for the best." He nodded his Play-Doh face up and down like a bobble head caught in a breeze.

He moved his face closer to mine. He exhaled a mix of cigarettes and cinnamon gum he most likely chewed to cover up his smoke breath. His office smelled like sadness and feet and the aforementioned desk was stacked with papers with no discernible organization.

"What do you think?"

Think? What did I think? I could barely breathe, let alone think. For starters, how about we open the door of this vestibule to Satan's orgy room?

The mom hopped on. "This way you can go door-to-door in the ministry full time."

They were both bobble-heading. The guidance counselor pasted on a smile to match the mom's. *Look, twins.*

His turn. "At this point you've missed too much time to move to the next grade, so if you don't quit you would need to repeat your grade. FYI."

The tacked-on FYI made me want to punch him. This guy didn't care what happened to me, FYI. He couldn't even fake concern convincingly, FYI.

Was there ever a time when he was good at his job? Did he start his career with real concern for all the children in his charge? Was there a time when he woke up excited and early, shirt pressed, tie straight, with all good intent to enrich the lives of his students? Did he work late and on weekends, determining the best ways to guide them? If he did, what changed? Or was it just me he didn't care about? Me, the loser, the loner. FYI.

I didn't look him in the eyes. I was afraid I would catch whatever *dontgiveashit* disease he was suffering from. Instead, I fixated on the chest hairs poking out from where his loosened tie met the opened collar of his wrinkled shirt. I summoned a contrived smile of my own.

What did I think about quitting?

It's interesting to note that when one is finally given the opportunity one thinks one wants, one suddenly begins to calculate the cost of getting it. My calculator powered up.

The reasons for quitting rolled around in my brain:

- I hated school. ***CHECK.***
- I didn't fit it. At all. ***CHECK.***
- I would have to redo a grade because of all the missed time. ***CHECK.***
- I was light years ahead of the curriculum. ***CHECK.***
- I could get a job and make enough money to get out from under. ***MAYBE CHECK.***

They were both smiling at me with plastic grins, waiting for an answer.

The reasons to stick it out popped up:

- I know what kind of jobs dropouts got in this town. ***CHECK, CHECK.***
- I wouldn't have to go door-to-door preaching. ***CHECK.***
- I would never become a world-saving scientist if I quit. ***CHECK.***

"Question?" I said, raising my right hand.

The fake grins slipped. The "guidance counselor" answered first.

"Yes, Cam, what?"

"If I drop out, can I still go to college?"

"Sure—" he began.

"This system of things won't last long enough for you to go to college," the mom said. "Jehovah God wants us to forget worldly things and spend our time in the preaching and teaching work. We have been over this many times and I don't know why you won't understand. You are so willful. You know this world doesn't have much time. You need to get on the righteous path, or you will find yourself dead along with all the wicked men at Armageddon. What will college do for you? After Armageddon, we will need real men. Real men who can clean, and build, and farm, not this fancy stuff that you read. And what money do you think we have for college?"

The counselor sat back from the intensity of the mom's response. His eyes went wide, and he looked confused. He nodded his head in agreement anyway.

I ached with the need to blurt out, "I could have gone to college with the insurance money you gave away." But I didn't.

Instead, I said, "I could get a job maybe, or go part time."

"Do you know how much college costs?"

"No."

"It costs a lot, and we don't have it, and you don't need it. You know I dropped out of school and I'm okay."

There it was. She wanted me to drop out. I looked to the guidance counselor. His fake smile went wider, showing some grey teeth.

I felt the promise I made to myself and to Dad slipping out of my grasp.

"You can always get your GED," he said. "Then you could go to community college."

Not once had this guy or one of his coworkers ever engaged me to discuss my future. Was it because of the mom and her religion? Was it because I was a social outcast? Was I marked as some sort of a loser? Was I marked as stupid? Why didn't anyone ever intervene? Where was this guy when I was insulted, hit, ignored, bullied?

I let the room grow uncomfortable. The words of my teacher, Mrs. Howse, rang in my head. "You are smart and funny and kind, and you can do and be anything you want."

Yea, Mrs. House, maybe. Maybe that's the nonsense you tell children to keep them hopeful. Maybe the die is already cast for us poor kids. More likely I was destined to become another statistic. Despite this school and the teachers in it, I knew math and I knew odds, and it wasn't looking good for me. Mrs. Howse, how do I keep the faith when everyone in my orbit tells me the world will end soon? How do I keep the faith when even the people paid to help me give up?

Hell, most days I believed Armageddon was going to happen just like the JWs said. Hear something enough, and it burns into your DNA. The drone from all the adults in my life was the same, and it sure wasn't, "Be anything you want to be." It was, "Keep your head down, don't think for yourself, obey what your mother and the Jehovah's Witnesses tell you, and maybe, just maybe, you will live to be on the post-Armageddon clean-up crew."

I dunno, Mrs. Howse, maybe I could be anything, but I'm not seeing the how of it. Mrs. Howse, I wish I could ask your advice. I wish there was somebody, anybody to ask. Sometimes books aren't enough.

Dad, I wish you were here. But you're not.

I'm so tired of the fight.

"Fine."

"Fine what, Cam?" the counselor asked with his I'm outta here at 3:01 pm, fake-ass smile. The more I thought about the near-zero level of help I received from the school, the angrier I got.

Could I have done more to fit in, to work within the limits of the school? Maybe. I dunno, I was a kid. Why did I have to figure all this out on my own? Why was I being pushed into quitting? Why no intervening steps? No advice, no real counsel, no special help, no advanced classes, no mentoring? Nada? Zero? Zilch?

My face was hot and getting hotter. Anger and bile were welling up in my throat. I wanted to break something. Maybe the Soviet-era desk, maybe the chair, maybe his doughy, ashen face. It took everything I had, but I pushed down the urge. It formed into a ball of steel in my stomach. The ball turned into a sun of clarity that cut through my body, leaving resolve in its wake.

Through clenched teeth I seethed, "I don't know where I'm going or how I'll get there, but I'm sure as hell not going to do it in this school, FYI. I quit."

The mom slapped the book from my hands, startling me.

"Always with a book in front of your face. Don't you dare think that dropping out means you can lay around all day reading, because it doesn't. Jehovah despises the lazy."

"Lazy? I've been looking for a job every day and everywhere."

And I had. I'd filled out countless applications. Outside of a few days as a laborer and one of the JWs hiring me to help him side a house, the longest job I'd found was a one-week gig helping conduct a parts inventory at a factory. To complicate the job search, I didn't have any transportation other than my beat-up bike, so any job I did find had to be close.

"If you don't get a job, you're going to have to go door-to-door full time."

I left the hot apartment.

I walked through the chilled retail air of the Oxford Valley Mall, past the Orange Julius, Merry-Go-Round, and Spaceport on the hunt for Help Wanted signs. I spied one at a kiosk called The Electronics Boutique. They sold calculators, digital watches, and Atari game cartridges. I approached the professionally dressed lady working behind the counter.

"Hi, I saw the sign. Are you hiring?"

"Yes, we are. You can fill this out, and I can interview you right now if that's convenient. We need someone right away."

Score, I thought, as she passed over a clipboard and pencil.

"That's great because I need a job right away."

As I worked my way down the application, I stopped cold at the education section: High School — Year Graduated. The accompanying *Yes* or *No* check boxes stared up at me, daring me. If only there was a third box: *No, but give the kid a shot.*

No such luck.

Such a small thing, checking the *Yes* box. Out of frustration, desperation, embarrassment, or all three, I checked it with a little deceitful check. As usual, one lie led to another, and I used the provided number two liar's pencil to write additional falsehoods on the application.

"Let's take a look. You live close, that's a plus," the woman said, working her way through my responses. "Not much work experience, but we are a young company and willing to train. You graduated last year so that makes you?"

Lies create more lies, and on and on it goes. "Nineteen," I lied.

"When can you start?"

"Today."

"Aren't you eager! I like that. Do you like video games? Do you know Atari?"

"I love Atari, and I know everything there is to know about Atari." On and on it goes, and where the lies stop, nobody knows.

"Looks great. We will give you a call to let you know."

The phone rang two days later. I became the newest Electronics Boutique employee. I was learning that you did what you had to do to survive.

Lies aside, things were looking up.

16

WORN BOOKS, NEW SHOES

"You're fired," Mr. Kim said.

The company owner, Mr. Kim, the regional manager, and a middle-aged woman clutching a large purse were standing at the kiosk shooting me a trio of angry glares.

"What? Why?" I said.

"This customer has been waiting to make a purchase for over an hour, and you weren't here to help her," he clipped, raising his voice.

"An hour? That's not possible."

But it was possible. I'm not sure what I expected, but sitting in a kiosk in the middle of a mall was awful. The first week, I sold one calculator and one Atari cartridge. The second week, I brought books to the store. I kept my book out of view, just below the counter. After three weeks of navel and novel contemplation, I was so bored, I took to locking up the kiosk and taking extended breaks to hang out with Stan, perusing books at Dalton Books and talking model making at Allied Hobbies. The surprise visit of the owner caught me playing hooky.

Stan Crowner was a friend I made at the Kingdom Hall. Stan was smart, and a reader. He was socially awkward, and he believed there were two classes of people, the "norms" and the "golden people." According to Stan, the "golden people" were the good-looking stupid people who always got whatever they wanted with minimal effort. The "norms," while smarter, were deprived of their just desserts by the unfair advantages held by the "golden people." He quickly categorized me as an ally in the norms vs. golden people war.

Besides a love of books, Stan and I shared a love of comics, music, and science fiction. He was a few years older than me, and he had a driver's license and a beater car. Regularly, we loaded up his car with snacks, drinks, and a stack of America, Steely Dan, Grateful Dead, and Eagles eight track tapes and took a drive to the Gwinit Valley Used Book Store. We spent the two-hour drive debating everything from the best episodes of Star Trek to what superpower was best.

The bookstore was a slice of heaven. I spent most of my browsing time in the Sci-Fi room, where thousands of well-read paperbacks were lined up on the rough wooden shelves. I was drawn to Sci-Fi novels of the 40s and 50s because of their bright covers depicting brave spacemen rescuing buxom blondes from many-tentacled aliens. The covers appealed to my burgeoning sexuality, jumping out at me like jewels amidst the darker-toned novels.

The bookstore sold paperbacks at seventy-five percent off the cover price, so I looked for the oldest paperbacks since they originally cost a quarter or fifty cents. The best part about the store was the trade policy. When you finished reading the books, you could bring them back for store credit. It was a perpetual loop of buying, reading, and returning. I read hundreds of books for an initial twenty dollar spend.

On one of our bookstore trips, Stan and I reignited our strongest superhero debate.

"I'm gonna go with Wonder Woman," I said.

"What? That's ridiculous. Last week you said Batman. and now Wonder Woman? Are you rotating through the Justice League to piss me off, or are you simple? How could Wonder Woman possibly beat Superman?"

I liked to mix it up just to mess with him.

"With her super-sexiness, of course, duh. She can get Superman to do anything she wants. Have you even seen Linda Carter? I mean, come on!"

"Even if I give you the Linda Carter version of Wonder Woman, there is no way Superman would do anything she tells him."

"Wouldn't you?"

"No, I wouldn't."

"Yeah, sure you wouldn't. If she were here right now and asked you for your car in exchange for an over-the-bra touch, we would be walking home, and you know it."

"Not a chance. I'm not like that."

"Whatdaya mean you're not like that?"

For the entire car ride, he shot answers back faster than a speeding bullet, and now he was slow to respond.

"Um, I'm not sure I'm into girls like that."

"What's that even mean?"

"I mean, I love the way they look and smell and especially how they dress, but...they couldn't get me to do things, I guess…is what I'm saying."

"So Linda Carter doesn't turn you on?"

Stan took another multiple minute pause before he answered.

"Not the way she turns you on, maybe. I don't know. Let's drop it."

"Well, she makes me crazy."

"I do like the way she dresses, especially the high-heel shoes and her boots."

"Aha! You're a leg man."

"Sort of. I'm not sure how to say it. It's the shoes and other things."

"So you got a thing for high heels?"

Stan was a hand grenade and I had pulled the pin.

"Oh, yeah. I love them. I imagine what it would feel like to wear them. It…I dunno…I guess it turns me on a little."

He glanced over at me, checking my reaction.

"No judgment here. How come?"

"I have no idea, but just looking at dresses and stuff and imagining them on me gets me crazy, to use your word."

"That's cool, I guess," I said, not sure what to say.

"It's not so cool. My dad caught me trying to put on one of my sister's shoes and beat me with it."

"That's screwed up. Why would he do that?"

"He said it's perverted, and Jehovah God hates that sort of thing. He called me a faggot and a freak."

"Wow, nice mouth on him. Stan, my man, you're none of those things. I'm sure God has some bigger things to worry about besides caring about what type of shoes you wear. Maybe pop your dad back once or twice next time he gets to hitting you."

"Yeah, maybe next time I will."

Stan's father was an Elder in the congregation. Elders were considered the local bosses in the Jehovah's Witness hierarchy, and they could decide whether you were accepted by the congregation or accepted by your own family. Elders were obligated to set a righteous example for the congregation and were supposedly chosen by God for the position. While Elders and their families were expected to be examples, in my experience, being installed in the position simply gave them an impenetrable shield to do whatever they wanted. In the case of Stan's Elder father, that was being an abusive monster.

I witnessed the abuse firsthand on many occasions. Not only did he verbally abuse his wife, Stan, and Stan's two sisters, I saw him dish out physical abuse as well. The second time I stayed over at Stan's house, I saw his father push his youngest daughter into a wall, repeatedly. She was caught snuggling and kissing a girl. Homosexuality was considered one of the biggest sins, and some parents tried to beat it out of their children. If the beatings, prayers, and lectures didn't work, they were thrown out of the religion and the house. I wanted to do something to stop the abuse, but I was afraid of repercussions.

After Stan shared his secret and realized I wasn't judging him, he became comfortable talking about it and more relaxed in general. One evening when the mom was out, Stan stayed over. He helped himself to some things from the mom's closet, then came out of her bedroom in one of her skirts, with his big feet stuffed into a pair of her shoes. He paraded back and forth in front of our hallway mirror, smiling like I'd never seen him smile before. I'll admit, I didn't understand it, and I found it sort of funny, but I thought, hell, if David Bowie could do it, why couldn't Stan? It made him happy, and besides the seams on the mom's skirt and the leather of her shoes, he wasn't hurting anything.

I didn't like someone being punished for being who they were, so I approached Stan's father after a meeting.

"Brother Crowner, why is it a sin to have sex with someone of the same sex?"

Brother Crowner fidgeted with his tie, and after several false starts, he said, "Jehovah God finds it abhorrent."

"I don't see what harm it does," I said.

"I am taken aback by your question. Surely you have been taught the reasons God hates homosexual behavior. The brothers have spoken about it many times during the talks. If we open our Bibles to Leviticus 18:22…"

He stared at me, neutral faced, waiting. That was my cue to take out my Bible and open it to the book and verse. It took me a minute.

"...you will see it says, 'You must not lie down with a male in the same way that you lie down with a woman. It is a detestable act.'"

"Yeah, I know the verse, but I'm asking why. Why is it a detestable act?"

"We are not to question the word of Jehovah God. Why are you asking about this? Are you feeling unclean desires toward men?" He took a step back from me like I might be contagious.

"No. I like girls. I want to understand why God hates it so much. It seems the Bible approves of a lot of awful things, like war and slavery, but the Bible and the publications make homosexuality seem like it's worse than murder."

"That type of unclean activity causes disease and death."

"But can't you get diseases from boy-girl sex? That's the same reason the Elders give for abstaining from straight premarital sex, right?"

"Yes, that's why you should stay a virgin until you marry."

"So if I understand what you're saying, if two virgin men have sex like a virgin straight couple, then the disease thing isn't an issue?"

"Maybe you should discuss this with your mother."

He turned a fine shade of pink and desperately looked around, hoping to find the mom. I pressed on.

"What about two women? That verse says men, right? So, is it okay for two girls?"

"Jehovah God hates the sin of homosexuality no matter if it's men or women."

"But it says men in the Bible."

"The book of Leviticus has many rules, and we must use the guidance of the Watchtower Organization and its heavenly representatives, the governing body, to understand them."

This was a non-answer, and I wasn't having it.

"Let me make sure I understand. We should obey the laws in Leviticus about men with men, and we should add in women with women?"

He shifted uncomfortably. "Yes."

Time to rip off the hypocrisy cover.

"So, then, what about shaving?" I asked.

"What? What about shaving? What does that have to do with what we're discussing?"

"Should men shave? According to the Bible, I mean?"

"If you're asking me if it's okay to have a beard, then no. We shave to show a clean professional look, to show glory to Jehovah, and show a good example to the world."

"But what about Leviticus 18:27, a few verses down from the men lying with men rule?"

I waited until he found the verse.

"Lemme read it for you, brother, and I am reading it directly from the Bible. It says, 'You must not shave.'"

He shifted his weight from side to side, like a scale trying to find its center.

"...um, not all of the laws in that chapter apply to us. Let us turn to ... um...that's not for us...hang on a sec...umm."

I pressed on. "Aren't they in the same book of the Bible? A few verses away?"

"Pray and Jehovah will guide you."

He snapped his Bible closed and hurried away. I had more questions, including one about not eating shrimp and lobster as another verse in Leviticus commanded, but Elder Crowner was done with me and the conversation.

That same month, a young girl from a local congregation went to the Elders for help. She was being sexually abused by her father, who was also an Elder. A judicial hearing was convened. Nothing happened to the girl's father. The police were not called, and he remained an Elder. According to the JW rules, you can only be proven guilty if there are two witnesses to your wrongdoing, and they both testify to your guilt. Of course, the poor girl was alone with her father when he abused her. According to the Elder committee, and JW law, no witnesses, no crime.

Not long after my encounter with Stan's father, Stan stopped hanging out with me. After I bugged him for weeks, he agreed to a trip to the used bookstore. Driving past the miles of farmland, Stan let me know what was what.

"My father doesn't want me to be friends with you."

"Why?"

"He says you are a bad influence."

"Me? What did I do?"

"Those things we did with the clothes were evil and wicked."

"We? If you recall, I wasn't the one who put on my mother's heels. What's going on here?"

"You need to promise me that you will never say anything about what happened."

"Of course I would never say anything to anyone. That's your business. Besides, my mother would know it was you that ruined her shoes."

I laughed, trying to break the serious mood that hung like smoke in the car.

"I'm dead serious. Jehovah God hates what I did, and I can never do that again."

"It's not a big deal—"

"Don't say that. It is a big deal. I will die at Armageddon if I ever do that again."

"Not sure I believe any of that Armageddon stuff, Stan."

"If you don't, then I can't be around you, and you will most certainly die at Armageddon."

I didn't know what to say to this version of Stan. We drove the rest of the way in silence with the music of Steely Dan filling in for our usual nerd banter. We barely spent fifteen minutes at the bookstore before Stan wanted to leave. The ride home was painfully silent.

As we pulled up to drop me off, I said, "Stan, I know you. You are not evil or wicked. You are not what your father says you are. What you did or do with the shoes and clothes is no big deal."

"That's Satan talking."

"It's not—"

"Get outta my car," he yelled.

I got out.

He reached over and pulled the passenger door closed with a slam and sped off.

Stan never spoke to me again. I saw him at the meetings, dutifully doing donation collection or sound mixing at the back of the Kingdom Hall. He never met my eyes, and I never once saw him smile. Word around the Kingdom Hall was that Stan wanted to be an Elder, just like his father.

Years later, I connected with Stan's sister. After their parents died, Stan withdrew, refusing to talk to anyone, even family members.

Stan spent the last years of his life living alone in his parents' home. They found him in one of the bedrooms, months after he died, surrounded by pill bottles, his Rhodes 88 electric piano, and stacks of hand-written sheet music of original piano compositions that no one ever heard.

When they found him, the paramedics couldn't tell where Stan ended and the carpet began. They were forced to cut him free. The wall next to his bed was covered with shelves. Filling those shelves were pairs and pairs of beautiful, designer high heels.

None of them were worn.

17

MEET CUTE

"Well, Buck, girls like to be impressed, but they don't want it to look like you're trying to impress them, and they will never let you know that they're impressed. They also want you to be in charge, but only when they want you to be."

It was the most confusing thing I'd ever heard. It was Sid's answer to my simple question: "How do you get a girl to like you?" Sid's answer was a mystery wrapped in a riddle baked into a puzzle.

"Huh?" I said.

You see, there was a girl, Marcy. Her light brown, curly hair bounced as she walked like it was trying to fly away but needed to return to kiss her delicate shoulders. Her smile made me think of Tinker Bell when she waved her wand and made the burst of sparkles on the *Wonderful World of Disney*. Her eyes radiated a soft kindness.

What I liked most about Marcy was the way she smelled. She left a scent trail of soap, perfume, shampoo, and just her that made me crazy. She smelled like the future. A future filled with a house, kids, family vacations, little league, dinner parties, and sex, lots of sex. Of course, I was a virgin, so that part was hopeful conjecture. Heck, I hadn't even kissed a girl yet, and the ladies were an absolute mystery to me.

I met Marcy, her brother Cal, and their mother at one of the conventions the JWs held a few times a year. Imagine four days of sitting in a big, hot convention hall while men on stage droned on and on for up to eight hours each day about how you'd better prepare for the death of everyone but JWs.

Cal and I talked a bit at the convention, and I was pleasantly surprised when he invited me to a party being held to celebrate Marcy's baptism. It was only the second time I'd been invited to a social event since the mom joined the JWs. I was not comfortable around groups of JWs. There was always a feeling that you were being watched because, honestly, you were. At the first sign of any behavior they considered "worldly" or unacceptable, or if you voiced a dissent to any of the teachings, you would find yourself in front of a "judicial committee" made up of the Elders in the congregation. They would pull you into their "court" when someone ratted you out for something as simple as wearing the wrong kind of clothes, listening to the wrong type of music, or, God forbid, messing about sexually. Being an independent thinker, I avoided these social events, but I considered Marcy's party worth the risk. If Marcy noticed me, the rest of the dream might fall into place.

What could possibly go wrong? I was a poor, seventeen-year-old high school dropout with limited social skills, dyslexia, a homemade haircut, and cheap, second-hand clothing. And acne. Did I mention the acne?

Guru Sid was my only hope.

"Brother, you can do this. All you have to do is wear your best clothes and remember to smile. You walk up to her and say —"

"Should I bring her a gift?"

"Yeah, girls love gifts and grand gestures. Aren't you flush with cash from the store gig?"

"Nope. I got fired, but I'll have a new job soon. Please continue. What do I say when I walk up to her?"

"First, start with a compliment, cause girls love those. Tell her she looks pretty, or you like her hair or somethin."

"I do like her hair. And the way she smells. What else?"

"Don't say anything else. Just drop one complement, smile, and walk away. That way it'll look like you don't care. For some reason they like that."

"That makes no sense. Why do they like it if you don't care? Are you sure about that part?"

"Buck, did you forget who you're talking to? I have no idea why, but it works, okay?" He smiled a toothy grin and nodded. "Also, talk to other girls and make sure she sees you do it. And laugh while you do."

When it came to love and the ladies, Sid did know. Sid had a way about him, a childish charm that made everyone, especially girls, instantly like him. He had an easy laugh that made everyone feel relaxed and intense, grey-green eyes that, when focused on you, made you feel heard. He was the most positive, easy-going person I knew. Since I'd dropped out, we were constant companions. We shared everything and trusted each other completely. He didn't believe the JW teachings either and was doing the absolute minimum to keep from getting pulled in front of a judicial committee and thrown out.

"You gotta bring her a gift. How much you got?"

"Maybe three or four dollars."

"That ain't gonna cut it, Buck. I'd give you some money, but I'm dead ass broke. Will your mom give you some cash for a gift?"

"No."

"Best get her a card at least."

The mom wasn't home. I made my move. I opened her wooden jewelry box, instantly memorizing the location of each piece so I could return things to their place. I lifted the top tray, revealing a small pile of costume jewelry in the bottom of the box. Surely the mom wouldn't miss one of these old broaches. I'd never seen her wear any of them. I felt a pin prick of guilt. I knew I should ask her before taking something to give Marcy, but if I did, I'd only be lectured about girls and the sin of lust and sex for hours and hours, and she would end up saying no. I selected a tin broach shaped like a daisy with yellow enamel filling in the pedals. Would Marcy like it? I had no idea, but it was something.

I hesitated for a moment, and almost put it back, but my guilt was pushed aside by thoughts of a smiling, grateful Marcy. Hopefully, she would see beyond its value. I wrapped it in a napkin and put it in my pocket with the card I'd bought her.

I parked my bike on the side of Marcy's house and took a moment to wipe the sweat from my forehead and smooth my hair into place. I'd made the seven-mile bike ride in record time, but the party was in full sway by the time I arrived. Cal saw me rounding the corner into the back yard.

He waved me over. "I'm glad you made it. Your pits are soaked. Do you want to dry off?"

I looked down at my sweat-stained armpits.

"Oh man, I can't let anyone see me like this. Can I use your bathroom?"

"Sure, come on."

I did the best I could to dry myself and make myself presentable. As I finished, there was a soft knock on the bathroom door.

"Hello, anyone in there?" came a gentle female voice.

"Yes, all done," I said, opening the door.

What a smile. It was brighter than Marcy's and framed by the cutest dimples I'd ever seen. Her eyes were a similar soft brown, bordering on hazel like Marcy's. She had a sprinkling of freckles across her nose and cheeks. She was thin, with an athletic build, and exhibited a sleek grace.

Marcy who? I thought and began writing reams of poetry to win her love, the words forming—

"Can I get past?"

"Oh, er, I'm... er, sorry…yes... sorry."

"Thank you," she said as I shifted to the side to allow her entry into the bathroom. As she squeezed past me, the same heavenly smell I'd associated with Marcy filled my head. I breathed her in as she pushed past.

She must have noticed me sniffing after her like a dog following a dinner bowl because she giggled as she closed the bathroom door. I was so taken with her that I didn't immediately feel the horrible awkwardness that was waiting for me and would hit in three, two, —

OH MY GOD, what is wrong with you? You sniffed her. AND SHE SAW IT. You are such a dork. Go. Hide. GO NOW.

I went outside into the backyard to see Marcy thanking everyone for the gifts and cards. Oh crap, the gift and card! I reached into my back pocket to find a wrinkled, damp card. I couldn't give it to her like this. Especially in front of everyone. I blew it. I crammed the card back into my pocket and backed away from the group as far as I could, trying to will myself transparent. I should have left. Instead, I stood there a frozen mess of anxiety and discomfort as the rest of the party socialized.

The girl I'd sniffed joined Marcy at the table in the middle of the yard.

"I want to thank my sisters, especially Trisha, for putting this all together," Marcy said. She turned and hugged the bathroom-encounter girl. So that was her sister!

Maybe I could talk to her.

No. Who did I think I was? Did I think I could come to a party like a normal kid? Who was I kidding, thinking a girl like Marcy or her sister would ever like me? Or any girl for that matter. I was a sweaty loser.

I got on my bike and left.

Sid was laughing. "So, Buck, are you telling me that you went there to hang out with Marcy, and you ended up liking her sister? That's something I would do."

"That about sums it up, yeah."

"Did you do the stuff I told you?"

"I never got the chance. I froze up and left. I blew it."

"Are you going to?"

"Going to what?"

"Man, are you deaf or just stupid? Are you going to see her again and go for it?"

"Who?"

"I don't know, Buck. You tell me. Whoever you like now, I guess." He gave me a deadpan look.

"Trisha. It's Trisha I like. I hope I get a chance to see her again. I'ma try my best to act normal around her."

"Good on ya, Buck! You deserve to be happy, but normal? You want to be normal? Forget normal, just be yourself. You know, one day you'll live at 10 Morning Glory Lane, and I'll live at 12 Morning Glory Lane, with our wives and kids. We'll be rich, fat, and happy, and every Sunday we'll barbecue together, and life will be grand. But until then, there are lots of girls that need kissing, so don't get locked down."

"I don't want any other girls."

"Oh boy."

"There's something special about Trisha. I don't know what it is, but since I saw her, I can't think of anything or anyone else."

"Wow, you got it bad. Okay, just be careful. You don't know how these things can go. I'ma look out for you."

"I wouldn't worry about it. We aren't in the same Kingdom Hall, so I'll probably never see her again anyway. Marcy comes sometimes, but I've never seen Trisha there. And I'm sure she doesn't want to hook up with a seventeen-year-old drop out."

The very next Sunday I was sitting in the Kingdom Hall, waiting for the two hours of doom droning to begin, when I looked up to see Marcy, Trisha, and her family entering a few rows ahead of me. Trisha was wearing a white blouse and a brown striped skirt, and I couldn't take my eyes off the way it clung to her thighs as she moved down the row. I looked up and she beamed a smile at me, releasing her dimples from their secret place.

I squirmed in my seat. Just a little smile made me want to jump out of my chair, sweep her up, and dance with her.

Act normal, Cam. You can do it.

The meeting started.

While the Elders droned on about Armageddon, I stole glances at the back of her head.

While the Elders talked of the millions of dead that would need burying, I fantasized about kissing her.

Act normal, Cam, act normal.

The meeting ended. I got up and made my way to the back of the hall and struck up a conversation with one of the more lenient JWs, a guy named Steve. We were talking about a new Stephen King novel we'd both read when Marcy and Trisha joined us.

Oh my god. What should I do? What do I say?

"Hi, ladies, this is my friend Steve. Not Steve as in Stephen King," I said.

What a dork.

"I love Stephen King's books," Trisha said.

She was a reader! Could it get any better?

"What book is your favorite?" I said.

Trisha leaned back against one of the folding chairs and I heard a rip. She smiled self-consciously and looked down at her leg. The chair had ripped a large hole in her stockings. She pretended it didn't happen and I pretended not to notice.

"Umm, I guess I'd say *The Stand*."

"That's one of my favorites. Have you read anything by Heinlein? There's this book called *Glory Road* that is by far his best, and wow it's great."

"No. Tell me about it," Trisha said.

I gabbed on and on about books and authors. She didn't run away. Instead, she fully engaged in the conversation and seemed to appreciate my book ramblings and recommendations. She even managed to slip in a few of her own when I paused for breath.

I suddenly remembered Sid's complement advice.

"I like your skirt," I said out of nowhere.

"Thank you. You are so sweet."

No one had ever called me sweet. It made me feel warm. Standing near her had a calming effect on my constant crush of self-criticism. For a moment I thought, maybe, just maybe, I had a chance.

The hall was emptying and it was time to go.

"Maybe we can talk again?" I said. "You know, about books and other things?"

"I would like that very much," Trisha said.

My heart swelled.

"Would you like to join us?" Trisha's voice over the phone line was like an angel's kiss on my forehead.

"Really?" I said. "You want me to go roller skating? With you?"

"Well, you know the way these things go. It will be a group thing, not just us. It will be Marcy, Jim, you, and me. Can we pick you up at 7:00?"

Trisha and I had spoken half a dozen times at meetings, and on the phone, but this would be a real live actual date. Or what passed for a date in the JW world.

"I would love to go."

Marcy's brown Plymouth Duster pulled up promptly at 7:00, and Marcy gave a little beep of the horn. I bounced down the stairs, stopping at the bottom to take a calming breath before opening the door. Marcy and Jim were in the front of the Duster, and Trisha was in the back. I joined her.

"I glad you could come," Trisha said.

"Thank you for inviting me," I managed to get out past my face eating smile.

"Have you ever skated at Rollarama?"

I had gone once and made a mess of myself, spending more time on the floor that on the skates. At six foot five, I was all legs, and I had a weird center of gravity.

"Oh sure. I've been plenty."

Trisha moved closer to me and our thighs touched. The heat of her leg warmed mine. Breath caught in my throat. Either she didn't know the effect she had on me, or she pretended not to notice. She lowered her hand and casually let her pinky touch my thigh.

"Umm…do you…umm…skate a lot?" I said.

She didn't answer right away. She tilted her head and moved her face closer to mine. I tilted mine until our mouths aligned.

I could feel the heat of her spearmint-scented breath on my lips as she answered. "No. Not a lot. But sometimes."

We inhaled as the other exhaled, the two of us sharing an infinite loop of breath. She moved closer, almost imperceivably.

"Oh." I moved my mouth closer to hers. "Only sometimes?"

"Yeah…sometimes."

I feared she could hear the beat of my heart as it quickened. Our eyes locked in an embrace and I swore I could see forever.

We kissed.

It may have been my first kiss, but I knew it was a perfect kiss.

We parted. I didn't want to.

"Wow," she said.

"Yeah. Wow," I said. "What now?"

"We go skating." She gave me dimples.

And just like that. I was in love.

18

THE GRAND GESTURE

In the months that followed, my calf muscles got huge from all the miles riding my bike to and from Trisha's house. Eventually, I saved up enough money from odd jobs to buy a beat-up Honda 550cc motorcycle that made the trip easier and expanded my job possibilities. Trisha was afraid to ride on the back, and anytime we wanted to go somewhere, we were required to have a chaperone, so we needed someone to drive us, a role usually filled by her brother Cal.

We spent countless hours talking and kissing. So much kissing. We talked about everything. Or, more accurately, Trisha would listen patiently as I went on and on about science, movies, art, and books. When our conversations turned to JW beliefs, she shared her terror at the thought of the "last days." Jehovah's Witnesses believed that before Armageddon, they would be locked up and tortured to try to force them to abandon their beliefs. The end of world teachings and fears that went along with them had taken deep root in her. If she had any doubts about the truthfulness of the teachings, she never expressed them. Selfishly, I didn't let her see my disbelief for fear of losing her.

In the JW world, you are only allowed to date if you're ready to marry. Dating for fun or pleasure was not permitted. We received flack for spending time together, but we countered by telling our parents we were never alone, and we were just friends.

Since Trisha was a true believer, I attended the meeting regularly. It made her happy, and it also took the parental and Elder surveillance down a few notches. Going to the meetings made the mom ecstatic, but it made me miserable. Sitting in the meeting hall listening to hours of monotonous end-of-the-world nonsense was torture. The only thing that made it survivable was allowing my hand to drift across the armrest of the chair and casually touch Trisha's hand. When I was particularly bored, I would close my eyes and imagine a time when we could be alone for longer than ten minutes. This had the unwanted effect of a swelling in my pants that was not easily hidden by the Bible on my lap.

Somehow, we talked Trisha's mother into allowing me to stay overnight at her house. We used the combo of "He's Cal's friend too" and "We want to go to the meeting together in the morning" to get the approval. I was shocked that her mom said yes, since I was certain she didn't like me. I got the vibe she saw right through my Jehovah's Witness believer-boy facade and was biding her time, waiting for evidence of my fraud.

After a pleasant day of hanging out with Trisha and her family and an evening of after-dinner TV, it was getting late.

"Time for bed," Trisha's mom said.

The family dog, a German Shepherd named Scout, got up from sleeping at her feet and yawned. No one made a move to get up.

"That means everyone. Let's go. We have an early start."

Trisha and Cal said goodnight and headed upstairs. Trisha's mom turned to me.

"We've got you all set up in the guest room," she said.

I headed into the guest room, and she followed, stopping at the door. As she was closing it, she gave me a look that read, *"Don't try any funny stuff."* Scout, sensing the messaging, added a side-eye look and a snuff.

"Sleep well," she said, staring at me to let the unsaid message sink in.

She closed the door, probably mentally willing it locked until morning. I imagined her as a dungeon master, casting *ARCANUS LOCKUS* with a wave of her wizard wand. The guest room door became a monolith of nope, protected by nothing more than motherly hope.

I tried to sleep. I really did.

The image of Trisha in bed only ten feet above my head drove me crazy. What was she wearing? Was she naked under her covers? Was she thinking about me? Was she as excited as I was?

How could I possibly sleep?

The idea hatched as an easily dismissed notion.

I should have dismissed it.

Nah, there is no way I could sneak up to see her.

Boy, oh boy, that would be amazing, though.

She is all warm and cozy in her bed. Probably naked or near enough.

No way I could do it, is there? Is there?

Boy, oh boy, that would be amazing.

Her mom is next store, and the stairs go right over her room.

But what if I COULD sneak up?

Boy, oh boy, that would be amazing.

I'd kiss her once real good and sneak back.

I would probably get caught. That would be bad.

Or would I? I'd be so, so quiet.

Couldn't I?

After fifteen minutes of silent internal struggle, a deep snoring emanated from Trisha's mom's bedroom.

Her mom was asleep!

Maybe it could be done.

I could always say I was going to the bathroom if I got caught.

Or sleepwalking.

Would she buy that?

Could I get away with it?

I imagined lying in bed with Trisha, her warm body pressed against mine, separated by the thinnest of pajamas. I imagined her smell, her soft, gentle hands touching me, teasing me as we softly and slowly kissed, her hand moving down my chest to the waistband of my sweatpants.

My body took over and I got out from under the blanket and went to the door. I placed my ear against it and willed my senses to detect each sound, every movement. I squeezed my eyelids tight, held my breath, and focused my will into a tunnel of detection. In that moment, I was superhuman with super senses. I was a nocturnal hunter on the prowl. I pressed my ear to the door. The thump, thump, thump of my racing heart, house creaks, and Trisha's mother's soft snoring found my ear. Nothing else was detectable to my super senses.

Was I going to stand there all night? I could still go back to bed. I should go back to bed. I wasn't yet committed to the quest.

My hand went to the doorknob. I paused and listened for changes in the sounds of the house. It took me five minutes to turn the knob fully to the left, my super senses hyper alert and tuned to the sounds of a waking mother. My heart was beating so hard that my T-shirt bounced on my chest in time. I felt like I was going to pass out. I wasn't breathing. I exhaled soundlessly and took in a new breath to hold.

With aching slowness, I stepped back from the door, pulling it open. I paused. No changes detectable in the pulse of the house. Do I dare leave the room? I really should stop my advance. So far I was not committed.

My body ignored the internal discourse and left the room, closing the door behind me. I walked one slow-motion step at a time into the living room. Another step. Another stop to listen. It took me ten minutes to walk the ten feet to the base of the stairs. I could still abort. I could make a dash to the bathroom if her mother woke up. But once I started up the stairs, there was no excuse in the world that would save me.

Again, my body dismissed all warnings, and without a conscious decision, my feet started up the stairs. I paused after each step and listened. My foot came down on stair number ten of twelve when—

CrEak.

Icy cold seized my body like a dive into a polar lake. Did she hear that? Was she awake? I couldn't hear anything over the beating of my heart.

Inside my head I screamed *ABORT, ABORT, ABORT*, but I couldn't move. My forehead broke out in a cold sweat. They would find me dead from a major coronary, frozen in a standing position, halfway to heaven. Trisha would cry when they found me. Her mom would nod a self-satisfied "*knew it*" as they took away my body.

I had to stop this madness. I turned around to start my return down the stairs to the safety of the guest room. A mound of what looked like clothing sat at the base of the dark stairs below me. How did I miss that on my way up? The mound moved. It wasn't clothing. Scout was sitting soundlessly at the base of the stairs looking up at me with a cocked head, tongue out. *Oh no!* If I went down would Scout let loose? One bark and no more Trisha, no more family, no more anything. One bark and I would be brought up on charges by the Elders and thrown out.

Every second I waited was a second closer to being caught on the stairs. I decided up was the way to go. As I turned back to make my way up the last two stairs, Scout padded up and passed me, stopping to wait by Trisha's bedroom door. Good boy, I telepathically messaged Scout. *Please, please, please, don't bark.* Scout nosed open the bedroom door and went inside. I followed.

I knelt next to the bed. Scout sat next to me. "What a good boy," I whispered. He licked my cheek.

"Trisha," I whispered.

She dimpled in the dim light of the room, her eyes closed.

"My mom is going to kill you, and then me, and maybe even Scout."

Scout made a quizzical woof.

"It's okay. I was quiet. So quiet."

"You're crazy."

The Cameron from the other dimension who knew what to say yelled over the fence. I listened.

"Crazy about you."

I swear she glowed.

Scout seemed to approve and hopped up on the bed. I followed him up and under the covers. Trisha pulled me in close. Every part of my body begged to touch every part of hers. Even in the dim of the room, I saw the sparkle in her eyes as we hugged face to face. I absorbed the smell of her and let it fill my soul. Her hand came up to rest on my cheek, my hand tangled into her hair. I drew her to me. We kissed the kind of kiss that connects more than just the lips.

"What now?" she whispered against my neck as she rubbed her thigh against me. I could feel her lips smile.

"What now?" I pushed back against her thigh.

I kissed her again. Longer.

Her body stiffened and she pulled away. Oh no. What did I do? Did I do something wrong? Did I read the signals wrong?

She yanked the side of my head to her mouth and whispered the last words any boy in that situation wants to hear.

The word came out like the hiss of a deadly snake.

"HIDE."

I'm not saying I actually have super speed or invisibility. But if a camera had recorded the events that occurred in the bedroom that night, it would have captured the fastest, quietest movement of a human ever recorded. Just sayin.

In one movement, I rolled out from under the covers and soundlessly lowered myself to the side of the bed not visible from the door. I somehow managed to fit all six feet four inches of myself under the bed. Now, if we were to examine the facts and footage, there was no scientific way I could have fit under that bed. I just did. Just sayin.

Seconds later, the room pressure changed as Trisha's mom opened the door to the bedroom. The light clicked on. I could see her slipper-clad feet from my impossible under-the-bed position.

"Are you awake?" her mother asked.

"Yes."

"Everything okay? I heard noises."

"It was just Scout. He woke me up."

Silence filled the room while Trisha's mother considered her daughter's answer.

"Okay…Goodnight then."

"Nite."

The light turned off. Her mother dallied in the doorway, listening and looking with her own super senses. She slowly closed the door. I sensed her on the other side of the door, silent, listening. After a few minutes, the stairs creaked as she went back down to bed. I had a terrifying moment trying to remember if I'd closed the guest room door. If I hadn't, I would know soon enough. I waited under the bed for over an hour before making my way back downstairs to the guest room.

The next morning at breakfast, nothing seemed out of the ordinary except Trisha wouldn't look at me. I was exhausted, and I was sure it showed on my face.

Her mother stared at me and asked the table, "How did everyone sleep?"

I returned her stare, trying to appear innocent and enthusiastic. "Like a baby."

Trisha's mother's gaze stayed on me. "How about you, Trisha?"

Trisha stared down at her breakfast as if the eggs held secrets. "Fine."

Later that day, Trisha got me alone.

"When we kiss, I feel so guilty. What we did last night is wrong. We're going to be destroyed at Armageddon for sure."

"I'm sorry, but I have to ask; do you believe that? Really? Do you believe God will kill us for kissing?"

"The Bible, the society and the Elders tell us —"

"Yes, but do you believe that? Seriously? Do you think the maker of the universe, the creator of the whole sha-bang cares if our tongues touch?"

"The Bible is clear. If we aren't married, then it's a sin and of Satan."

"What if we got married?"

"But we aren't."

"We could get married."

"We can't do that. My mother would never allow it."

"Aren't you old enough to make that decision for yourself? Do you love me?"

"I do love you."

"And I love you. Isn't that what it's all about?"

"Marry you? Like for real? I can't do that."

"Why not."

"I just can't. My mother..."

"Your mother what?"

"She doesn't like you."

There it was. I already knew it, but there it was, out in the open.

"Why?"

"She says you're not spiritual enough and you don't follow Jehovah's ways and the society's teachings. She says you will never be a good provider or a spiritual leader in the congregation."

I guess my acting wasn't as good as I thought.

"I see. Do you feel that way?"

She wouldn't answer, but I did see. She was a prisoner to the JW beliefs and to her mother's approval. Despite that, maybe her mother was right. I was a high school drop-out with nothing to my name. Trisha could and probably should find someone better.

Only six months had passed since we first met, but my love for her was as real as anything I knew. I couldn't bear the thought of losing her.

"I know I'm young and I don't have anything now, but I will. I may not be the best spiritually and all that, but one thing I know is that I love you, and I would do anything for you, and that's got to mean something, even to God and your mother. These past six months have been the happiest I've ever been. That's because of you. I think you feel the same way. I'm sorry you feel so guilty when we kiss. I didn't know how that made you feel."

I hugged her and continued. "I couldn't help myself last night. You make my body and heart sing, and I had to be close to you. I love your kindness, your gentleness, your grace. Through your eyes I've seen myself differently, and that's reinforced my desire to become more than I am. I know this is special. I know it in my heart."

"You're special to me and I do love you. I just need time." Her eyes were wet.

"Sure. How much time?"

"I don't know."

"An hour? A week? A Month? Ten years?"

"I...I don't know. Please lower your voice."

"Can I see you next Saturday night? Is that enough time? We can talk more then?"

"Sure, I mean, yes."

I was not going to give up on a future with her without a fight.

Saturday night came. Trisha's brother Cal drove us into the Pennsylvania countryside for our 7:30 reservations at the Cock n' Bull Restaurant.

"This place is fancy and expensive," Trish whispered with her hand over her mouth.

"Don't worry, I have it covered."

"Thank you," Trisha said, ever the proper lady.

In fact, I didn't have it covered. I had borrowed money to cover the evening.

I ordered us two glasses of champagne. It was the first time I'd ever ordered alcohol. I was grateful that our waitress didn't ask me for ID.

I raised my glass and offered it for a clink. "To us."

"We don't do that," she said, shaking her head no.

"We don't do what?"

"We don't toast. It's pagan and Jehovah's people don't do it."

"Oh, I didn't know. Sorry."

"That's okay."

This rule was a new one to me. So many rules. Could I really obey them all for the love of a woman? I lowered my glass and smiled, trying to put the slip-up behind us and keep the mood right. A little small talk later, and the champagne combined with the warmth of the fireplace near our table was putting just the right amount of distance between us and the real world. We both relaxed into the evening.

"Last weekend I made you feel uncomfortable and I'm sorry for that," I said.

"It wasn't all your fault. I was there as well."

"I want you to know that I love you for more than, you know, more than the physical things. You have been so kind and patient with me. I love how you look at the world and how you look at me. I like how I feel about myself when I'm with you. Does that make any kind of sense?"

Trisha blushed. I continued.

"I've been thinking a lot about us this week, and I realized that when I brought up the subject of marriage it wasn't done in the best way possible."

Trisha dimpled up and giggled.

"Maybe not."

I reached into my pocket and brought out the grand gesture I'd purchased on borrowed money. I pushed my hand to the middle of the table, took a deep breath, and opened the ring box.

"Trisha, will you marry me?"

19

MONIKERS

Sid didn't believe his ears. "You did what?"

"You heard me."

"I was hoping I heard ya wrong. Are you crazy?"

"No. Just in love."

"Same thing, Buck, same thing. What'd she say? As if I can't tell from your face."

"She said she couldn't."

"Way I see it, there's only two answers to that question. It's a yes, or it's a no."

"No, then, I guess."

"I'm sorry, Buck. I know you feel a lot for the girl. You okay?"

"No."

"You will be, you will be. Can you get an ID?"

"What do you mean?"

"A fake ID. You need to be nineteen for what I got in mind. Can you get one?"

"I don't know how to get one. Do you? And why?"

"Don't worry about it. I got peeps. Lemme see what I can do."

A week later Sid handed me a real New Jersey driver's license. Different name, but based on the listed personal details, he could have been me, minus a few inches of height. A picture on your license was not a thing at that time, so virtually anyone with access to a license that fit their description could use one as a fake ID. I was now Kevin Folmer, born on December 26th. I bet his parents were upset that he missed being a Christmas baby by one day, and he had to be miffed that his gift count was reduced by his birthday's proximity to Christmas.

"Do not lose that. I have to give it back next week."

"I won't."

"I finish work at seven, so be ready to go tomorrow night around nine."

"Go where?"

"You'll see. By the early hours of Saturday, it will be Trisha who."

Sid pulled up at 9:45 and hit the horn of his cherry-red Gran Torino. It was identical to the car from *Starsky and Hutch.* Sid worked hard for that car. He was the new guy at *Hooker Chemical,* and the new-guy job was cleaning out chemical vats. Each day for eight hours, ten with overtime, Sid put on a protective suit with an air hose and wooden soled shoes. They lowered him into a giant metal vat, and it was his job to scrub down the walls. They couldn't let the vat cool below a certain temperature or the sludge of chemicals on the vat walls would harden and ruin the vat. Because of the heat and toxicity, Sid could only spend ten minutes at a time scraping the walls down with an industrial sized squeegee before they had to lift him out. His workday was a rhythm of ten minutes in the vat, and ten minutes out to let him and the shoes cool down. He repeated this all day, with two fifteen-minute breaks and thirty minutes for lunch.

"How was work?"

"Sucked. If I don't get offa vats soon, I'm gonna quit. I can't do it anymore."

"I bet. I couldn't do what you do."

"No shit, you're too tall. And besides, white boys don't have to do it. White boys get an easier job when they start. It's only brothers like me that get stuck on the vats."

"That makes no sense. Why do they make the brothers do it?"

"Are you for real right now?"

"That's not fair. Everyone should have to do it. That's just wrong."

"Yes, my brother, it sure as hell is. Enough of that shit. You got the ID I gave you, right?"

I pulled it out of my pocket and held it up.

"I'm guessing we're going to a bar?"

"We sure are, Buck. First, a little quiz. When were you born?"

"February —"

"Wrong! When was the other you born?"

"Oh. December 26th."

"Good, what's your name?"

"Easy, Kevin Folmer."

"Good. What's your address?"

"Crap."

I pulled the license closer to read it in the dim car.

"Yea, crap. If you get asked this stuff and you don't know it, they will not let you in, and they'll take Kevin's license, and that will not be good for either one of us." Sid turned on the cab light. "You have about fifteen minutes to learn all about the new you."

"You could have given a brother some notice?"

"Didn't I give it to you near a week ago?"

I read and re-read the driver's license info, committing it to memory.

"I got it now. Go ahead and test me."

"What's your sign?"

"My what?"

"Your astrology sign. What's your sign?"

"I have no idea. Will they ask me that?"

"They might. Bouncers like that one. It trips folks up. Let's just hope they don't ask, cause I don't know December's either."

"Where we going?"

"We're going for pizza."

"Then why do I need this ID? I thought we were going drinking?"

Sid laughed. "We are. We're going to Pepe's Pizza and Beer," he said. "After ten, they clear the tables and make room for dancing. They have a killer sound system, a great DJ, and the girls are smokin. Gonna make you forget all about Trisha."

"Dancing?" Anxiety gripped me. "I don't dance."

"You will."

"I don't think so, no."

"Yeah...You will."

The door into Pepe's was filled by a wall of flesh. A name on the flesh wall's shirt identified it as Tiny, because of course. All that concern about getting me past the door was unnecessary. Tiny barely looked at "my" license as he nodded his chin beard toward the inside. Sid was next up. Sid handed over his license. Tiny did not give Sid the same nod, because of course.

"Where are you from?"

Sid gave Tiny his best "I'm no threat" smile.

"Right up the street in Willingboro."

"I've never seen you here before."

"I was here last Friday. You weren't at the door."

Tiny considered this.

"What's your sign?"

"I don't think we're compatible."

"What did you say?"

"Aquarius. I said Aquarius." SMILE.

"Driver's license number?"

Sid rattled off his license number.

Tiny looked from Sid to me and back. "Okay, funny guy, are you and your boyfriend here going to be a problem?"

I shook my head *no*.

Sid laughed. "Only if you run outta beer."

Tiny looked trumped. He handed Sid back his license and waved him in.

"What was that all about?" I asked, as we made our way to the bar.

"You still don't get it, do you? If you weren't with me, he probably woulda found a reason to not let me in."

"How do you put up with that bullshit?"

"Practice."

We went to the bar.

"Hi, I lima kaddasy," she yelled at me over the bass throb of "Another One Bites the Dust" by Queen.

"What?" I yelled back.

She gripped my arm like her hand was a carnival claw machine and my arm was the prize. She pulled my head to her mouth.

"I'm Kathy," she yelled, blowing out my right ear. Her breath smelled of wintergreen gum and beer.

"Oh. I'm Cam."

"Hi Ken, nice to meet you," she yelled, ruining the remaining hearing in my ear.

"No. Cam, not Ken."

"Right. Ken. Got it."

"No, it's...never mind."

Her grip tightened on my arm. She dragged me toward the dance floor.

"No, I don't..."

No use. I was in the middle of the dance floor trying not to spill my plastic cup of beer while being struck by a whirlwind of dancer's arms. The boom of each bass note hit me in the chest, and each *"Hey Hey"* from Freddie Mercury's lips pierced my head. Illuminated by the flashing dance floor lights, I caught a glimpse of Sid through the crowd. His eyes were closed, and joy was etched on his face as he danced.

My mother's voice played in my head. *"Don't be like worldly people with all their drinking, and drugs, and sexy dancing. That's the way Satan gets you."*

The beer was winning, and my mother's voice was getting fainter. Maybe it was the alcohol, the look on Sid's face, Freddie's lyrics, or the smile of my new friend, but I gave in and danced. Timidly at first, then with more confidence when I realized nobody was watching or judging. I moved my feet and legs to the beat and tried to duplicate the moves of the dancers around me. As the song played, I gave in to the beat. I discovered I liked dancing. On second thought, I loved dancing.

Queen's, "Another One Bites the Dust" changed into "Take Your Time, Do It Right" by the S.O.S. Band. Somehow, maybe by magic or some other yet unknown voodoo, the DJ seamlessly changed the song, keeping everyone dancing on beat. As the chorus dropped, the entire dance floor cheered and sang along. Kathy threw her head back and sang along at the top of her lungs. As the chorus ended, she returned from wherever the song had taken her and gave me a hungry-eyed look. She came in closer, grabbed my ass with both hands, and pulled me against her crotch. I was overcome by embarrassment and pulled away. I looked around. No one was looking. No one cared. There was no judgement here, just joy.

We danced for thirty minutes until Kathy gave me a head nod to leave the dance floor. Her hands all over me, she led me outside.

"Ahh, the air feels so good. It's so hot in there. You're a great dancer, Ken."

"Thank you. So are you," I said looking down self-consciously.

"Oh my God, are you blushing? Did I make you blush? Are you a shy boy?"

"I dunno, I guess, maybe?"

"Come with me, shy boy."

She grabbed my arm and coaxed me to the side of the building, out of the sight of the doormen at the entrance. She grabbed my head with both hands, locked a leg around me, and kissed me. Beer and wintergreen overwhelmed me. I was certainly no kissing expert, having only kissed one girl, but I wasn't a big fan of what she was doing. Her mouth was looking to swallow mine, and her tongue was a separate living thing, pushing in like a snake through leaves. Her kissing was so wet and slobbery that my nose got wet. She pulled back to spit out her gum. I tried to say something to extradite myself from her wet attack, but before I had a chance, her tongue was back inside my mouth, everywhere all at once.

"Time," I managed to mumble out past her tongue as I pulled away, making the letter T symbol with my hands.

"What's wrong shy-boy Ken?"

"Nothing's wrong. I just —"

"You have a girlfriend? It's okay, I have a boyfriend, so we're even-steven."

"Um, no. It's just that I want to dance some more."

"Oh. Okay, shy-boy Ken, let's go dance some more, but you need to buy me a drink first."

"Sure, and my name is Cam, not Ken."

"Whatever, shy boy."

After dancing to a few more songs, Kathy must have sensed my disinterest and drifted off to find someone else more likely to enjoy her slobbering. I made my way through the crowd to the DJ booth and parked myself next to it to watch the DJ.

"Excuse me."

The DJ gave me the one-minute finger as he changed the song.

"What do you want to hear?"

"Nothing. I want to know how you do that."

"Do what?"

"How do you make two different songs go together and keep the beat the same?"

"Mix?"

"Yea, mix. How do you do that?"

"With the mixer."

"What's a mixer?"

There are some moments of kindness that change our lives.

The DJ opened the half door entrance into the DJ booth.

"Come on in and I'll show you. I'm Joey."

"Cameron." We shook hands.

"These are the turntables and this, in the center, is the mixer. You use the mixer to raise the volume of one record as you lower the volume of the other."

"How do you mix them so they sound like each other?"

"That's the fun part."

Joey spent the next hour showing me the basics of DJing. He explained how to line up two different songs using the instrumental intros and breaks put into dance records. He explained how you can increase and decrease the speed of the records through the night to control the dance floor energy. He did this while juggling requests and drinking a fair amount of vodka.

"It looks like you love this."

"Do you know any other jobs where you get paid to drink, play music, and talk to girls?"

"Besides rockstar? No, I don't. How do you get a job doing this?"

"Get yourself a set of turntables, some records, and practice. Practice a lot. When you're ready, DJ a few house parties to see how you do with a crowd."

"How did you get this job?"

"The owner had no choice."

"How's that?"

"My dad owns the joint."

On the drive home from Pepe's, I announced my new career intentions.

"I'm going to be a DJ."

"Good on ya, Buck. What's your plan?"

That's what I loved about Sid. There was never even a word of doubt or disbelief. If I'd announced that I was going to be a rocket, he'd have built me a gantry and started a countdown.

"I'm gonna get two turntables, a mixer, and some records, and I'ma practice mixing. I'll get good, and then I'll find a place that will let me DJ. I need to go listen to more DJs and learn all the music."

"I like it. We need to hit some more clubs. When you get your first gig, I'll come and get all the ladies dancing. We will rock it Sid and Cam style."

"Deal."

"Deal."

We shook on it.

"My DJ name is Cameron Alexander."

"Alexander? Why not use your real last name?"

"It's my middle name and my dad's first name."

"I love it."

DJ Cameron Alexander was conceived.

20

YELLOW BRICK ROAD TRIP

The grungy white awning of 315 Bowery advertised the space as CBGB and OMFUG. I had no idea what it meant, but it sounded exotic. Studded-leather-jacket-wearing punks, "normies," and what could have been homeless people but might have been band members of the next big thing crowded the street in front of the entrance.

"Yo, bros, this place looks sketchy as hell," Sid said.

"So, what does CBGB mean? Is it short for something?" Gordon asked.

"I don't know what it stands for. All I know is Jerry said we should check it out," I replied.

"Do they let brothers in there?" Sid asked.

"Look, that guy coming out is black," I said.

"Yea, but he's got a mohawk," Gordon said.

"Can you two get your hair into Mohawks real quick?"

"Sid can, cause his fro is big as hell," Gordon said.

"Don't be busting on my fro, son. Look at your nappy-headed ass," Sid said.

"This isn't nappy." Gordon ran his hands over his hair. "This here is Nubian natural, and the ladies love it."

The New York City trip became an obsession of mine after a conversation with Jerry the DJ at an after-hours club. He said that if I wanted to understand the club scene, I had to go to New York City and feel it live. He rattled off a list of clubs to check out from disco to punk.

CBGB was our third try of the night to find a place to party, and we were frustrated. Our first stop was Studio 54. What we didn't know, and Jerry didn't know, is that Studio 54 had closed its doors for good. I should have verified the list before convincing Sid and Gordon to go on a road trip, but there we were, banging around New York City like the country bumkins we were. Gordon didn't care about Studio 54 being closed, but Sid and I were bummed.

Gordon was Sid's friend from work. I was introduced to him at one of our Friday night hangs at a local bar called the Woodshed Inn. Gordon and I hit it off instantly. If there was one word that summed up Gordon, it was charming. Gordon's smiling eyes, perfect teeth, and happy mannerism were magnetic and contagious. Sid joked that Gordon was so charming, he could "charm the habit off a nun."

Our second stop of the night was a place called Electric Circus on Fifth Avenue. Despite what I'd been told about New York City's door policies and strict dress codes, we got in easily. We realized why as soon as we walked into the club. It was three floors of nearly empty space. We ordered some overpriced drinks and sipped them, waiting for more people to arrive. After forty-five minutes of navel gazing, we bid a goodbye to the lone girl dancing on the cavernous dance floor and headed to the next club on the list.

We joined the CBGB door line. When the door opened, a crash of music pushed out like a Rottweiler straining against chains. The discordant sounds of guitar, drums, and synthesizer grabbed me and pulled me like a magnet pulls rusty iron filings.

The three of us traded glances. Sid and Gordon did little "no" head shakes while I counterpunched with an enthusiastic "yes" nod.

"Can we give it ten minutes?" I asked.

They looked like their minds were made up.

"Come on, guys. Just one drink and we're out. Please?" I pleaded.

"Yeah, okay," Sid said. "But you owe us big time for this trip and especially this place."

"And we need to talk about your list at some point," Gordon added.

We entered CBGB.

To say the place was dirty and loud is an injustice to the words *dirty* and *loud*. I wasn't prepared for the smell. Stale beer and cigarettes were the main notes. Added to the bouquet were subtle hints of hairspray and body odor. Rounding out the scent was what could best be described as wet, dirty wood. The floor held my feet with a sticky pull. It was the most revoltingly wonderful place I had ever seen or smelled. The raw, blaring notes flooding off the stage were the perfect soundtrack for the club's flyer and graffiti covered walls.

Without a look back at Sid and Gordon, I forced my way through the crowd to get closer to the stage. The band was playing what in some other multiverse might be called jazz. The melody, if you could find it, was random and unpredictable. The front guy was playing a small synthesizer. He stopped and picked up a clarinet and started, well, *wailing* is a better term than *playing*. Another band member played a horn as if he were responding to the clarinet. The guitar player looked down at his guitar to accuse it of not knowing how to play in tune and launched into a rhythm riff that might have been part of some other thing. The drummer sped up the beat and they finished close to the same time. The audience delivered a respectable amount of applause led by a small, vocal group directly in front of the stage.

The band kicked off the next song. It was a soundscape of bass and synth riffs with a thick funk beat. The guitar filled in a rhythm layer, and the crowd started to sway. I swayed with them. The clarinet player was doing a half-spoken, half-singing overlay. I didn't have a label for what I was hearing. It was new to my ears. New, like the first time you eat Sushi new, when, not knowing what it is, you smear the green stuff onto the piece and take a bite. The wasabi burn is off putting, but then the sweet, clean taste of the tuna comes through, joining with the burn. I loved what I was hearing.

I closed my eyes. The colors took over.

Ever since the tar can incident, music induced vivid light shows in my head. Most music brought on a show, but some music was more stimulating than others. Jazz produced the most intense light shows. I could add this new music to the list.

After the explosion, I described my new experience of music to a doctor:

"Beats and notes looked like squares, circles, dots, and lines that burst into color like fireworks, then disappear with a poof, leaving a rapidly cycling rainbow of color. Drumbeats are mostly shades of grey and white, and sometimes black against white. Cymbals and hi-hat hits are brilliant blue triangles. Synthesizer tones are yellowish and look like a smushed square. Horns can be any color and changed shape, depending on the tone and range. Bass notes are always red, and guitar is orange. Piano notes are usually white, but they can change color depending on the scale. The colors and shapes play out like a scrolling roadway in my mind. The more complex or discordant the music, the greater the show."

I discovered it by accident when a few weeks after the tar can incident, the mom put on Tchaikovsky's "The Firebird Suite." I closed my eyes, and the show began, better than any fireworks I had ever seen. The finale took my breath away. Lying on the living room floor with eyes closed, I played "The Firebird Suite" repeatedly until the mom put an end to it by calling me weird and pushing me out the door to play "like a normal boy."

The band finished their song and the colors faded. The clarinet player said, "We're Gray." The members started breaking down their gear. I hung out while the stage was changed for the next band. A guy in a leather biker jacket but no shirt standing next to me struck up a conversation.

"You a DNA fan?" he asked.

"A what?"

"DNA, you know, the next band."

"Um, I don't think I've ever heard them."

He laughed. "First time here, huh?"

I laughed back. "Does it show?"

"It's cool. You're in for a treat. Arto is the real deal."

I had no idea what he was talking about.

The three members of DNA took the stage. DNA was nothing like Gray, but they sounded like they could be a leaf on the same musical tree. DNA was more discordant and disjointed than Gray, but I could see why they were booked for the same night. At first, my ears didn't know what to do with their sound, but after it settled into my brain, I got it. If Marcel Duchamp had been in a band, this is surely how it would have sounded. Listening to DNA, I felt special. I felt smart.

The song ended. Sid appeared next to me and shoved a cold beer into my hand.

"Do you like this stuff?" Sid asked, waving his beer in a tight circle over his head.

"I do. It's…it's something…it's new."

"New? It's weird is what it is."

"It is, and I'm okay with that."

"You crazy."

Gordon found us. "I was talking to the black dude from the last band, and he said we should go check out a place called the Mudd Club. He gave me drink tickets." He held up tickets.

"Free drinks?" I asked.

"Yup."

"Hells yes, let's go," Sid said.

"He said it's close enough to walk," Gordon said.

"Nah, let's drive. I wanna check on the car anyway," Sid said.

The car was still there. We loaded in and made the short drive to the Mudd Club.

"Oh man. Look at that line," I said as we walked toward the mob at the front of the club.

"This here is the pretty crowd. Are we gonna get in?" Sid asked.

"I got this." Gordon waved the drink tickets over his head like a victory flag and advanced. The doorman waved him forward.

"How many are you?" the doorman asked.

"Three, we got three." Gordon said, pointing to himself, Sid, and me.

"Who are you with?" the doorman asked.

"Huh?" Gordon said.

"Who gave you the tickets?" The doorman looked at Gordon like he was simple.

"Jean-Michel hooked us up. We just checked out his band over at CBGB."

"Was the band named Gray? You mean Basquiat? The painter?" the doorman said.

"Yeah, him," Gordon answered.

The doorman laughed and gave the three of us the once over. His expression was as obvious as the yellow on a NYC taxi. It rang of *You three aren't Mudd Club type of clientele.* With a hand wave of resignation and a slight shake of his head, we were in. As we passed cries of "Really?" and "Are you kidding me?" and a shouted "You let the eggplants in?" went up from a loud guy at the entrance. We made our way past the chain, paid the cover, and went in.

I never considered myself hip. In fact, I pretty much knew I was the opposite of hip. I was a tall, gangly, dorky, overly friendly, smile-for-no-reason, poor-white-trash flavor of anti-hip. If I had ever experienced a self-deluded moment of believing I was hip, walking into the Mudd Club erased that thought permanently and confirmed that I was, in fact, not even a member of the solar system of hip. At best, I was a chunk of space debris that accidentally found itself, ass on fire, streaking through the hip system, not even permitted to slow down enough to orbit the lesser of the hip planets.

CBGB was raw and angry; the Mudd Club was the opposite. The physical space wasn't anything special, but it had a special vibe. And it didn't stink, so it had that going for itself. While CBGB lit up my emotional core, the Mudd Club and its denizens appealed to my head space. Oh, sure, at its basic level it was just another place to drink, dance, and try to get laid, and it was populated by a fair share of posers, but it felt smarter. Maybe it was all just country boy goes to the big city but being inside the club made me feel like painting, writing, and starting a band.

"Now we're talking. Look at these honeys," Sid said as we made our way deeper into the club.

Sid was right. The women were beautiful and dressed like they'd just stepped down from a runway. A few people wore what, to my suburban filter, appeared to be Halloween costumes. I was wearing the best clothes I owned—black pants with a well-worn grey belt, a black button-down dress shirt, and rough black dress shoes that had seen better days. Even though the men around me weren't dressed much differently, I felt under dressed. Inadequate. Poor.

The DJ was playing a James Brown song, and the dance floor was jumping. We pushed our way to the bar to turn in our tickets for some free drinks.

Sid made his drink disappear in a fast gulp and grinned. "Last one in the pool pays for gas home."

Gordon and I watched Sid make his way into the middle of the dance floor. He inserted himself between two very blonde, very tall girls and started doing what Gordon and I called the Sid dance. Sid was a great dancer, but he had a distinctive way of snapping his fingers when he danced that made Gordon and me laugh. We mimicked him when he wasn't looking, and sometimes when he was. At first the very attractive, very tall blondes were not happy about Sid busting up their twosome groove, but before James sang *"Get up offa that thing"* two times, they dropped the cool shields and started dancing with him. Sid motioned for us to join. Gordon headed over, but I waved off to explore.

I nestled into a good vantage point to watch the DJ. There didn't seem to be any thematic programming in the DJ's playlist. His music selection jumped from genre to genre without much concern for mixing or beat matching. Despite that, it was obvious his finger was on the pulse of the place, and he knew what worked. Cheers went up on every song.

After watching for a while, I looked around for my crew and found Gordon and Sid talking with Jean, the guy from the band, Gray.

"Do you guys want to go upstairs?" Jean asked.

Gordon looked up. "What's upstairs?"

"Some art," Jean said.

"Sure," I said.

We followed Jean upstairs. There was a bathtub of ice and beer, a makeshift bar like the ones at weddings, booths like you find in diners, and a few couches spread around. Hanging on the walls were posters and paintings. What pulled my attention most was a human-sized cage in the middle of the room.

"Are you into art?" Jean asked.

I spoke up. "I am."

"Do you like these?" He nodded around the room at some of the art on the walls.

"Some of them."

"Which ones?"

"That one." I pointed to one of the pieces made up of black and red cartoon-like illustrations.

"My friend Keith did that one. What do you like about it?"

His question caught me off guard.

"I like the way the figures and lines fit together, puzzle like. Connected. Like its all dancing together. It makes me feel hopeful."

Jean-Michel looked me hard in the eyes.

"It's for sale. Do you want to buy it?"

"How much?"

"That one is $200, I think. It's a good one. All of Keith's stuff is good, but that one is great."

"I like it, but I don't have $200 right now."

"Okay, cool...cool, it's cool. There's more you might like."

"What's the deal with the cage?" Gordon asked.

"It's just a thing they have here," Jean said.

A middle-aged lady dressed in a shiny green dress waved in our direction from across the room.

"I have to go see someone." Jean zipped away toward the lady.

We went to the bathtub bar and turned in our last drink tickets.

"Apes belong in cages," a voice said from behind us.

We turned as a group. It was Mr. Eggplant commenter from the entry line.

"Yeah, you heard me. Both of you belong in there," he said, pointing to the cage.

Sid's smile flipped down into a clench. It took me a minute to figure out what Mr. Eggplant was saying.

"You too." He pointed at me. "All apes and their monkey lovers should be in cages."

I got it. It took me longer than it should have, but my brain wasn't in that space. It's like when you ask for a Coke and they bring you a Dr. Pepper. At first you think, hmm, I thought I ordered Coke. Is this Coke? Then you take another sip and realize, hey, someone replaced my happy-go-lucky fun night with a racist verbal attack on me and my friends.

I considered him. A feeling I hadn't felt since a night long ago in an abandoned mansion flooded back. I decided.

"Fuck you…you racist motherfucker," I said, squaring up in front of him.

Gordon and Sid looked at me, their eyes wide and jaws open.

"What did you say?" Mr. Eggplant asked, taking an aggressive stance.

"Really? That's your response? Do you need me to repeat what I just said, you dull-witted chump. Do you need it repeated so you can use the time to cook up an even more lackluster line of racist drivel? I'll tell you what, you syphilitic sack of horse excrement, how about I keep talking until your molasses filled cranium can figure out something more interesting than, 'What did you say?' You just hold up your small-fingered hand when you've whipped up a response worthy of our time."

Mr. Eggplant's face flip-flopped between confusion and anger. People nearby turned toward the fuss.

"Nothing?" I said. "While we're waiting, let's dissect your racist statement. As racists predictably do, you likened my black friends to apes. Here are some facts for you while the hamster wheel in your head spins up a response, you pathetic miscreant. Did you know that we share 98% of our DNA with apes? Yeah, you do as well, you uneducated dullard."

From the crinkling of his brow and the redness of his cheeks, I guessed anger was winning the war.

"Nothing? Still nothing? This guy…" I threw a thumb in his direction.

I continued. "Did you know apes have the same blood types as humans? That's right, the stuff they bleed is the same as yours. Who knows, we might get a chance to see yours tonight… Still nothing, tough guy?"

A crowd formed around us like an elementary school fight circle. The crowd was chuckling at the exchange. Mr. Eggplant was turning the same shade as his namesake.

"I'll keep going, cause it seems you share another trait with apes. They can't speak either. Of course, they have an excuse. They don't have a voice box. Your problem is that you lack a developed wit, I said.

The crowd was laughing. At him.

"Did you know that they taught an ape named Koko sign language? Yea, it's true, and her favorite things to sign were curses. For instance—"

I signed with my fingers. "This means you're an asshole," I said.

I signed with my fingers. "This means you have a small dick."

I signed with my fingers. "This means you have a poo face."

"And Koko's favorite." I stepped closer, and my fingers flew in front of his face. "This means you are a stupid, racist, small-witted moron and we're done wasting our time with you. But before we end this encounter, as requested, I will repeat my original statement. Fuck you, you racist motherfucker."

The crowd roared.

He leapt.

His weight hit me full in the chest, knocking me onto my back. He pulled back and rained blows down on my head. Gordon and Sid were on his arms before he landed anything serious, but they couldn't pry him off. Eventually, a big wall of flesh pushed Sid and Gordon aside, reached down, and lifted the racist clean off me. The wall then carried him toward the stairs like a sack of groceries. Gordon helped me to my feet.

A bouncer came over and grabbed Sid and me by the collar.

"You guys gotta go," the bouncer said.

"Why? That guy attacked me."

"Yeah, yeah, but that's the rules," the bouncer said.

"Fine, fine," I said. "But for the record, that's not fair."

"Life's not fair. Get gone."

We headed out and made it to the car without incident. Sid started up and peeled out.

"I'll bet this kind of bullshit doesn't happen in Europe," Sid said.

"Maybe the next place will be better," I said.

Sid shook his head. "I've had enough big apple for one night."

"I hear that," Gordon agreed.

"But we have time to hit at least one more spot," I said, pulling out my list of clubs.

"Lemme see that list," Sid said.

I handed it over. Sid rolled down his window and thew it out.

"Damn, Sid, that's cold blooded," I said.

"I'm serious. I can't wait to get the fuck out of here. Every goddamn place we go some racist bullshit happens," Sid said.

"I hear that," Gordon said.

"But, I mean, how do you know it's different in Europe?" I asked.

"I've got family over there. When I talk with 'em they tell me about how much better it is for a black man over there. They don't look at us the same way. Here, white people look at us with old master eyes."

"I'm sorry you feel you have to leave, but I get it," I said.

"Besides, have you seen the women over there?" Sid said, changing the mood.

"No." I smiled. "But I'm pretty sure you haven't either."

"Maybe not, but I can imagine. One day, Buck, you'll see," Sid said. "You'll turn around and ask, 'Hey, where did Sid go?' and I'll be in France writing you a postcard telling you about the woman I hooked up with."

"You wish."

"Damn, you really sliced that guy up with words," Gordon said.

"He deserved it," I said.

"He deserved worse, but if you'd have let it go, we would still be hanging with the hotties," Gordon said.

"How do you let that shit go?" I asked.

"Practice, my brother, practice," Sid said.

The drive home was quiet except for Gordon's snoring from the back seat and the drone of the freeway against the tires. I stayed awake to keep Sid company and make sure he didn't nod off at the wheel.

Nearly home, Gordon woke up.

Gordon asked between yawns, "Yo, Cam, where the hell you learn sign language?"

I smiled. "What are you talking about? I don't know sign language."

Our laughter is still echoing down the New Jersey turnpike.

21

COURT JESTERS

"Do you go on all the Kingston ski trips?" she asked.

"No, this is my first. My friend Sid is the trip guide." I motioned toward Sid standing at the front of the tour bus.

My seatmate nodded and brushed her short blonde hair away from her face.

"Oh, sure, I know Sid. Have you skied Killington before?"

"No. In fact, this will be my second time skiing. My first time was on a bunny hill in the Poconos, and that didn't go well because I didn't have the right clothes and I nearly froze to death."

"Oh my God, you're almost a virgin." Her eyes moved like blue lightning, making me feel suspicious of her intentions. If she only knew how right she was.

As the ski trip guide, Sid could often bring friends along at no charge. Sid gave me and two other JW friends, Colin and Kent, the entire trip, including gear rental and lift tickets. That was the only way someone as poor as I could go on a ski trip. Heck, I couldn't even afford ski pants, but I got lucky at the local Goodwill and found a pair for five dollars. I got a scratched-up pair of ski goggles for a dollar more.

"I am a virgin, but I'm hoping to lose it on this trip. Ski-wise, that is."

She grabbed my arm. "You be sure to let me know if you need help with losing that virginity. Ski-wise, that is."

"I'm Cam."

"I'm Val. Nice to meet you, Cam." She gave me a quick peck on the check, leaving behind lipstick.

She rubbed it into my cheek. "Oops. I didn't mean to mark you." She giggled and snuggled against me.

We spent the rest of the six-hour bus ride talking and drinking the cheap wine being shared around.

I spent the next morning on the bunny hill. Thanks to my "new to me" ski clothes, I wasn't frozen after one run down the hill. I gained confidence with every run, and before the morning was over, I'd graduated to a beginner trail. After a morning of runs, I ran into Sid and some of the other beginners at the base of the mountain.

"Hey, Buck, I'm going to take this group up to the top and take the Four Mile Trail down. Wanna go?"

"Can I ski it?"

"Yeah, you can. It's easy. I watched you come down on your last run. Looking good, brother."

The view from the chair lift on the way up to the peak was incredible. Overnight, a storm had dropped at least a foot of fresh snow. The sweet mountain air was replacing the suburban air in my lungs and clearing my head, giving me a fresh outlook on life.

"Thank you again for all of this," I said.

"You're welcome," Sid said. "I'm glad you came. Fun, isn't it?"

"Hell, yes."

"Hey, by the way, don't let Colin and Kent hear you curse. Those two are full in, and they'll report you to the Elders in a heartbeat."

"Why did you invite them if they're narcs?"

"They're good dudes. Just a little too far down the JW rabbit hole."

"I'll be fucking careful around them."

Sid shook his head at me.

We unloaded at the top of the lift and headed over, twelve strong, to the entrance of Four Mile Trail. When we got there, we found it blocked by red flags and a member of the ski patrol waving his arms.

"Sorry, gang," the ski patroller said. "Four Mile Trail and most of the other trails on this side are closed. Last night's snow caused some drifting, and they aren't passable."

"How about Great Eastern?" Sid asked.

"Also closed," the patroller said.

"I've got a bunch of beginners here. What's the best green trail down?"

"There are no passable green trails down right now. We got a ton of snow last night."

Sid unfolded and studied his trail map. After some considering, he said, "Follow me."

He skied off, and we followed.

Four hours later, the Killington Ski patrol finished getting the last of our group down from the mountain. Turned out, the only way down from the peak was via double-diamond mogul fields. Some of the group walked down, and some tried to ski it and hurt themselves. Others stopped halfway down, afraid to move. I took a shot on the expert mogul trails and spent most of the runs sliding down on my ass until the trail turned into an intermediate trail.

"It turned out okay in the end," I said to Sid as we sat commiserating later that night at the Pickle Barrel, a popular bar in Killington.

Sid took a swig of his beer. "I messed up big time. Someone could have died."

"But no one did. Someday, we'll tell the story of how your clients had to be snowmobiled down a mountain and laugh. Lemme get you a shot."

Sid gave me a death look.

"Bartender, two shots of tequila, please," I said.

"What, no shot for me?" Val, my bouncy seatmate from the bus appeared at my side. "Or do you two big-time ski instructors want to be alone?"

"I guess you heard," I said.

"Are you kidding? Who hasn't?" she said.

"So not funny," Sid said.

"Yea, it is. A little. Hey, at least no one died," Val said.

Sid looked downcast. "You both suck," he said.

After an hour of drinking and listening to a Led Zeppelin cover band, the weight of the day won, and the three of us shared a cab back to the hotel. Val followed us to our floor.

"Where's your room?" I asked Val.

"Right here," she said, nodding at our door.

"That's our room," I said.

"Wow, you aren't very bright, are you?" she said.

"He's kinda slow," Sid said.

Val smiled. "Do you have any wine?"

"Oh. Yes," I said, embarrassed. "Would you like to join us for a drink?"

"I thought you'd never ask," Val said.

I poured her a plastic cup of wine. She took it and hopped into my bed, patting the mattress next to her.

Sid got in his bed and turned off the lights.

"I'm wiped. You two have fun, but please keep it down," he said.

"Can you be quiet, Mr. Cam?" Val asked.

"Like a mouse," I said.

She passed me the wine glass and took off her shirt and pants.

"What are you doing?" I whispered.

"What do you think?" Val said.

"I don't want to be rude, but…"

"Oh, shit, you aren't attracted to me."

"No, I am. You're really cute. But…"

"Oh my God, you're gay. Is Sid your boyfriend?"

"No, we aren't gay," Sid said. "Can you two please shut it so I can sleep?"

"Sorry, Sid," we said together.

"Do you have a girlfriend?" she whispered.

"Nope," I said.

"Then I don't get it. Why are your clothes still on?" She put her hand under my shirt.

I gulped down the wine.

"It's just that… I want the first time to be with someone I love."

"No way. You're a virgin? Like a for real virgin?"

"Come on, you guys," Sid said.

"Sorry, Sid," we said.

"It's no big deal. I'm a virgin, so what?"

"You could have told me before I took my clothes off."

"In my defense, they came off pretty fast," I said.

"So, it's a no?" she said.

"Sorry."

"This is crazy. I'm the one that says no. I can't believe you're an honest to goodness vir—"

"Cam, will you please fuck her so I can get some sleep?" Sid said.

"Sorry, Sid," we said.

"Can I sleep next to you? I promise I won't try anything." She giggled. "I can't believe I just said that to a man."

"I'ma come over there and fuck the both of you if you don't shut it," Sid said.

"Sorry, Sid," we said.

She tried. I didn't.

A 6:30 am knock on the door interrupted a sex dream involving two women.

"We don't want housekeeping. Come back later," Sid yelled from under his covers.

"It's Colin. Open up." The doorknob jiggled.

"Hang on a sec." Sid turned to us. "Better hide Val."

"Hide Val? What the hell does hide Val mean? I don't think so," Val said.

Colin knocked again. "Who's that in there with you guys?"

"It's Cam's friend. She came by to meet us for breakfast," Sid said.

Val got out from under the covers and stood up in nothing but a bra and panties.

"Val, please put on your clothes," Sid hissed.

Val lasered Sid a look hot enough to boil water. "Hide Val? That'll be the day."

We moved to block her, but what could we do? Neither one of us thought it appropriate to tackle a girl in her underwear. Plus, she was really fast. She opened the door.

"Hi Colin, I'm Val," she said to a slack-jawed Colin. "Come on in."

The lack of windows and proper ventilation made the Kingdom Hall basement hot, moist, and cloying. Brown paneled walls, blue carpeting, and cheap folding chairs made for a chef's kiss of visual discomfort that complemented the stiflingly thick, stale air.

Three Elders were seated in a semi-circle on a raised stage at the front of the room like some cut-rate Spanish inquisition. They directed the mom to wait outside and asked me to take a seat on a chair they'd placed in front of the stage. I was eye level with three sets of legs in worn polyester pants and shoes that had seen better days.

Jehovah's Witnesses spoke of these hearings as a way to get help for sinners in their midst, but, in application, they were anything but. You could be brought into a judicial committee for a huge array of offenses, from something as small as smoking a cigarette, to major crimes, like abortion or murder. The Elders acted as judge, jury, and executioner, singularly deciding your fate. Punishment could be as simple as a private admonishment, all the way up to *disfellowshipping,* where you are cut off from your entire family and all your friends until the Elders decide you're repentant enough to return. The amount of ass kissing required to be considered repentant was legendary.

I knew all three Elders and their reputations. They didn't care for me. At all.

Elder "Walnut" was dressed in five shades of brown, from tie to shoes. He thought of himself as an intellectual, his lack of fundamental reading and comprehension skills in no way diminishing his belief that he was everyone's mental superior. He proudly told anyone who would listen that schools were full of demon-controlled teachers, and anything you needed to know could be found in the pages of the Bible.

Elder "Tight Pants" earned his nickname the obvious way. Maybe his pants had fit at some point, but after surviving hundreds of trips to the dry cleaner, they must have shrunk. That was my hope, because if he'd chosen pants that tight, I had questions.

The third Elder was Stan's father, Elder Crowner, but let's call him Elder "Abuser" to keep track. The fact that this man whom I'd witnessed physically and mentally abuse his own children was going to judge my morals made me insane.

I wanted to scream at these charlatans, but I knew the second I did, it would be all over for me. I sat jaw-clenched, silent, the muscles in my frame tensed with rebel energies.

Elder Walnut began, "Before we begin the judicial committee, let us pray together that Jehovah God guides us with his spirit."

The *bla, bla, bla* of his prayer droned on and on. I shut down my ears and thought of what I was about to go through.

Stories were abundant about the mistreatment people suffered during these meetings. It wasn't possible to get up and leave. Defendants were persuaded to stay against their will for hours until either their will snapped or the Elders ran out of methods to break them.

The prayer concluded. "In Jesus's name, amen," said the three Elders in unison.

"Cameron, the reason you are here today is because Colin reported to the Elders that a worldly girl was in the room you shared with Sidney Brown during a ski trip. Is that true?"

"Let me ask you a question. Was Colin the only person who allegedly witnessed this?" I asked.

They looked at each other the way TV cops do when their suspect asks for a lawyer.

"Cameron, we're interested in your eternal life and Jehovah knows what happened. Also, we ask the questions," Tight Pants said.

"Was Colin the only person that reported this to you?" I repeated.

Elder Abuser's right leg bounced up and down and his face screwed up. "Don't you want to see your dead father again in the new system after Armageddon?"

This asshole. I focused all my energy on his face, hoping it would melt.

"Why won't you answer my question? Was Colin the only witness?" I asked.

"Sidney Brown was also present at the assumable place," Elder Walnut said.

I knew Sidney would not and did not say anything. Bad bluff, Elder Walnut.

"The word *assumable* makes no sense in that sentence. Now, will someone answer my question?"

"Young man, why are you so rebellious?" Tight Pants asked, narrowing his eyes and pursing his lips. "Jehovah tells us that we are to be sheep, and yet you're acting as a goat."

"Was Colin the only person that came forward? If he was—"

"Enough. Yes, he was the only person that lovingly came forward," Abuser said.

"Well, brothers, I think we're done here," I said, standing up.

Elder Abuser's leg twitching turned to a stomp. He stood up. "Sit down. We are not done here."

Elder Walnut placed a hand on Elder Abuser's arm. "Brothers, please, be calm. Please sit down."

I sat back down but only after the Abuser sat.

I let them work me over for an hour. They asked me if I touched the girl on her vagina or breasts. They asked if she touched my penis. They asked me if we engaged in sexual contact. They asked if Sid joined in. They asked every disgusting, intrusive question they could think of to get me to admit to a sin. I sat silent. They became a morass of loosened ties and sweaty brows.

Tight Pants smacked his Bible down on his knee and gave it one last shot. "We're deeply concerned for your eternal life. You have not been cooperative with us. Jehovah God knows what happened, and he will judge you according to your deeds."

I made a move for the door.

"Please send in your mother," Abuser said.

The following Sunday, Brother Walnut took the podium just before the closing prayer.

"This is to inform the congregation that Cameron Gilchrist has been reproved for conduct unbecoming a Christian and his congregational privileges are removed."

The judging stares of everyone in the Kingdom Hall were on me. The Elder had informed the congregation that I was effectively an outcast. While the two-witness rule kept them from disfellowshipping me, removing privileges was just as bad in most of the minds of the members. Since the congregation members didn't know the details of the charges, they would assume the worst, make up stories about what I'd done, and a whisper campaign would ensue. The mom's face was a combination of hurt and hate.

They were right, I was no sheep. No longer would I pretend to be clay for their 2000-year-old molds. I'd had enough of the hypocrisy, the pedantic rules, the judging, the hate wrapped in concern, the anti-intellectualism. I was done with all of it and all of them.

They, however, were not done with me.

22

SLEDGEHAMMER

"There they are." Sid nodded toward Evette, his girlfriend and a tall leggy blonde heading in our direction from the parking lot. Evette's friend reminded me of a mermaid.

"Who's her friend?" I asked.

"That's the future Mrs. Gordon," Gordon said.

"Nah, she's too tall for you," I said.

"Yeah, but everyone knows that blondes love brothers. You don't stand a chance, white boy," Gordon said.

"Maybe she's the exception to the rule and she prefers pale," I said.

"Ain't you a virgin?" Gordon said, delivering his Cheshire grin. "You wouldn't know what to do with her."

Thursday night was Rainbow night at Emerald City, and the line was long. Sid, Gordon, and I were at the tail end of it. Friday through Sunday nights, the club featured top-40 dance music, but on Thursday nights, the club played punk, or what passed for punk in the suburban town of Cherry Hill, New Jersey.

Evette gave Sid a quick kiss in greeting.

"Hi, babe. Hi, guys. Guys, this my friend, Katie," Evette said.

Gordon stepped between Katie and me and took her hand.

"Hi, Katie, I'm Gordon. You've probably heard of me. I am most pleased to make your acquaintance."

Gordon half-bowed over her hand, kissing it in the process.

Katie did a little curtsy. "Nice to meet you, Gordon. Who is your attractive, tall friend behind you? Can you introduce us?" She looked around Gordon to smile at me.

We all burst into laughter.

Gordon held onto her hand and hit her with his flirtiest smile. "You know, I can't wait until tomorrow."

"Oh, yeah? Why's that, Mr. Gordon?" Katie asked.

"Because I get better looking every day. You might wanna be around to see it," Gordon said.

"Wow, look at the confidence on you. Can you introduce me to your friend now?"

"Damn…that always works…so cold." He took Katie's hand and placed it into mine. "Your loss. This here is pale Cam."

Katie gave my hand a squeeze. "Hi, Cam."

"Hi, Katie. Nice to meet you, and just to be clear, I'm sure you haven't heard of me, and I will look pretty much the same tomorrow."

"Maybe I have…heard of you." Her honey brown eyes darted a glance toward Evette.

"Really? What have you heard?" I asked.

She pursed her lips into a small o and made a zipper move across them. "I'll never tell."

It was our third time at Emerald City. The first time, a new artist named Prince performed. His song, "I Wanna Be Your Lover" was a favorite of mine. Prince and his band played with enough energy to fill a stadium. I picked up his album the day after the show.

The second time we went we met up with college friends of Sidney's to see a band called The Cure. They were a big deal in England, but hadn't made much noise in the States. It was their first live appearance in the US. I was always down to hear new music, so I planted myself right in front of the stage for the sparsely attended show. I liked a few songs, but their performance didn't move me. Sid hooked up with Evette that night and they started dating.

There we were, back again, this time to see Wendy O. Williams and the Plasmatics. I didn't know what to expect, but word was their show involved nakedness and a chainsaw. My kind of band.

We entered the club and grabbed some chairs at one of the long tables in the main room. Evette and Katie knew everyone, and before long, our table was filled with a big crew, drinking, talking, and laughing. The Thursday-night DJ played mostly punk, postmodern, and new wave, but every so often he would drop in a disco song. The throb of "Knock on Wood" by Ami Stewart started and Katie jumped up.

Katie made grabby hands at me. "Dance with me, Mr. Cam."

Gordon leaned close and said, "If you don't get up and dance with this girl, I'm going to personally kick your ass."

Katie kicked back into an arms-crossed, challenging stance. "Cam? Is it okay with your boyfriend Gordon if we dance?"

"Yeah, he said it's alright, but no kissing," I said, straight-faced.

"Your loss." She pulled me up out of my chair.

We danced for thirty minutes straight through "Knock on Wood," "Rock Lobster," "The Wait," "Life During Wartime," and a few other songs. We were a sweaty, breathless mess at the end. We headed back to the table hand in hand. She sat on my lap.

"Sorry, Gordon. He's mine now." Katie ruffled my hair. "You had your chance, but I like him and I'm gonna keep him." She kissed me on the top of my head.

Gordon laughed. "You can have him. He's no good in bed, anyways."

"Hey, don't I get a say in this? Maybe I'll date you both," I said.

"Nah, you'll have to leave Gordon if you want to be with me."

"Fine. Sorry Gordon. Can we still be friends?"

"No. We are done," Gordon said.

"Hey, The Plasmatics are starting in ten. Let's head over to the lounge," Evette said.

The Plasmatics took the stage like an army of invaders. Their sound was a punky wall of guitar sound. The lead singer, Wendy O. Williams, moved like a nuclear bomb, endlessly exploding, over and over again. She never stopped moving, touching her breasts and crotch repeatedly. During one of the songs, Wendy took a sledgehammer and paraded it up and down the stage over her head, offering it up to the rock gods. Sitting on the middle of the stage was a tube TV. She brought the sledgehammer down onto the TV, sending pieces across the stage. She grabbed a chainsaw and started it up. The smell of gasoline filled the air. Looking at me with concern, Katie pulled on my arm and led me out of the live music room. We made our way back to the table in the main room.

"Sid and I were talking," Evette said, looking to Katie and me. "My mom is out of town this week, so the four of us could head to her place and hang out. What do you say?"

"Sure," Katie said.

"I'm down," I replied.

We weren't at Evette's house more than ten minutes before Evette and Sid peeled off and headed upstairs, leaving Katie and me alone on the sofa.

"Is someone taking a shower or running water for a tub upstairs?" Katie asked.

"Sounds like it," I answered.

"We did sweat up a storm."

"No kidding. A shower sounds like a good idea right now."

"I like my men sweaty." She moved in and licked my neck. "Mmm, salty."

"Careful, that's my kryptonite."

"Yay! What happens if I do this?" She kissed my neck, sending little shocks through my body. "Or this?" The kissing changed to sucking.

It drove me crazy. We kissed.

Splashing sounds came from the upstairs bathroom.

"Yup. It's the bathtub," Katie said.

The splashing sounds got vigorous, soon turning to grunts and moans.

"Oh my, they are having fun. I hope they don't flood the upstairs," I said.

"Maybe we should take a bath. A shower at least. We're kinda sweaty."

"And dirty."

"Yeah, so dirty."

We went back to kissing. Her hand went inside my pants and found my hardness.

"Maybe we should skip the shower and do something with this."

"About that," I said.

"About what?" Katie said, pulling her hand away.

"I've…I'm…I never."

"You've never?"

"No."

"Wanna know a secret?"

"Yes, always."

"I've never either. I mean, I've fooled around, but I've never, you know, gone all the way."

"We must be the last two virgins in the world."

"Certainly, the last two in this house."

Katie's hand went back to rubbing me.

"So, virgin, what have you done?"

"I've kissed, obviously."

"Obviously. What else?"

"I've touched a girl, and she touched me."

She opened my pants and took me out.

"Like this?"

"God, that feels so good."

"It's supposed to, silly. What else?"

She lowered her head.

"Did she ever do this?" She licked me and looked up at me.

"I, ah, no."

She pushed me back into the couch and took me in her mouth.

"Oh my God, that feels so good."

"Again, it's supposed to."

"I want to make you feel good, too."

"No more talking."

The moaning from upstairs was getting intense. Katie and I added our own. The entire house moaned.

I moaned loudest.

"That was amazing."

"I'm not certain, but that may have counted as group sex," Katie said. We laughed.

"But what about you? You're the odd girl out."

"Let's find a bed."

We found the guest bedroom. I sat on the edge of the bed and slowly took off her shirt and bra. I kissed her neck to her breasts. I pulled her pants and panties down and followed a line down between her breasts with my tongue. Her hands tangled into my hair as I slowly worked my way down.

"You've done this before."

"No, I haven't."

"That's not true."

"Yes, it's true."

"Then how do you know how to do that?"

"I read a lot." I laughed.

"I'm a lucky girl. Are you sure you don't have a girlfriend?"

"No more talking."

I put my mouth on her. Her giggles transformed into a low deep moan.

She became still and the grip on my hair turned painful as she let out a guttural scream.

"Stop, stop," she said pulling away.

"What? Did I do something wrong?"

"No, no. It's sensitive now."

"Did you come?"

"Yes, you silly boy. You couldn't tell?"

"I'm kinda new at this."

We collapsed into bed. She laid her head on my chest, her long blonde hair spread out over the two of us like a golden sheet.

"Your heart is beating so hard," she said. "So, about this virgin thing. Do you swear you're truly a virgin?"

"How many times do you need me to answer that? Yes. I am a virgin."

"Why? How?"

"It's a long story, but my mother is a Jehovah's Witness. Sex or even fooling around before marriage is considered a big sin. In fact, they say that you give up eternal life if you have sex before marriage. Technically, I'm not even allowed to date unless I'm looking for someone to marry. I'm certainly not allowed to do this."

"Allowed?"

"If the Elders in the church ever found out about what we just did, I would be thrown out of the religion or *disfellowshipped,* as they call it. If that happens, no one can speak to me, not even my family."

"That's stupid. Actually, I take that back. That's evil. And that's why you're a virgin?"

"Mainly that, but I like to think I'm a romantic. I want to wait until I get married before going all the way. You know, save something."

"But what if you and the future Mrs. Cameron hate having sex with each other?"

"I won't have anything to judge it against, so wouldn't it be fine?"

"I guess so."

"What about you? Why are you still a virgin?"

"Enough talk. How about we get some sleep. I'll rub your back."

"Yes, please." I detangled and turned over.

She rubbed my back and I slipped off to sleep.

I was floating on a sea that stretched on forever on all sides. The waves gently rolled under me. A pillow of blue air kept my head inches above the slowly rolling water. I was mid-point between asleep and awake. A regular rocking from the real world was pushing me toward the dream shore.

Consciousness returned. Three things struck me.

1. Strands of long blonde hair were brushing against my nose and mouth.
2. Two hands were rhythmically pushing down on my chest.
3. I was inside of Katie.

Katie lifted from my chest and arched her back, causing me to push deeper inside her. I reached down to feel where I was and confirmed what I already knew.

Two more things struck me.

1. We were no longer virgins.
2. According to my mother and God, I had committed a big sin.

"Hey, y'all, my mom will be home any minute. You guys gotta go," Evette yelled from the other room.

Sid and I were dressed, out the door, into his car, and driving away in record time.

"I heard quite a bit of splashing last night."

"Cleanliness is next to godliness." Sid winked. "I'm hungry. You hungry?"

"I sure am."

Evette's house was a few blocks from the Echelon Mall. Sid parked and we went inside.

The mall had just opened and was empty except for a group of colorfully dressed, elderly mall walkers. We ordered donuts and sat on a bench watching them fast-walk past us in their sun-visors, sweat-bands and Velcro secured sneakers.

"So, how was it?" Sid asked between bites of chocolate eclair.

"How was what?"

"Oh, you gonna do me like that? How was it with Katie?"

"I don't kiss and tell."

"Sounded like more than kissing to me, Buck."

"How could you possibly hear anything last night with your ears all full of water?"

"Didn't need to hear anything, Buck. I knew what was gonna go down with you two."

"What do you mean you knew what was gonna go down?"

"Maybe I just happened to tell Evette that you were a virgin. And maybe she said she had a friend that would like you."

"You two planned it? Scratch that. Did you three plan it?"

"Well…"

"Are you kidding me?" I yelled. A couple of startled elderly mall walkers made a wide berth past our bench.

"You're scaring the blue hairs. It's no biggie. She liked you and you liked her. It worked out."

"Hold on, hold on. So, Evette went to her virgin friend and said, 'Hey, my boyfriend's best friend is a virgin. You two should de-virgin together?'"

"Something like that."

"For real? Last night was planned?"

"Why are you so angry?"

"I don't know, but it all feels weird. It's like some sort of weird virgin match game."

"About that…"

"About what? What now?"

"Katie's not a virgin."

"Son of a bitch."

23

DANCE HALL DAYS

"Don't you have any Jethro Tull or Aerosmith?"

"I'm sorry, I don't."

The bar customer hitched up his pants, revealing a rebel flag belt buckle, grumbled and shuffled back to the bar.

There I was, wearing a dress shirt, tie, and grey suit jacket on a Friday night in a blue-collar bar in National Park, NJ. One long bar ran down the length of the left wall. Folding tables and chairs were spread haphazardly about the place. Filling the tables were locals who worked at the plant in town. They were a rough, hard-drinking lot, and pitchers of beer and shots of whiskey looked to be the drinks of choice.

By my side was Sidney, who, true to his word, showed up to my first-ever DJ gig to both show his support and act as taxi for me and the DJ equipment. Sid was also wearing a tie and jacket, only his jacket was white. He was the only black person in the place and we were nervous.

I brought exactly two rock records: *Born to Run* by Bruce Springsteen and *Led Zeppelin IV*. I alternated between those two records for thirty minutes. Soon I would have to break out the dance music or start the two-record rotation all over.

The crowd was getting drunk and antsy, and it was going to get ugly if I didn't figure out what to do. Thank God "Stairway to Heaven" was eight minutes long. It gave me time to figure out what to play next.

Paul, the regular DJ at the Woodshed Inn, had a small crew of people he booked to DJ parties, weddings, and bars. After many Friday nights of proving my ability to work the equipment and dance floor (and buying him many beers), I convinced Paul to give me my first shot at being a paid DJ. The place was not exactly the kind of place I envisioned when I embarked on my journey to become a DJ.

An intimidating, biker-looking dude covered with what appeared to be prison tats walked up to my table and pawed through my record crate.

"Can I help you?" I asked.

"You got any good shit?"

"What kind of good shit?" I smiled, hoping to disarm him in advance.

He smiled back, showing a mouth deprived of most teeth, either from poor dental hygiene or swinging hands. I thought it best to tread carefully or my mouth might look similar in short order.

"You know, good shit my girl can dance to."

He motioned with his beer glass to a girl at a table six feet away. Her smile revealed a similar tooth situation.

"I can play anything you see in there that she might like."

He looked up from paging through my records and said, "Who's the black guy? Your agent?" He laughed at his own joke. "And why are you two wearing jackets and ties? Are you gay or something?"

"No. We're not gay, just overdressed."

"You look gay. Gay Jerry over there is gay, and even he wouldn't wear a jacket and tie to this place. You look like a couple of asshats."

He had a point. Sid and I took off our ties and jackets.

"Play this one." He held up my copy of "Ladies Night," by Kool and the Gang.

"You got it," I said.

I took the record out of its sleeve and placed it on the turntable and cued it up.

Sid whispered, "Give me the mic."

"What? Why?"

"Just give me the mic, Buck. Trust me."

I passed him the microphone.

"Start the song when I tell ya."

Sid threw the switch on the mic and I turned up the microphone volume.

"Hey, y'all. I hope you're ready to party, cause this here is DJ Cam, and I'm MC Sid, and we're going to get the dance floor poppin. Who's ready to dance?"

Crickets. I swear a tumbleweed rolled by and tobacco hit a spittoon.

"I said: Who's ready to dance on this Friday night!?"

A few small whoops went up from the crowd.

"Now, I know y'all didn't work your asses off all damn week at the plant just to sit there sippin beers. Let's get this party started."

Sid nodded to me. I jammed up the volume and let the needle drop. As the first beats of "Ladies Night" boomed from the speakers, the biker's girl leapt up from her chair, knocking it over and splashing beer over the table. They started a jerky dance in front of our makeshift DJ table. They had zero rhythm, but they had enthusiasm. They were going for a dirty dancing type of thing combined with a born-again rapture thing. It was terrifying to watch. I couldn't look away.

The biker cupped his hands and yelled to the nearby tables, "Get your asses up."

Either from intoxication or fear of an ass whupping, entire tables of people got up at his command and joined them. He yelled his dancing order to the rest of the room, and before the song was half over, the floor was packed with dancing.

Sid and I gave each other a *"How about that?"* look and went to work. For the next few hours, Sid worked the microphone, and I worked the turntables. The dance floor was packed the entire time, and everyone was having fun. The crowd got drunker and drunker, and the biker couple even pulled Sid onto the floor to dance with them and their friends.

The party was jumping, and people were bumping into the table, causing the record to skip. *"BOO"* went up from the crowd. The same drunk girl was working on her fifth bump into the table when the biker appeared.

"What the fuck, man?" the biker yelled at me.

"She keeps falling into the table." I shrugged.

The biker approached the girl. "Hey, Diane, stop fucking banging into the table."

Diane's dancing partner was not happy with the biker's tone.

"Yo, don't fucking talk to her like that," Diane's partner said.

"Who the fuck do you think you're talking to?" the biker said.

"You is who, motherfucker," Diane's dancing partner yelled.

Diane banged into the table and the needle bounced off the record with a speaker-shaking *scrrreeaacchh.*

"Goddammit, Diane," the biker yelled into the now silent room.

"Motherfucker, I told you, don't talk to her like that." The dancing partner threw a punch at the biker's face. The biker sidestepped the punch with ease. The biker smiled. He lived for this.

In every Western movie ever made, there's a bar scene where someone disrespects the hero or the hero's woman, or someone cheats at poker and a fight breaks out. A quiet, tension-filled pause occurs just before bottles, bullets, and fists start flying. I recognized the pause. It hung in the air like a layer of cigar smoke.

"Sid, get down!"

We ducked under the table.

With a bearish roar, the biker smashed his attacker in the chest with both hands, throwing the guy backwards into the crowd. Chairs, bottles, and pitchers flew through the air. MC Sid and I cowered behind the table.

"The owner said you did a good job," Paul said, handing me forty dollars.

"Thanks."

"I got another gig for you if you're interested. It's a place called The Beernut. Can you DJ this Saturday?

"Before I say yes, is this place like the last place? If so, I'm going to need a bouncer with me." I laughed.

Paul chuckled and said, "You'll be okay. The Beernut is a regular bar with a real dance floor. They have their own equipment, so it'll be an easier gig."

"Thanks Paul. I appreciate it."

"You earned it. Is it true you brought a black guy with you and you both wore suit jackets and ties?"

"Yep."

"You brought a black guy to that bar in that town?"

"He's my friend and a hell of an MC."

"I dunno if you're stupid or just ballsy."

"If someone has a color problem, it's on them."

"Fair enough."

Paul liked me, and the bar managers and owners sent back good reviews, so Paul gave me regular bookings. On the weekend nights when I didn't have a DJ gig, Sid, Gordon, and I were out and about. After a night of dancing and flirting, we would usually end up at an after-hours club called the Coliseum. The Coliseum was located above the ice rink where the Philadelphia Flyers practiced. If you came early enough, you could sit at one of the multiple bars and watch people playing hockey on the rink. The club didn't get busy until after the other bars and clubs closed. Peppered among the "one-more-drink" crowd, the bartenders, wait staff, managers, and DJs, were the people who actually powered the nightclub industry: the drug dealers and mobsters.

All the clubs were full of drugs, but none more so than the Coliseum. Cocaine was the main drug of choice, followed closely by meth. Most people I met in the clubs did coke. Minutes after meeting a DJ or bartender at the Coliseum, I would get one of three questions: "Do you have any?" "Do you wanna do some?" "Do you know who has some?" In the men's room, the persistent sniff of lines going up noses was louder than the repeated flushing of toilets designed to cover up the sound.

"Cam, this here is Tony. He's a friend from high school," Gordon said.

Tony looked like he'd just walked off the set of a mobster movie. His black shark eyes and slicked down wind-tunnel-tested hair made him look years older than Gordon. His way-too-tight black suit and white dress shirt opened two buttons too low contributed to the effect. Around his hairy neck was a Mr. T starter set of gold chains. Hanging among the shrubbery, a gold cross and a Catholic medal peeked out.

I reached out my hand to shake. "Hey, Tony."

Tony ignored my hand and gave me a shoes-to-eyes once over. "Hey. Nice to meet ya. Whadda you do?"

"I'm a DJ."

He rubbed his nose and pulled his shirt cuffs out from under his sleeves, flashing gold cufflinks and a gold watch.

"No shit. I have, let's say, an interest in a few clubs. Where do you spin?"

"I do a night at The Beernut and some other spots."

"Don't know that joint. You any good? Gordon, is he any good?"

"Yea, Tony, he is. He keeps em dancing all night."

"You need anything?" Tony asked.

"What do you mean?" I asked.

Tony laughed. "Party supplies. You guys good?" He looked back and forth between the two of us.

I looked at Gordon and gave a little shrug.

Gordon answered, "No, we're good Tony, but thanks."

Tony pulled a business card out of his inside suit pocket. On it was nothing but a phone number. He handed it to me.

"Any friend of Gordon's is family. You ever need anything, anything at all, you gimme a page. Good luck with the DJ thing."

I took the card. We shook hands.

"Thanks, Tony."

Tony faded into the crowd like smoke.

"What's he do? Is he in the club business?" I asked.

"Sorta."

"Do you think he would hook me up with a gig at one of the clubs?"

"I'm sure he could, but if I were you, I wouldn't ever use that number. It comes with strings. Strings you don't want."

"Like what?"

"Nothing's free. Like he'll ask you for a favor that could land you in jail. Or worse."

I stashed the card in my wallet and headed up to the DJ booth.

"Hey, Rick," I said.

"Hey, Cam. Do me a favor and mix for a while. I gotta hit the head and grab a drink."

The club and dance floor were packed. From the DJ booth vantage looking down into the club, I recognized managers, radio and club DJs, and bartenders in the thick crowd. Rick had let me mix some nights when no one was there, but never when the club was packed.

"Are you sure?" I asked.

"You got this. Just don't blow it." He laughed and walked out, closing the DJ booth door behind him.

"Do You Wanna Funk" by Sylvester was playing, and it had about two minutes to the break. A break is the part of a dance song where it breaks down into a drum solo. That's the best and sometimes only place to mix in your next song. To keep the energy up and keep everyone dancing, it's imperative that you align the beats of both songs to keep the rhythm the same between songs. Keeping the dance floor packed and full of energy requires solid song selection and smooth transitional mixing. I once watched the entire Coliseum dance floor stop, face the DJ booth, and boo because they didn't like the song, so the pressure was on.

Sixty seconds left. I had to pick a song, cue it up, match the speed, and get ready to mix it in. I pulled out "Babe Were Gonna Love Tonight," by Lime. I beat matched the songs and, with milliseconds to spare, dropped the instrumental synth opening over the top of the drum break in the Sylvester song. A scream went up from the dance floor. The dancers were pumping their fists in the air and yelling. Boos avoided.

Song after song, I mixed for an hour straight. The dance floor was wall-to-wall for my entire set.

The DJ booth door opened and one of the Coliseum bartenders came in.

"Hey, man, it's closing time. You gotta give last call."

I picked up the microphone. "Last call for alcohol."

I faded out the music and turned off the equipment. I walked out of the DJ booth and down the short flight of stairs through the security door into the club. Waiting just outside the DJ booth were Sid, Gordon, Rick, and a collection of DJs I knew. They were applauding. Someone pushed a shot glass into my hands.

Rick slapped me on the shoulder. "You broke your cherry. Good job, kid. Drink up."

"Where did you go? I was as nervous as hell."

"I was talking to a girl and lost track."

Rick took me aside. "Listen, Sunday nights may be opening up if you're interested."

"Are you kidding me? Yes!" I said, as the sting of the Mezcal shot hit me.

"You guys wanna keep going?" Sid asked.

"I'm kinda beat," I answered.

"Come on, Cam. Let's go to Paul's for one more drink," Gordon said.

The Coliseum closed at 4:45 am. Paul's opened at five am. Paul's Tavern was the last stop on the clubbing road trip. Or the first stop for a small cadre of aged alcoholics who would park themselves at the old school padded bar promptly at 5:01 am to drink beer in little glasses. By 5:15, Paul's would be full up with the hardcore, one-more-drink drinkers and addicts continuing their eternal quest for that ever elusive good-as-the-first-time high.

"Come on, Cam, let's celebrate you popping your big-boy DJ cherry," Sid urged.

"Yeah. Who do you think you are to deny yourself one more drink?" Gordon said.

The crew chanted, "Cam! Cam! Cam!"

"Stop already. I'll go," I said.

We loaded up a few cars to make the drive to Paul's. I squeezed into the back of Sid's car with Gordon and a guy I didn't know.

"Wanna bump?" the stranger said, digging a key into a small clear baggie.

"Nah, I don't do that," I said.

"Okay, whatever. Gordon, you want a bump?" he asked.

"Hell yeah." Gordon snorted the coke from the end of the offered key.

"What's that like?" I asked.

"Carl gets good stuff. You should get in on it," Gordon said, pinching his nose.

"What does good mean?"

"Can't explain it, buddy. Just do a bump."

Carl dug the key back into the baggie and came up with another small pile. He pushed it up under my nose. "Jesus Christ, just fuckin do it already."

I snorted the pile of white powder.

My nose lit up with a chemical smell and something else unidentifiable.

The smell turned into taste and hit the back of my throat.

I coughed. "That's awful," I said.

A laugh went up in the car.

The smell passed.

I swallowed.

My throat went numb.

The wheels in my brain engaged into a new gear.

I was awake. Extremely awake.

My vision was sharper. Edges were crisper.

I felt good. No. Forget that. I felt great.

The continual murmur of judgement that played in an endless loop in my head went silent. The quiet was delicious.

I wanted to move, dance, talk, fuck, all at once. Most of all I wanted to talk. Words tumbled out of my mouth like water from a broken faucet.

"What a great fuckin night you guys are the best I'm glad to hang with you all I can't wait to tell everyone about tonight do you guy want to go out tomorrow night wow I feel great."

The car laughed.

My lips had more. "Tonight was so cool I can't believe I got to do a full set at the Coliseum me DJing at the Coliseum so cool tonight was the start of something nothing can stop me now I'm gonna get some great gigs next stop New York City...Love you guys."

"Yo, Cam. This is what I mean by good," Gordon said.

"What?" I said.

The car laughed.

"Yo, Buck, you're high," Sid said.

"Nah, I'm just having a good night," I replied.

"Whatever you say," Gordon said as the car broke into a new round of chuckles.

Was Sid right? Was I high?

My mind was a million-point plane. Thoughts raced and banged into each other, hopping over each other to get to the front. My hair tingled. Maybe it was because of all the zooming thoughts trying to get out. My mouth was as dry as the journal of a Bedouin monk.

I felt strong, invincible, towering. Nothing could stop me. I was king of the world.

Like a drowning, desperate cat, trying one last time to sink claws into the side of a life raft, the mom's voice came. "You are out there doing drugs and drinking. Jehovah God will destroy you at Armageddon."

Maybe, but not tonight, Mom, not tonight.

Tonight, I am king.

The bass throb of "Don't Stand So Close to Me" by The Police played on the car's radio.

"Yo, Sid, turn that up," I said.

"No backseat DJing," Sid said.

Sting's voice filled the car. I sat back deeper into the car seat.

Sid looked back at me in the rear-view mirror. "You good, Buck?" His brows creased and he radiated concern.

"Yeah, I'm good. Thanks, brother." And I was good.

Was it the accolades and attention for doing something I loved? Maybe it was the friendship of a makeshift family made up of friends and strangers or the simple joy of hanging with the crew.

At that moment, I felt better than I ever had in my life.

Carl offered up the key. "Want another bump?"

But. What if it was the coke?

I woke up the next morning to a headache, an awful taste in my mouth, a stinging nose, and the mom standing over me.

"You can't live here anymore. Get out."

JOB

24

WHAT HE TAKES AWAY

"Where will I go?"

"You should have thought about that while you were out galavanting and doing worldly things with your worldly friends," the mom shot back.

"I was with Sid. I'm learning how to be a better DJ. You should have seen me last night, I—"

"Until three am? You can't just come and go as you please. This is not a hotel, and no matter what, I am still your mother and I say who lives here."

"That's when the clubs are open. What if I was working nights at some factory somewhere? I guess that would be fine with you if I came home late from working my ass off in a factory?"

"Stop cursing. You don't respect anything. You are going to die at Armageddon if you don't turn your life around. Sid's mother told me you two are messing around with girls."

"I'm not hurting anyone. I have to work, and we need money. All I'm doing is dancing, listening to music, and watching DJs. I love playing music, and I'm good at it. People like what I do. I'm working all day and night right now to make something happen in my life. Last night I was given an opportunity to work at a spot that will open up lots of gigs for me."

"Jehovah God does not approve of you playing that demonized music with people gyrating like they're possessed. That music is demonistic. And all the whores, drugs, and alcohol…"

"What have I done that is so bad, so evil that I deserve to be thrown out?"

"You have to go."

"Do you even care what happens to me? Where will I sleep?"

"With the people that love what you do. Or stay with one of the whores. This is for your own good. Maybe you'll reconsider your life and change your ways. If you do, and if you start going regularly to the meetings and out door-to-door, then we can talk about you coming back."

"Are you serious? Are you really throwing me out because I came home after midnight? Is that what this is about? Would Jesus throw out his family into the street? Is this the love that the Bible talks about, that Jesus talked about?"

"It's for your own good. I prayed on it and prayed on it, and the Elders said it was best."

"Oh, now I see. The Elders said to do this."

"They are chosen by God."

"You mean that bunch of cheap-suited window washers and janitors that can barely speak a three-syllable word? The same Elders that beat their own children and let rapists go free? Those Elders tell you it's a good idea for you to throw your teenage son into the street and you do it?"

"You have to go."

"What god agreed with this plan? It surely wouldn't be the God of love you keep going on and on about."

"Get out."

"If Dad was alive, this would not be happening."

The look the mom gave me bordered on hatred. No. That's inaccurate. It was not on the border. The look had a full-on citizenship with all rights and privileges to Hateville. I contemplated the person who had birthed me, searching for any sign that love, or at least mercy, was present. There was nothing but righteous disdain.

"You're possessed. Satan has you," she said.

There it was.

She thought I was chock full o'demons. She would rather believe I was possessed than accept that I didn't believe what she did. The late nights weren't the problem. My lack of faith was the problem.

Years of burying my true beliefs or lack thereof and going along to get along were over. All my filters and deception were done.

I let out the sickly warm breath I'd been holding in like a poisonous cloud ever since she dragged me to the first Jehovah's Witness meeting.

"That's bullshit. I just don't believe what you believe, and you can't handle that."

I didn't want to be on the street. I certainly wasn't making enough money to get a place. I stood still and quiet, hoping she would soften and change her mind.

She sat down on the couch, picked up a copy of the Awake magazine, and started reading, or pretending to read. On the cover was a smiling, happy family. The irony of that cover made me burst out a quick laugh. She glared at me.

"Mom."

She would not look at me.

"Can I at least stay for a few weeks to save some money so I can get a place?"

"No. That's it. Get out." She didn't look up from her sacred magazine.

This was it. The eighteen-year battle of wills was over. All that was left on the battlefield was a damaged woman who'd given up her individuality and all she ever was to a strict, fundamentalist faith and a boy dying to be heard past the choke of those beliefs. A boy trying to strike a bargain between what a heart-broken, terrified mother told him he had to be and the space he needed to become a man.

It was clear that a peace treaty would never be signed and there could be no winners. Only pain and fear and anger were left, pounded into the mud under the canons of ego and hurt. Nothing I could do would reverse her decision.

I went to my bedroom and packed the little clothing I owned into a duffle bag. My eight-year-old brother, Sean, was sitting on the bed watching me. The mom had blocked most of my attempts to have a relationship with him through the years because she feared my individuality would rub off on him, and our age difference didn't help. I felt bad leaving him, but I didn't see what, if anything, I could do. Maybe one day I could come back for him.

I gave him a hug. "No matter what, never lose who you are."

He sat quiet, unresponsive. I went to the mom's side.

"I'll be back for my records. Bye, Mom."

No response.

I left.

I sat on my motorcycle in the parking lot of our apartment building. My brother peeked out of the window. He gave me a little wave.

Reality sunk in. I was an eighteen-year-old high school dropout with a low-wage job, no skills, and now, no family and nowhere to live.

Adrenaline pumped through my veins and a feeling of panic and nausea punched me in my gut. I was incapacitated, unable to decide what to do next. My motorcycle seemed to start and drive itself to a safe place. I needed time to think. I needed a plan. As always, the library gave me both.

I sat at my favorite table for hours, bent over, head in hands. The librarian passed by and asked me if I was alright. I managed an up and down shake of my head under my hand-covered face. I didn't want her or anyone else to see me crying. She brought over a paper cup of water and set it on the table.

"You aren't supposed to have food or drink in here, but..." She drifted away when I didn't respond.

Her kindness poked a hole in my sadness.

Enough. I took a deep breath. I wiped my face. No more wallowing. No more feeling sorry for myself. What was done was done. I had been here before. In fact, it was at this very same table, surrounded by these very same books, that I gave myself permission to be happy after my father died.

Maybe getting thrown out was exactly what I needed. And really, could it have gone any other way? My soul had been crying out for the freedom to do and be something of my own choosing. Here was my chance. I was now the lone master of my future. But I was scared. All I had was a beat-up motorcycle, a bag of clothes, and a few crates of records. What if I couldn't do it? What if I wasn't brave enough, strong enough, smart enough?

I missed my dad.

Head up, I looked around at the shelves, thick with books. Maybe I wasn't alone. In reality, I had friends and family an arm's reach from where I sat. Bound up in cardboard and leather, stories contained in these plastic-wrapped books had guided me for over a decade. My head and heart were crowded with characters from every book I'd ever read—from Johnathan Livingston, Socrates, and Nietzsche to artists Picasso, Duchamp, and all their Dadaist friends, to Edison, Einstein, and the greatest thinkers and scientists and poets from all of history. All their struggles and triumphs, joys and pains, poems and teachings were part of me and always would be. I also had two great friends in Sid and Gordon. Not many people could claim friends as good or as loyal.

For the first few weeks after getting thrown out, I stayed at Sid's house, riding my motorcycle to my job as store manager at an import-export store in the Cherry Hill Mall. Considering the hours I was required to work, it didn't pay well, but I was grateful to have it.

Having a motorcycle as my only transportation presented a challenge, and that challenge's name was *weather*. Sid and both of his parents worked, so I couldn't ask them for a ride. Besides, I was inconveniencing them enough by staying at their home. I also needed a car to carry crates of records to my DJ gigs. Getting rides was wearing thin, and leaving my records at the clubs was risky. I needed a car, and I needed one right away.

I walked into a local car dealership down the road from Sid's house with no down payment money and non-existent credit and somehow drove away with a used Toyota Celica. Although I had no idea what I was signing and the salesperson didn't spend any time explaining, I signed for an $8,000 car loan with an insane 25% APR. The worst part of the deal was that the car was only worth $2,000 and it was a lemon. Bad breaks, bad tires, bad carb, and the list went on. The salesman, as a "favor," had his cousin sign me up for car insurance that was 25% higher than if I'd purchased it directly from an agency. Yeah, they got me good.

Driving back to Sid's house with my overpriced lemon, I was excited. I wasn't sure how I was going to make the monthly payment, plus insurance, but I had plans. If I picked up one more night of DJing in addition to my mall job, I would be set. Hell, I could land one more gig. I felt it in my bones; things were turning around. I would get through this. I would do more than just survive. I would build a life worth writing about.

I pulled into Sid's driveway with my new ride, excited to show it off. I knocked on the front door. Sid's mom appeared, looking like she'd just tasted something bad.

"Hi Judy." She looked upset. "What's wrong?"

"Your mother called. You can't stay here anymore."

25

ADVICE FOR THE RECENTLY DISPLACED

My duffle bag was on the hallway floor. It was packed.

"Your mother told me that the Elders said she should ask you to leave home. She said you don't believe in the teachings of the Bible and of Jehovah's organization. Is this true?" Judy asked.

I chuckled. "Asked me to leave? Is that how she put it?"

"You know I follow Jehovah God's representatives on Earth, and I need to follow the Elder's advice."

Unbelievable. It wasn't enough that the mom threw me out. Now she was making sure no one would help me.

"Thanks for letting me stay with you. Please tell Sid I'll be okay and I'll catch up with him later."

"I will. Take care of yourself."

"Seems I'm the only one who can."

There are so many things you take for granted when you have a home. A place to shower. A place to go to the bathroom. A place to clean and hang your clothes. An address to receive mail. The worst part of being without a place, besides the constant stress, is feeling like you no longer exist. You know that disconnected from society feeling you have when you go camping or hiking? It's like that, but in a bad way, and without the fresh air. Most days I felt like the invisible man, floating around the real people as they went about their daily lives.

In the first months after leaving Sid's, I worked out the big technical challenges. I had a cash deal with the manager of the local gym, so I had a place to shower. As a side benefit, I was getting in great shape. I learned to time my eating to avoid having to go to the bathroom while "in the wild." I grabbed a PO box for my mail and bills. I found the laundromats in town. Laundromats are great. While my clothes were in the dryer I could grab a nap, read a book, or talk to the interesting denizens of the day.

When I first slept in my car, I parked behind strip malls or in parking lots at the library or public parks. All bad choices. The police regularly patrolled those places and used the spots themselves for twenty-minute on-duty naps or late-night hookups with their girlfriends.

I shifted to sleeping in residential areas. Apartment complexes were best, but they had their own risks. There were often assigned parking spots or a shortage of spots to start with.

Warm. Snug. Wrapped in a soft white cocoon of lovely. If I stayed in it long enough, I was sure to emerge something better, but something evil was fingering the cracks, prying at the edges with metal fingernails. A persistent TAP TAP TAP on my carapace was splitting the peace of my good place. NO! LEAVE ME BE! TAP TAP TAP. Please, just five more minutes Dad. TAP TAP TAP. It wasn't Dad. Dad would not take me away from this holy place. Besides, Dad went on to the next thing years ago. It had to be other. Evil other. TAP TAP TAP. Lifting now, cooling. As I floated up and looked back, the cocoon morphed into the front door of my childhood home on Chestnut Lane. Apple pie and pine tree smells drifted up from the visage like cartoon vapors teasing Sylvester.

Tap. TAP.

"I'm awake, I'm awake," I said, relinquishing the warmth of my dream.

The light of the cop's Maglite scorched my face. I reached down and put my seat up.

"Hands on the steering wheel. Open the window," the cop yelled at the glass, making a circle motion with his flashlight.

I wasn't sure how I could do both at the same time, so I put my right hand on the wheel and opened the window with my left. I was careful and slow to avoid escalation. I knew how fast these things could turn.

Sid and Gordon had shared with me their hard-learned lessons on the safest way to act when encountering the police. Their advice was based on dozens of "Driving While Black" stops. Sid laughingly called it DWB, but it was the kind of laugh that covered over something else. Sid joked that white boys like me probably didn't need "The Lesson," but it was better to be safe than sorry.

Sid's Ten Rules for Getting Pulled Over:

1. Smile at the officer. Then smile some more.
2. Stay calm and move slowly.
3. Only do what they ask you to do.
4. Do what they ask while repeating their exact command.
5. Do not ask questions.
6. Say "sir" and "yes, officer" and nod your head up and down a lot.
7. Keep your license and registration in your upper pocket when you drive. Do not reach into your glove box or center compartment, ever, for any reason, unless you ask for permission first.
8. Watch your emotions, words, and your body language, even if they are treating you unfairly.
9. If they decide to arrest you, go limp and compliant. Even the smallest movement away from their intended direction of your body will be considered resisting.
10. If they beat you, cover your head.

"Why are you sleeping here? Are you drunk?" the cop said.

"No, sir. I'm just very tired sir. I didn't want to fall asleep driving, so I was just grabbing a quick nap."

"You're drunk, aren't you?"

"No, sir, officer, sir." Big smile.

"License and registration."

I got my license out of my wallet, then requested and received permission to pull the registration out of the glove box. I handed them over, making a mental note to keep both in my pocket going forward.

The cop went back to his car.

I never understood the immediate suspicion I received when a cop found me sleeping in my car. Not once in all my wake-ups did a cop ever ask if I needed help.

The officer returned. "Step out of the car."

"Yes, officer, I am stepping out of the car."

"Walk heel-to-toe nine steps, stop, then walk back the same way."

"Yes, officer."

I walked heel-to-toe.

"Follow my finger."

I followed his finger as he moved it from side to side.

"Recite the alphabet backwards."

Uh oh.

"Officer, I have not been drinking, but your request is gonna be tough for me. I have dyslexia."

The officer stepped back three feet.

"What's that? Can I catch that?"

"No, officer, it's a disability that causes me to mix up the order of things."

"Yeah. Sure."

"Honestly, officer, it's a thing."

He considered me for a moment and pushed the button on the radio microphone attached to his shirt.

"Fourteen to dispatch."

"Go ahead, Fourteen," came a female voice over his radio.

"Beth, you ever hear of something called dyslexia?"

"Yeah, my neighbor's kid has that. It's a retard thing."

"Thanks, dispatch."

"You don't look retarded. Are you lying to me?"

"No, sir. I will take any other test you care to give me."

He handed back my license and registration.

He took out his baton and cracked me across my upper arm. Pain shot through my arm and chest, driving me back against the car. I fell to the ground, clutching my arm and braced for another.

"Go sleep at home, retard. Cars aren't for sleeping. If I catch you here again, I'll give you a real beat down."

Fuck you, officer asshat. Fuck you and your dispatcher for your ignorant, degrading comments about people with disabilities. Fuck you and your baton. Fuck you for hitting me when I was just trying to grab a few hours of sleep. Fuck you for ignoring the fact that I am a human just like you or your brother or your kids. Fuck you, your violence, and your authoritarian douchebaggery.

I didn't want my ass dead or in jail, so instead of saying all that, I gave him a big fake smile as I was taught and said, "Thank you, officer."

26

RESPITE

"It's okay. Just admit it. I won't judge," Lori said.

"But I'm not," I said.

"Really, it's okay. You can admit it. My best friend is gay. He's single. And cute. I'll introduce you, maybe you'll hit it off."

"But I'm not gay. I like women."

"Then why won't you fuck me? Guys would never say no unless…"

"I'm exhausted. You're very sexy, but I need to sleep. Is that okay?"

"It's okay to be gay. Just admit it."

Lori couldn't imagine a man not wanting to be with her or being too tired to get busy. I imagined the reverse happening, and how annoyed she would be if I insisted she was a lesbian because she wouldn't have sex with me. It seemed like a rash of people lately had been asking about my sexuality. Why did people automatically associate being different with being gay? It was confusing and silly. Granted, I should have been honest with her at the start of the evening and told her that I wanted her for her bed, not her body.

I'd met Lori at the club and gone home with her. After debating with her for thirty minutes, I decided there was only one way to get some shut eye.

"You're right Lori, I am gay. Thank you for letting me come out to you."

"See, I knew it." She clapped her hands like a toddler given cake.

"Can we just hold each other and sleep now?"

"I'm so proud of you." She hugged me. "You and I will be best friends."

When I left in the morning, she gave me her friend's number in case I needed someone to talk to about my new "out" life. She also invited me to brunch and shopping with her girlfriends. Did she think all gay men were into brunching and shopping? Were they? I wondered if gay men found stereotyping as annoying as I did. I made a mental note to ask a gay man if I ever met one.

I was as horny as any other young man at eighteen, but I had only been with one girl up to that point. I'm not saying I didn't fool around occasionally, but I managed to not go "all the way" with the girls I went home with during that time. In fact, I became a bit of an expert at avoiding sex.

When asked where I lived, I would tell them I lived at home and my mother was a religious nut that didn't approve of me dating. A few times I cracked and let the truth slip. The first time was with a girl named Laura. I met her while DJing on a Friday night. She'd come to the club with her coworkers after finishing her waitressing shift at a local restaurant. She chatted me up in the DJ booth and we hit it off. She invited me to her place.

"In my car," I answered.

"What do you mean, in your car?"

"Just that. I've been living out of my car for a while now."

"What? You poor thing. Why?"

"It's a long story."

"Got somewhere to go?"

I laughed. "Ouch. That hurt. No, I guess not."

She kissed my cheek. "I'll get us some drinks."

She filled two chipped glasses with whiskey from her modest bar set up.

She plopped down on the couch next to me. "So, let's hear it."

For the first time since I was thrown out, I opened up, wide. I turned off the filters, raised the curtains, and let go. Most people don't listen. Instead, they wait for the other person to finish speaking so they can say their piece and find a way to relate it back to themselves. At best, most folks listen halfway, until they think they know what you're saying, then they start mentally formulating their response.

I prided myself in being a good listener. Laura was like me, an active, patient listener. I told her about my suburban upbringing, the death of my father, and the mom joining a cult. I shared the abuse, both physical and mental, that I'd experienced at the hands of the mom and others. I told her about the guilt and almost paralyzing fear that permeated my waking moments. I confessed that, despite not intellectually believing in the whole Armageddon thing, it would sometimes still hit me like a baseball bat to my stomach. I told her about my reading disability and the insecurities as a result. I went wide open.

Letting it all out with someone who truly listened was glorious, and the sharing went both ways. She had issues of her own, and she poured them out to me, telling me about her tough childhood and challenges she'd faced after being adopted in Korea and taken to America. I guess we both sensed in each other the need to be heard, to be seen, to be understood. I couldn't figure out why we trusted each other so soon after meeting. I considered that maybe it was because we were strangers and figured we might never see each other again. That might have been it, but I think it was more than that. Something about that night, that time, aligned for us to connect. We talked for seven hours straight. By morning, we had burned half a bottle of cheap whiskey. We were emotionally spent, voiceless, and more than a little tipsy. We moved to her bed. In silent agreement, we fell asleep in each other's arms, wrapped up like lovers on her twin bed.

We slept until three the next day. It was the deepest sleep I'd had in a long time. We lay in bed after waking, groggy, unwilling to move, the sun cutting through her window blinds like laser beams making a cross hatch of light across us. I detangled myself from her and made my way to the bathroom to dispense the whiskey and morning breath back to the hell from whence they came.

I was finger brushing my teeth when Laura said through the closed door, "There might be an unopened toothbrush under the sink."

I rinsed. "I'm good. I've got my trusty finger brush with me."

A giggle came through the door. "You know what?" Laura said.

"You're considering throwing away your toothbrush and joining me in the all-natural finger brushing movement?"

"No, silly. I'm firmly in the toothbrush camp as God and the good people at Crest intended."

I opened the door. Laura was sitting up in the bed, white sheet pulled tight against her naked body. Errant beams of sunlight fell across her, highlighting her breasts and thighs under the sheet. She brushed her long, black hair away from her face, sweeping a few stubborn strands away from her lips, looking at the strands as if they had intentionally betrayed her.

The morning light revealed her beauty. *Exotic* is the word most would have used to describe her, but that didn't cover it. Her mother was Korean and her father was German, and I could see both in her face. Laura had almond-shaped eyes that shone with inner hard-won confidence. Her eyes were framed by high cheekbones. The relaxed way she lay in bed couldn't hide a self-aware, almost formal posture.

I found enough breath to squeak out, "You were asking?"

"Huh?"

"You asked me if I knew what."

"Oh yeah. You know what?"

"I do not, for certain and true, know what, so please tell me."

"Come here." She patted the bed next to her.

"Yes, ma'am."

"I like a respectful, obedient man." She flashed me a gigawatt smile. I tried hard to hide what it did to me.

I sat on the bed. Her nipples, hard against the white sheet, pulled my gaze.

"Um, my eyes are up here, thank you." She laughed.

"I know exactly where everything is, thank you. So, you were saying?"

"Yeah, so, we didn't even kiss last night."

"We were using our lips for talking and drinking whiskey."

"We should have been using them for other things."

"It's never too late. Maybe we should shut up?"

"Yeah, maybe."

I leaned in and we kissed, tentative at first, expanding into a deep passionate kiss. It was the kind of kiss where you lose yourself. The kind of kiss where the outside world ceases to exist, and everything focuses down to just the two of you. She ran her hands through the hair on the sides of my head and pulled me down into the bed. After a few minutes of intense kissing, she pushed me away.

"Thank God," she said.

"What's that mean?"

"A kiss can tell you everything you need to know."

"I think I know what you mean."

"Dammit!"

"What's wrong?"

"I wish we'd started this earlier. Damn, damn, damn. I have to go to work. I have a double shift that starts in half an hour."

"So quit." I laughed.

"I wish. Unless you have room in your car for the two of us, I have to get a move on."

"I'll trade it in for a van. A big one with a girl riding a dragon painted on the side."

"I'm in."

She put her face, nose to nose, against mine, and gave me a quick kiss. The breathless thing happened. "Damn, damn, damn." She kissed me again, jumped up and headed into the bathroom.

The shower started with a hiss. "You can stay here and clean up before you have to head out," she said. "There's stuff in the fridge if you're hungry."

She came out of the bathroom, freshly showered, wearing nothing but a towel. I wanted to restart the kissing.

"Thank you for trusting me," I said.

"If I didn't trust you, I wouldn't have invited you over. I've learned to trust my gut, and so far, my gut hasn't let me down. That doesn't mean I won't do a background check on ya." There was that smile again.

"When can I see you again? Provided I pass the background check and buy a van of course."

"I should be done with my shift by midnight. We can get together after, or, heck, you could just stay right where you are."

My turn to shine a smile. "I have to DJ tonight, but I should be done by two?"

"See you after?"

"Yes, after is good."

"Great. It's a date."

She dressed in a hurry, giving me fan-dancer flashes of her lithe body. She kissed me one last time. Hard.

"Here's my number. Lock up on your way out. I'm looking forward to after."

As I lazed alone in her bed, I felt fully relaxed for the first time in a while. The night of connection and promise of more gave me the space to forget the bad stuff for a minute. I took in a breath and slowly let it out. I hadn't realized how much I was physically holding in until some of it escaped. The balloon of stress that filled the spot where my heart used to be wasn't quite as tight. My connection with Laura felt like a beginning. The romantic in me wanted to start imagining a future with her.

Stop it. You don't know enough about her to go down that road.

Yeah, but she knows everything that's wrong and she still wants to see me again. I'm a loser.

Yep. You are, but she could be serial killer, you don't know.

Nah, serial killers are never good kissers, are they? How could they be?

Probably not, but then again, I don't know many serial killers.

I bet that kid who tried to kill us under the big tree grew into one.

Oh, him? Most definitely. Probably killing someone right now. Anyways…she sure is a great kisser.

Oh my, yes. I want more of that.

Tonight.

Yes, tonight.

How about we get up and take a shower like a real boy, maybe get some food in us to soak up the whiskey?

But this bed feels so good.

Five more minutes. Deal?

Deal.

I left her house feeling more positive about life than I had in a long time. I couldn't wait for our date.

27

WHISKEY LULLABY

I floated through the rest of my day, checking off errands, including picking up a bottle of whiskey to replace the one Laura and I had polished off. I stopped at the laundromat to get my clothes smelling nice and fresh. While waiting for the dryer to finish, Boo Boo showed up. I'd met Boo Boo on my first visit to the laundromat. A veteran, he'd had been on the street for years, and he spent a fair amount of his time at the laundromat.

"Yo, Cam. What's good?"

"Got a date tonight so I gotta clean my duds."

"Yeah, me too." He laughed in his helium pitch. "Where did ya meet her, and does she have a sister for me?"

"At a club, where else?"

"You got a place yet?"

"No, still living at the Toyota Inn."

"Better than what I got." His smile faded.

Boo Boo was street homeless. No car or couch for Boo Boo. He had a few regular outdoor sleeping spots and made food money from recycling cans, panhandling, and occasional labor jobs. I gave him a few bucks when I had a few to spare. When he found out I was going through it, he offered to show me how it was, how to get by. He told me about some rescue missions and he even offered to show me a few spots where I could bed down if it ever got to that.

Boo Boo got his nickname because his voice was high pitched like Boo Boo from the Yogi Bear cartoon, but the name and voice didn't fit him. He was a burly dark-skinned guy, over six feet with a crescent-shaped dent in his forehead. He had what he laughingly called a resting murder face.

"No regular bed yet?" I asked.

"Nah. I went up to the shelter a few times but some shit went down. Plus, the boss up there, he an asshole."

"Sorry, Boo Boo. Wish there was something I could do."

"No wups. I appreciate it. You got your own shit, I'm sure. So, how'd an ugly ass white boy like you get a date?"

"Dunno. Just found one that didn't look too closely at me. In her defense, it was dark in the club."

Boo Boo smiled. When he did, his resting murder face turned semi-angelic.

"I bet she's blind. You stole her cane, didn't ya?" Boo Boo cracked himself up and doubled over laughing at his own bust.

"Promised it back if she went on a date with you, didn't ya?" He was howling now. His laughing switched to a body-wracking cough.

"You're gonna kill yourself with your own jokes."

"Maybe," he said, catching his breath. "But it's not the worst way to go out."

"What's the worst way?" I said, setting him up for his next delivery.

"Waking up in bed next to your ugly ass and dying cause of the shame."

Boo Boo was in a full bent-over, cough-laughing spasm. Seeing the big guy doubled over laughing like he'd inhaled helium was quite the sight. A lady with a baby on her hip dragging a laundry bag opened the door to the laundromat and froze in the doorway, trying to figure out the tableau before her. Safety calculations occurred in real time on her face. She must have decided that the stinking bag of baby clothes she was dragging exceeded the risk to her personal safety and came in. She maintained a careful, side-eyed glance at both of us as she set up.

"You good?" I asked Boo Boo. "Do you need some water or something?"

"Naw, I'm good. Phew, that's some funny shit."

"You really crack yourself up."

"You gotta laugh or it will get ya."

"Truth. On a serious note, you doing okay?"

"What can I say? I'm getting through. Some days, better than others. Some days, worse."

"Did you ever connect with your cousin?"

"Yeah, but he ain't got much room for me, and his girl won't have none of it."

"Gotcha."

"You know, Cam my man, I can deal with most of the shit, but you know what gets me the most?" he said, the last of his humor draining.

"What's that?"

"The way folks look at us. Or worse yet, how they won't." He looked down at his shoes. "Sometimes it's like I'm the invisible man, get me? When they do look at us, like this lady here, they look at us like you gonna do something bad. I ain't never hurt nobody in my life. Not even in the Army, when they pushed a rifle on me. It ain't right. I'm a good man. I ain't a bad man, I ain't invisible neither, I'm only homeless."

"I see you, Boo Boo." I gave him a smile.

"I wish you'd stop looking at me with that ugly mug of yours!" Boo Boo went back to laughing and coughing.

The bar was packed that night, and the energy was great. My mixes and music were on point, and the owner gave me a smiling nod when he passed the DJ booth. After closing, I couldn't pack up my records fast enough. I skipped my after-work beer with the bartenders and made a beeline for Laura's. Her car wasn't in front, and it looked like she wasn't home yet. Just to confirm I knocked on her door. Nope, not home yet. I went back to my car to wait.

The clock rounded 3:00 am, then 3:30 am. My heart sank as the clock ticked off the minutes. I was getting stood up. Even if she'd gone out for a drink after her shift, there was no way she should be getting back this late. I guessed she could have gone to the diner to get something to eat and lost track of time. But she knew I'd be at her place by 2:30, didn't she? Had I imagined our connection? Did I get the details wrong somehow? Was it the whiskey? I waited some more.

The clock rounded 4:00, then 4:30. Still no Laura. Yea, she stood me up. But it made no sense. Why would she do that? Was she staying away from her own home just to avoid me? No, it couldn't be that. She must have met someone else, or she had a boyfriend that she didn't tell me about and she was with him.

I knew it was too good to be true. No one wanted to be with a guy in my situation. I understood. I left her parking lot before someone called the police on me for sitting in my car. I drove to one of my safe spots and tried to catch some sleep before the sun came up.

I slept a few broken hours in the car. I went to my gym to work out and take a shower. I found a payphone and called Laura's place. It rang and went to voice mail. I didn't leave a message. I spent the rest of the day oscillating between being upset that she'd stood me up and an increasing feeling of confusion. It didn't make sense. Like a stalker, I drove past her place to see if her car was there. It wasn't.

I should just leave it all be, I thought. If she wanted to see me again, she knew where I DJ'd. I tried, but I couldn't let it go. I found a payphone and called her house again. No answer. Against all my instincts, I drove to the restaurant where she worked.

"Hi, just you today?" the hostess asked.

"Is Laura working?"

"Uh, no I'm sorry, she a, she's, um..."

"Is she off today?"

"Can you hold on a minute?" The hostess disappeared toward the back of the restaurant.

A man came out to the hostess stand. His name badge said Manager Tim.

"I'm sorry, Laura is not here. Can we seat you with someone else?"

"No, thank you. I'm a friend of hers and I was just stopping by to say hi."

"I am so sorry. So, so sorry. You didn't hear?" he said in a lowered tone.

"Hear what?"

The manager took me by the shoulder and led me into a part of the restaurant that was unoccupied.

"I'm so sorry. Laura was in an accident after she left here last night."

"A what? You mean a car accident? Where is she, what hospital, where?"

"You should talk with Laura's family."

"I don't know her family. Where did they take her?"

"I don't know where they took her, but we heard earlier today."

"Heard what? Heard where they took her?"

"I'm so sorry. We heard…we heard she passed."

"Passed? What the hell does that mean? *What is passed? Passed what?"*

Nothing made sense. I couldn't breathe. What was this Tim guy even saying? He made no fucking sense. I didn't feel right. No air. No air. I needed air.

"Passed away."

"No no no no no no. NO. That's not possible. Don't say that. You...you got it wrong."

"I'm so sorry."

I left the restaurant and drove to the closest hospital. The front desk wouldn't or couldn't tell me anything because I didn't know her last name. I called the restaurant and spoke to Tim. He wouldn't tell me her last name. I went to all the local hospitals within a twenty-mile radius and spoke with admissions, the front desk, and anyone who would talk to me. Nothing. I couldn't think of anything else to do other than camp out in front of her place, and that was a bad idea. That would lead to cops.

I needed my best friend. I needed Sid.

"Hey, Buck," Sid said as he opened the door. "Come on in." He hugged me. "I guess you heard."

"Heard what?"

"About Gordon. I stopped by the store yesterday, but you were off. Where you been staying, anyway? I need a way to reach you. I left a message with them to give to you when you came in."

"What are you talking about?"

"I thought maybe you found out from his sister."

"I haven't seen his sister. Found out what? What are you talking about?"

"Gordon is dead."

I stood there unable to speak. Nothing made sense. None of this was real. It wasn't a dream, so I was probably being held down somewhere getting drugs shot into me. It had to be a hallucinogenic fever dream.

I was still at home and both of my parents were standing over me, worried because I wasn't going to make it to my first day of college, but it would be okay because the doctors were treating me and soon I'd be right as rain, and I would kiss them both and go off to college, graduate with honors, and go on to help researchers unlock the secrets of curing cancer. After falling madly in love while on a trip to a conference in Paris, I would marry and we would have two children and I would go to the museums and jazz clubs and have the most amazing time, and we would all go to sleep safe and secure in the home we built together, so full of love, and the next day we would have all of our friends over for a barbecue and we would love and support each other as we talked about our goals and future dreams. Our children would grow into the most wonderful and unique people, overflowing with tolerance, love, and intelligence. They would be the kindest people, and everyone would love and respect and admire them. And Sundays were always the best days. Sid and his family would come over and we would listen to jazz, talk of books and music, and cook together. As night approached my family would go to sleep, safe and secure in the big house full of love, ready for whatever the new week threw at us because we had each other's backs. We were family and that's what families did.

But none of that was true. There was nothing but death on Sunday. Death and a black vacuum that sucked the goodness away from the warm soul of the world. It wasn't worth it anymore. I was out of fight. Maybe it was time to go. I was half gone already. What would actually change if I left? I was barely a scratch on a tiny ball in a vast universe of who gives a fuck. Sure, Sid would miss me, but he would be okay.

Fuck it. Fuck it all. Fuck it all straight to hell.

The world went black.

I went down.

Two funerals in one weekend.

Both closed caskets.

The sensitive girl I'd held in my arms and my beautiful friend who'd spread joy with nothing more than a smile were both destroyed so thoroughly by this world that their faces could not be seen one last time by the ones who remained, by those who loved them. They were just...gone.

After I'd regained consciousness on Sid's floor and rejected an ambulance, Sid moved me into the guest room. There, Sid told me that Gordon had died in a car accident while working on a turnpike repair crew. When I finally collected myself, Sid's mom said it was time for me to go. Sid objected, but she couldn't be swayed. I lied and told them both I had somewhere to stay.

I checked the newspaper every day that week, sitting alone in my car scanning the obituaries. Gordon's and Laura's appeared next to each other on the same day. Their pictures looked so full of life and joy. The connecting line between them was me. I felt guilty, as if it were my fault. Maybe if neither of them had known me, they would still be alive.

Gordon's family was sitting in the front row of burgundy chairs at the funeral home. I passed his mother, father, and sister. I'd never seen such despair so close. Shadow traces of smiles flashed across their faces, rising upon seeing a familiar face, then receded immediately under the weight of reality. The hardest sting was reserved for the look on Gordon's girlfriend's face. She was five months pregnant with their child. She was blank. Sid knelt in front of her and took her limp hands in his. There was no response. He tenderly kissed her hands.

"Whatever you need, we got you," Sid said.

She looked up and past him to the closed coffin. Sitting on the lid was a picture of Gordon in a silver frame. She expelled a sharp burst of a laugh. It passed and the blankness returned.

A low, scolding murmur went through the attendees. Maybe they didn't understand the laugh, but I did. There was nothing anyone could ever do to fix her need. Her life course was permanently altered. Nothing could change that. All her hopes, dreams, and plans for her unborn child were now dust. In that second, I understood why people need gods.

Sid asked me to come back to his house for the night, but I couldn't be in a place where I wasn't welcome because of the Jehovah's Witnesses. I'd rather have died on the street. It wasn't Sid's fault; it wasn't anyone's. It just was what it was.

The next day, I went alone to Laura's funeral. I was welcomed by an usher who handed me a piece of paper and a small pencil like the kind you use at bowling alleys to keep score. Friends and family were being asked to write a note that would be placed in the coffin.

I was an imposter. I didn't belong with the people who really knew her, loved her, and were infinitely changed by her loss. The blank paper looked back at me accusingly. I wrote a message anyway and got in line. As I neared the casket, I shook like I'd been dipped in freezing water and left, naked, to dry outside in winter. On top of Laura's coffin were photos in frames. Someone had forgotten to remove a price sticker from one of the frames. I wanted to scratch off the sticker, but I didn't. If the photos were to be believed, she came from a big happy family.

My hand shook as I placed my note on top of the others in the ornate box next to the coffin.

Laura,

Thank you for listening. Thank you for accepting. Thank you for the time you shared with me. I wish you had more, but wishes are never enough. - Cam

So, this is how it goes? One second you're here, and the next second you're...what? Gone? Gone where? Somewhere? Nowhere? What are we doing here scratching away at life like a chickens pecking at the ground for grubs while the farmer sharpens his knives? What did it all matter? What a fraud.

28

CARDBOARD

I woke up to chilled air blowing across my face and human stink from a man holding my car door open. He smelled of piss and sweat, and in his hand was a knife. Red-rimmed eyes over a scraggly beard looked down at me. "Get out of the car," he said.

"You deaf? Get outta of the car." He waved the knife at me.

Adrenalin snapped my hungover head into the now.

"Easy, easy. I'm getting out."

"Red Eyes" backed away. My passenger door opened. There was a second one. This one was younger, thin, with acne scars and a stubbled, shaved head covered with unreadable tattoos. "You heard him. Get out," he said, revealing a mouth of mostly gums.

With hands up, I swung my legs out of the car. My head throbbed, and my mouth tasted like both of them had slept in it. I stumbled standing up. The whiskey bottle I had done my best to finish the previous night after the funerals of two friends fell out of the car with a clatter, spilling the last mouthful on the ground between me and Red Eyes. I considered picking up the empty and bashing him in the head.

He must have read it on my face. "Don't even try it," Red Eyes said.

My head felt like it was going to explode. I sat down in the dirt. The hilarity of it all hit me. I, who had nothing, was getting robbed. I laughed at the ridiculousness of my life as a wave of nausea roiled through me. How had it gotten to this?

"Empty your pockets." Red Eyes waved the knife like he was filleting a flying fish.

I stood up and turned them inside out. Seven singles and some change hit the gravel. He picked it up.

"Where's the rest of it?" Red Eyes asked.

"You picked the wrong person to roll. That's all I have."

For a second, I thought about jumping him to get the knife, but something about the way he held it told me he knew how to use it and probably had. I played out scenarios in my hung-over head, and every way I ran it, I ended up perforated. I was in no shape to risk getting stabbed for my meager possessions, but given the chance, I would have killed both of them with my bare hands for one aspirin.

They loaded themselves into my car. Gums turned the key and was met with the rapid "click, click, click" of a dead battery. In my drunken state, I must have left the radio or the heater on all night. After several more attempts and copious amounts of cursing, they gave up. I just sat in the gravel laughing like some kind of idiot.

"You think this is funny?" Red Eyes spat.

"Don't you?" I said.

"Something's wrong with him," Gums said. He threw my keys in a high arc into the overgrown grass next to the warehouse's parking lot. "How bout that? You think that's funny?"

"You don't get it, do you?," I said. "It's all a farce. This is a comedy show to entertain the gods. The poor steal from the poorer while the masters run it all."

"Shut your hole," Red Eyes said.

"Live a good life and good will come to you? Right? Isn't that what they say?" I said. "It's a bullshit story made up for children. Just like Santa Clause and the Easter Bunny. What a joke."

"No shit, Sherlock," Gums said out of the side of his mouth as he and Red Eyes beat feet outta there, leaving me alone with my dead car.

I crawled around in the grass until I found my keys, then sat in my car until most of the nausea and the worst of the pathos passed. If I was going to get my car moving, I needed a jump or a battery, and they weren't going to magically come to me. I didn't even have a quarter to call for help. What I desperately needed, more than a solution to my battery problem, was water. I left on foot to find some.

Boo Boo was sitting on the curb in his usual spot in front of the laundromat. "Yo Cam, what's good?" he asked.

"Nothing."

"Oh mama, look at you. What's happened?"

I told him, then followed him to the back of the laundromat where he got me aspirin from a first-aid box hanging near the manager's office.

"Here you go. The owner won't mind," he said. "Me and her got an arrangement. You can get water from the rinse sink."

I drank like it was an elixir sent from the gods themselves.

"You're such a dummy," Boo Boo scolded. "I showed you the safe places. Why didn't you do like I showed you?"

"I dunno, Boo Boo, I dunno. I thought I was safer in my car."

"Trust me. I been on the street a long time. People see you in a car and figure you got stuff. People being people an all, they gonna try and take your shit."

He looked at me the way you'd look at a child who'd just tried to pet a feral dog. "You ever go to the Sunday Breakfast mission like I told you?"

"I don't remember you ever talking about breakfast."

"Let's go. Get on up. We going."

"But I don't need breakfast. I need a battery or a jump."

"Later. Let's go."

"Where?"

Boo Boo grabbed me and lifted me to my feet like I was a doll.

"To the Sunday Breakfast Mission. They got beds."

"Okay, okay. I'll go with you. Put me down."

"What's the magic word?"

"Please?"

"Good white boy." A huge grin softened his face as he lowered me to the ground.

We hopped the speed line in New Jersey and got off at Eighth and Market in Philly. I slogged behind him through the city for ten blocks. Boo Boo stopped in front of an old, well maintained, tan brick building. If it weren't for the group of people milling about in front of it, you would have thought it was a nice hotel. Over the entry was a sign that read Sunday Breakfast Association.

"This here is the mission." Boo Boo pushed me inside the vestibule.

"You know you can't stay here, Boo Boo. Not after last time," Terrance the intake manager said through the metal grill.

"That shit wasn't my fault T, and you know that."

"Language Boo Boo, language. This is the Lord's place."

"Sorry, T. Look, I ain't here for me any old way. Someone threw away this perfectly good white boy, and he needs a bed for a few days to get himself right."

"All full up for tonight, but he can get on the list."

"Give him your name," Boo Boo said.

I gave Terrance my name.

"Be outside at 4:45. If we call your name, you get a bed. If not, you can try again tomorrow. God bless," Terrance said by way of dismissing us.

"Boo Boo, I appreciate what you're trying to do, but I need to get some cash for a battery before someone takes my car."

"I hear ya. Probably no bed for you tonight anyway." Boo Boo rubbed his chin. "Alright, let's go."

"Where are we going now?"

"For someone that ain't got nowhere to go, you sure ask a lot of questions. Come on."

Boo Boo walked me to a bench and pulled out a marker and some pieces of cardboard from his army green backpack.

He handed me a piece. "Here, write you a sign."

I took the cardboard from Boo Boo, noticing his dry, white, cracked knuckles, worn from exposure to the street and its weather. I wondered what I looked like after sleeping in my clothes, getting mugged by the stink breath twins, and rolling around on the ground and grass. I made a minimal effort to smooth out the worst of me.

The cardboard sat in my lap looking up at me. I took the black marker in hand. I knew what Boo Boo had in mind. I didn't want to do it.

If I committed words to the cardboard sign, something inside me would change. Once the black ink met the brown cardboard, a fundamental shift in my reality would occur, and when my writing was done, the way I thought of myself would be permanently altered. I popped the marker cap, the sweet chemical smell giving me a memory wash of easier days.

For more time than I wanted to admit, I'd refused the common label for what I was going through. I told myself that because I sometimes slept in beds or had a place for a few months when I could find it or afford it, that I wasn't. I told myself that because I had a car, a job and kind friends that gave me occasional sanctuary, I wasn't. I had refused the word, the ugly word. I played justification word games in my mind, never allowing it, hopscotching over and around it. I knew a thesaurus of alternates to the word.

I didn't want to, but I knew I had to. It was true and it was time. I wrote the word on the sign.

Homeless

Boo Boo led me to a freeway on-ramp. He pushed me closer to the light.

"This here is the sweet spot," Boo Boo said. "You take it." He went back a few car lengths.

The cardboard must have transmuted into a new heavier element, or maybe the gravity of the Earth had quadrupled while we walked over. Despite its weight, I held up the sign, hiding my face behind it. The dirt kicked up by tires joined with the grey exhaust and I pretended it was the reason for the tears in my eyes. I allowed myself that one last self-delusion.

An older man in a freshly washed luxury sedan shook his head at me and mouthed, "You people."

A twenty-something girl looked at me in horror through her closed car window and turned up her radio.

An older man on the passenger side of a van waved me over and gave me a dollar and a half-eaten McDonald's hash brown. "God bless," he said.

A middle-aged guy in a white utility truck yelled, "Get a fucking job, bum."

A twenty-something guy with long hair in a beat-up car handed me three dollars and said, "Here you go, brother."

A little girl in the back seat of a BMW asked her mother, "Why is that man there?" The window motor engaged, and before the windows finished rolling up, I heard her mother say, "Don't look at him, honey." The little girl smiled and waved at me with her tiny perfect fingers.

An uncountable number of uncomfortable people locked their gaze forward and either by choice, lack of awareness, or because of the callous that builds up on a soul from seeing daily suffering, did nothing.

I didn't blame them. Really I didn't. I was guilty of the same throughout the years. I'd looked the other way, gone stone faced, pretended not to see, not to feel. To do otherwise would have allowed in the possibility that it could happen to anyone, and that was unthinkable. That thought had to be kept at bay at all costs, even if the cost was as high as refusing to acknowledge a soul in need.

For some folks, it eases their conscience to blame the unfortunate for their lot in life—to believe people on the street are there because of choices they've made. I'd met people who said being on the street was their choice, but it wasn't the kind of choice people think. They didn't choose between a house in the burbs and being homeless. They chose the street over living with an abuser, or being raped, or beaten, or having their few possessions stolen at a shelter. The majority didn't have the capacity to care for themselves, having been turned out from a mental health facility or tossed onto the street after a hospital stay.

"How much you got brother?" Boo Boo yelled over the car noise. "About $10, maybe $12."

"I got $15 for you. That enough for a battery?"

"I don't want your money."

"It's nothing. You'd do the same for me."

Together, we got enough cash for a battery. We found a gas station and bought one. Boo Boo trudged it back with me in case the stink twins came back. Together, we got it installed. My home was drivable again.

"Can you drop me off at the hospital back in Philly? I wanna go see a friend of mine."

"Of course I can, but I think it's too late. Visiting hours are probably over."

"It's no never mind. I'll catch a nap in the ER waiting room until morning and go up to see him...if he makes it."

"What happened?"

"Someone tried to light him on fire while he was sleeping in a doorway. He's in a bad way. No one did nothin for him until the cops came, and they just asked his smoldering ass to move on. It's like we are invisible, even if we on fire."

"Thank you for all the help today. I'll never forget this. If you ever need anything, all you need to do is ask."

"It's nothin', brother Cam, nothin' at all."

I wondered if I'd ever driven past Boo Boo and pretended not to see him. Had I contributed to making him feel invisible? If not him, surely I'd done it to someone. Shame. I felt shame more for that than for my situation. On the street, how long does it take before everything you are fades away like car exhaust in the wind?

After I dropped Boo Boo off, two words from the Bible played in my head on a loop.

Jesus wept.

29

KYRIE ELEISON

I slammed my foot down on the brake pedal with everything my calf muscles had to offer and yanked up the emergency brake handle at the same time. With the last bit of rubber on my brakes gone, the *creech* of metal on metal came from my wheels. My car wasn't stopping this time.

The front of my car punched into the yellow Camaro with a crunch. I pitched forward into the steering wheel with a snap. My forehead cracked against the top of the wheel, white sparklers popped, and I was treated to a Fourth of July fireworks show.

I had almost made it back to Harrison's, my Margate DJ gig. *Goddamn it. Just when I was getting it together,* I thought through the glittery haze. Just when I had nearly enough money to get a place. All to shit now.

I was okay. Shaken but not completely stirred.

Panic.

Thankfully, the other car wasn't that bad. The driver glared at me from his car. He looked okay. Pissed, but okay.

But still, PAnic.

Expired license.

PANic.

No insurance.

PANIc.

Expired registration.

PANIC.

At a minimum, this would be thousands of dollars in ticket money I didn't have. Hell, I couldn't afford new brakes, let alone tickets. My expired license and I were scheduled to visit the DMV on Monday. So close, yet far too late. At best, I'd just lost my transportation. At worst, the Margate PD were gonna lock me up.

PANIC. Time to go.

I backed up and drove my car around my victim and raced off as fast as my bent up, steaming front end would allow. Sure, he ran the stop sign, causing me to hit him, but I knew who would be blamed. I was only a few blocks from Harrison's. I could park behind the bar, outta sight. Two blocks away from the scene, steam billowed out of my engine.

Come on car, a few more blocks, just get me there!

Thirty feet away, with a wet spit, my car gave out. I coasted into an open parking spot in front of Harrison's like a snorting dragon at the finale of a Chinese New Year parade.

Harrison's was only a few blocks from the police station, and the sirens coming down the street had to be coming for me. Did I really think I could hide? I was stupid. And I was fucked. This wasn't just my transportation; it was my bedroom.

The cop came to a stop behind me. I got out of the car and stood next to my bleeding home.

"Were you just involved in an accident?"

I looked to my dented, steaming car and back to the cop. Now was not the time for wiseassery.

"Yes, officer. He ran the stop sign and I couldn't stop in time."

"Turn around and put your hands behind your back."

Oh great, matching bracelet time.

"Why are you cuffing me?"

"You fled the scene."

"I just needed to get outta the intersection. I work here at Harrison's, and I was going to go in and call you guys."

"You work for Carl and Barry?"

"Yes, officer. I'm the DJ."

"I go here with my girl sometimes. Carl and Barry are good guys."

"Yep. They are."

He stopped fitting me for jewelry, slid the cuffs back into their belt pouch, and spun me around.

"Lemme see your paperwork."

I handed over the little I had.

"My license and registration are expired, and I don't have insurance."

"Have a seat on the curb."

He went back to the squad car. I thought about running, but where would I go? I had to be back later that night to work, and they would just grab me when I showed up. Better to face it all now.

The officer eventually came back from his car and a tow-truck pulled up. After a whispered discussion with the tow truck operator, my car was hooked up. I watched from the curb in horror as my home, my transportation, was towed away. I swear I heard taps playing. Without another word to me, the officer got back in his squad car and drove off.

Was I free to go? What just happened? Besides the crates of records I'd left in the bar, everything I owned was in that car.

With a bolt I screamed, "My money!"

In the back seat under the floor mat was the $760 I'd managed to scrape together toward getting a place before the cold set in. Without my car and that money, I was down to the clothes on my back and $16. Thank god my records were in the DJ booth.

I went around to the back entrance to the bar. Carl was loading in cases of beer for the Memorial Day weekend.

"What's up, Cam?"

"Nothin good, Carl. I just trashed my car."

"What happened? Is that what the sirens were all about? Are you okay?"

"Some guy cut me off and I hit him. The cops towed my car. It had all my money and stuff in it."

"Oh shit, so those sirens were for you? How's the car? Can it be fixed?"

"Dunno, hope so. They towed it and didn't tell me where they were taking it."

"No tickets?"

"No."

"That's a good thing. I'll take you over and see if we can get it back."

The lady at the police station reception desk was arguing on the phone when we came up. She slammed down the receiver.

"Yeah?" she said.

"I was in an accident today and they towed my car. I'd like to know what I have to do to get it back."

"Name?"

"Cameron Gilchrist."

She shuffled through a stack of papers on a clipboard.

"Nothing here under that name. What kind of car was it?"

"Silver Toyota Celica."

More shuffling. She turned to a terminal, and after a spate of typing with the tips of her long-manicured nails, said, "Nope. No Celica taken in. Maybe the paperwork isn't in yet. Stop back or call tomorrow."

I tried "tomorrow," and the next day, and many days after that. I went to the impound lot, checked at all the gas stations and mechanic's garages and any place with a tow truck, including the ones used by the Margate PD. I went to the police station twice more and was told that there was no record of an impounded Toyota Celica. After a week of looking and asking, it was clear that my car had been "disappeared." My last resort was to find the officer who'd had it towed. After some careful consideration, I didn't do it in case he had a stack of tickets, or worse, waiting for me. In the end, I just let it go. I wouldn't be able to pay to get it fixed, so what would I do with it if I got it back?

I spent the summer splitting my time between Margate, NJ and Voorhees NJ, a distance of 50 miles. I worked Friday and Saturday nights at Harrison's, sleeping on the bar floor or occasionally at a girl's house or on a sofa in the upstairs apartment where Carl and Barry stayed. On Sunday afternoons, I would take two buses and a train ride, four milk crates of records in tow, to get to the Coliseum in time for my shift.

After my Sunday night shift ended, I would shut down all the equipment and dance floor lights. When most of the bartenders and waitstaff left, I would turn off the DJ booth light, lock the door, and duck down. The DJ booth was elevated over the club, so it was easy to hide. Sleeping on the DJ booth floor was the best sleep I got during the week.

The Philadelphia Flyers practiced on the ice rink at the Coliseum, and they had a state-of-the-art gym. I would get up early, just after the cleaning crew arrived, and head downstairs and grab a shower. The cleaning staff saw me, but I learned early that when you act like you belong somewhere, no one questions you.

That left Tuesday, Wednesday, and Thursday nights. On those nights, I couldn't sleep at the club and I was on the street, and not metaphorically. I found a spot in the woods not far from the Coliseum, away from people and the police. I used an old blue tarp I'd salvaged to keep me and my records safe from the rain.

During the day, I walked a few miles to the Echelon mall to grab someone's lunch leftovers and clean up as best I could in the food court bathroom. If I timed it right, I could evade the security guard's bathroom checks and quickly wash some of the free promo T-shirts I'd grabbed from bar promos to replace my "disappeared" clothing. I was determined to stay presentable, not to mention it wouldn't be a good thing if I arrived for my DJ shifts dirty and stinking.

Weeks into this routine, standing at a bathroom sink washing out one of my T-shirts, alert for mall security, I caught a glimpse of myself in the cracked bathroom mirror. I was tired and worn. I no longer recognized myself. I was disappearing. My cheeks had sunken in. I had lost at least thirty pounds. Above my sunken cheeks, my eyes looked like they hadn't seen the inside of their lids in a thousand nights.

Maybe it was time to stop the bullshit and let it all go. I was saving money so slowly that I would never have enough for a place. I was living in the woods. For fuck's sake, why bother anymore? I was tired. I was done. I packed up my wet clothes and left. Maybe, it was time to quit it all. No one would miss me. At least not for long. On the walk back, I pondered the way I'd do it. There were plenty of trees in the woods. I wondered if the straps I used to tie down my record crates could hold my weight.

I returned to my spot and found a guy about my age with long straggly hair sitting on the ground going through one of my record crates.

Sitting next to him was a worn backpack with a smiley face patch on the front flap. Judging by his worn sneakers, dirty clothes, and presence in the woods, I guessed he was an unwilling camper like me.

"Hey," I yelled in my most intimidating voice. "Those are mine."

"Can you kindly provide proof, sir?" he said, looking up at me from under a shock of hair.

"What? Get away from my records!"

"But sir, how am I to know these are yours?"

"The 11th record in that crate is "Let the Music Play" by Shannon."

He counted through my records, pulled out number eleven, and held it up. It was Shannon.

"That could have been luck, sir." He flashed a toothy grin.

He was playing with me. Why was I letting him?

"Are you nuts? Do you know the odds of someone guessing that? They're mine, now get outta them."

"May I kindly request more proof? What record is number thirty-five?"

"No more games. Put down my shit and get the fuck out of here."

His head lifted from my crates. He had the strangest eyes. They were pale blue, reminding me of a huskies', and they looked younger than the rest of his face.

"Sir, I ask this with all respect due. Are you a dangerous man?"

"When I need to be."

"Do you need to be, kind sir? Right now?"

"I guess that depends on you."

"Nothing here depends on me. Everything, sir, depends entirely on you."

"Fine, whatever. Leave my stuff alone. It's all I got."

"These records? This tarp? I'm as certain as we breathe that you have much more."

"I have four T-shirts, one sweater, one pair of jeans, two pairs of socks, these sneakers, one coat, that tarp, that hand truck, and those fucking records."

"See."

I was tired of his bullshit.

"See what?" I took an aggressive step toward him.

"See, when you thought about it, you realized that the records were not *all you got*. And you have more. I'm certain there is more— much more that you have not yet acknowledged."

"Oh yeah, what else do I have? I don't have any money if that's what you're after."

"Lord no, sir. I have no need of your money."

"Then what more do you think I have?"

"You have your life."

I stopped advancing. "Is that some kind of a threat?"

"More of an observation, sir."

"Threat, observation, what-the-fuck-ever. I'm tired of your bullshit." I took another step toward him and my records.

He stood up and backed away from the crates. "No need for anger, sir.

None of this should be cause for violence." He made a grand sweep of his hands over my crates, then spun around, pointing to the trees, bushes and ground.

"With respect, sir, do we really own anything? All we do is rent things while we are in this form. All of this is nothing but distraction."

"Easy to say," I said as I stacked my record crates onto the hand truck.

"Why yes, it is easy to say, sir. Maybe you might say it? Try it on for size?"

"You're delusional."

"I prefer illusional."

I was tired of this forest philosopher.

"Look, one of us has to go. Will you leave, or should I? What are you even doing here?"

"That's the real question, isn't it. What are any of us doing here?"

"I meant specifically, like here in these woods, right now, messing with me and my shit."

"I'm shadow boxing with your perceptions."

"How's that going?"

"I believe, kind sir, that I see an opening. I just need to sneak in a quick left jab and get a good crack started."

I sighed. "Can you please stop. I've had quite enough. Of everything. I'm too tired for this." I sat down on the tarp.

"Yes, sir." He sat down against a tree. "This..." He pinched himself on the upper arm. "Can be tiring."

I sighed. "Do you always speak in metaphorical riddles?"

"Sir, I speak in whatever language is required by the circumstances."

"Is that so?"

We sat across from each other in the clearing, staring at each other. Maybe if I didn't engage, he would drift back the way he came. He dug around in his backpack and came out with half a loaf of French bread wrapped in paper. He ripped off a chunk and offered it to me.

"No, thanks."

He nodded and gnawed on the bread. The smell of his bread mingled with the smell of the woods. Something about the combination was soothing.

"What's your name?" I said.

"If we are to be friends, then you may call me David," he said between chews. "If we are to be foes, then kindly address me as Michael."

"Uh huh."

"What do they call you?"

"Cameron."

"Well chosen and well met, Cameron."

"Where are you from, David?"

"Here and there. Mostly there, but now I'm here and here is what matters most."

"That sounds like a line from *Alice in Wonderland*. Let's start simple. Where were you yesterday?"

"It's no use going back to yesterday because I was a different person then."

"That one I recognize. It's from *Alice in Wonderland* for sure."

"It is indeed, my good sir, but that does not make it any less true."

"You're certainly curious and curiouser. Do you have a home?"

"I am like the aether that flows."

"So that's a no?"

"The earth is my alter, the sky is my dome, my mind is my garden, the heart is my home, and I'm always at Om."

"More Alice?"

"No sir. That is from friend Ahbe from the better coast."

"You're from California?"

"From? No sir. I've walked the western dirt. As will you, one day."

"Is that so. How do ya know that?"

He smiled and went back into his bag, pulling out a few sci-fi paperbacks and pieces of paper, littering them on the ground between us. In the pile was one of my favorite childhood books, *Glory Road,* by Robert Heinlein. I must have read that book twenty-five times. I hated seeing a book in the dirt, especially that one.

"Aha!" He pulled out a wrinkled dollar and held it up toward me. "Here it is, sir. See. Look. Proof."

"See what? It's a dollar."

"Kind sir, this is how I know you. This is the very dollar you gave me when you were in California. I never forget a kindness and I must, by necessity, repay all kindnesses."

"That makes no sense. How could I have given you that when I was in California? I've never been to California."

"Gave, given, give. Sometimes I use the wrong tense. You will give it to me. I believe it was—will be a Monday."

"Okie dokie. So, you're a time traveler, huh?"

"Sir." He looked indignant. "Time is an illusion. Except for teatime. That is most real."

"You're bonkers."

"Most observant, sir. All the best people are."

"You're not wrong about that."

I was starting to like the guy, even if he imagined himself a time-traveling mad hatter.

"So…" I played along. "You came here from the future to do what? Bother innocent strangers in the woods?"

"I am here to repay your future kindness," he said, straight faced.

"For the dollar? What does a dollar get me?"

"Kind sir, it's not the amount, it's the kindness behind it that counts. What do you want most?"

"A bed to call my own would be a nice start. Do you have one of those in your bag?"

He looked at me with a deadpan seriousness. "Don't be silly, sir. There isn't room in my bag for a bed."

"You asked me what I most needed. That's what I need right now."

"Are you sure that's what you need most at this moment? Is that your true heart's desire?"

"Considering that I've been sleeping under a tarp in the woods, I'm gonna go out on a limb here and say yes, a regular place to sleep is what I need right now. I'd settle for a bed or a sofa. Can you make that happen?"

"I will see what I can do."

"Yeah." I laughed. "I'm sure you will."

"If I may offer an opinion, I believe what you most need, tonight, and I say this respectfully, sir, is hope."

"Do you have that in your bag?"

The deadpan look returned. "Sir, hope is only found within. You have much hope, but I sense that perhaps you have forgotten where you put it?"

He wasn't wrong. I had given up. Was it that obvious? Was it written on my face? Why was I still playing word games with the guy?

"And you can help with that, huh. How can you help me find my hope? Did you bring me some from the future along with the dollar?"

"Perhaps you will allow me to remind you of the things you already know."

"Such as?"

"Such as the fact that nothing is permanent, especially not this unfortunate situation you find yourself in. You must not give up hope."

"You don't know anything about my situation."

"Sir, if I may, I do know some things about you. I know you're sleeping in the woods. I know that you love music. Judging by the way you looked at my offered bread, I know you're hungry. Judging by the way you refused it, I know you have pride. Judging by the look of horror on your face at the sight of my books in the dirt and your knowledge of the classics, I know that you are a lover of the written word."

"A+ for observation, but you don't know I will get through this. No one does."

He held up the dollar over his head with two hands.

"Oh yeah, the time-traveling dollar bill." I sighed and shook my head.

David collected his books and papers and stuffed them back into his canvas backpack. When he finished, he slung it over his back, stepped to me, and placed the dollar bill at my feet.

"For when we meet again, sir."

"I don't want your dollar."

"It's not my dollar, sir."

"Yeah. Okay. Thank you, I guess."

David's face took on a different look in the failing light. It appeared to morph ever so slightly.

"Sir, you must always get back up. This is no time to quit. Your journey has barely begun. Even when you are in the dark of it, you must keep your hope and wits about you and find the door."

Without another word, he turned and walked away into the woods.

The encounter used up everything I had left after spending two nights in the cold, damp clearing. I lay down on the tarp, thinking every crack and rustle in the woods must be David. Was he waiting in the wood for me to doze off? Would I wake up to him kneeling over me? *"Sorry, good sir, but I must slit your throat, sir. Also, kind sir, I will be, did take, your records to the future where I will be was, a time traveling DJ."*

Better get up and find a new spot was my last conscious thought before exhaustion beat my fear and sleep took me down. I dreamed of bedrooms and doors and flying above a suburban landscape of neatly kept homes. I awoke in the early light with a jolt, happy to find my throat still intact and records within arm's reach. I shook off the sleep and the dew, jumping up and down to get my blood moving.

After a quick inventory, I gathered and secured my stuff and made the long walk, train ride, and bus ride back to Margate. Jim the bartender had previously offered up the couch at his place in Margate if I ever got desperate. I was going to take him up on that offer. His friends and their after-work parties went late, but I needed some solid sleep. At least for a few days.

After my shift, we closed the club and I went to Jim's place. The after party wound down around five am, and I dug into the couch for a warm, safe, indoor, crazy-person-free sleep.

I woke up to a knee on my chest and a gun pointed at my head.

The knee drove the wind out of me.

"Don't move," the man attached to the knee said.

Maybe accepting Jim's offer was a mistake.

30

PASTA AND HERB

The first time you have a gun pointed at your head is special. It's a singular sensation unlike any other, and you will never forget it. We all like to think we're heroes. That goes poof when you can smell the gun. It's true, you can smell a gun if it's close enough. It smells like a car mechanic reading a detective novel.

"Put your hands over your head," Gun Man said, driving the last of my breath out of me.

I did.

Another man locked a pair of handcuffs on my wrists. They were cold.

Gun Man lifted his knee off my chest. "Sit up."

I did. I drew in an emergency breath.

"Don't move."

I didn't.

"Don't talk."

I didn't.

Jim's girlfriend. Anne, dressed only in a long WHAM! T-shirt, was sitting in the recliner facing me, legs clamped together, hands cuffed behind her.

A swarm of blue wind-breaker jacketed men were moving through the house. White letters across their backs identified them as DEA. Several of Margate's finest were standing with their thumbs in their belts, trying to look involved and failing. Strangely, a brown-outfitted UPS man was standing off to the side of the front door, holding a box and a clipboard.

I really had to get my own place.

Next up on the handcuff parade was Jim. He was escorted out from the back bedroom and placed on the couch next to me.

"That everyone?" DEA agent #1 said.

"No," DEA agent #2 said.

"Who's missing?" DEA agent #1 asked.

"The sender," DEA agent #2 answered.

"Wasn't he supposed to be here?" DEA agent #1 asked.

"Yes. Someone screwed up," DEA agent #2 answered.

"Typical," DEA agent #1 snorted.

"Clear except for the second bedroom. It's locked from the outside," DEA agent #3 (aka, Gun Guy) stepped up and added.

"Is that the sender's room?" DEA agent #1 asked.

"Unknown, but likely," DEA agent #3 answered.

DEA agent #1 crouched down in front of Jim. "Where's your roommate?"

"I dunno."

"Don't be stupid. Where is he?"

"Dunno."

"The room with the gate latch on the door. Is that his room?"

"Yes."

"Is he in there?"

"Don't think so."

DEA agent #1 nodded to DEA agents #4 and #5 standing to either side of the locked bedroom door. DEA agent #6 came forward with a crowbar and, with a pop, the latch was off. Agents #4 and #5 rushed in.

"Clear," came from the room.

DEA agent #1 pulled a bunch of papers from a back pocket and dropped them on Jim's lap.

"That there lap warmer is a warrant," he said.

"For what?" Jim asked.

DEA agent #1 looked around at no one in particular, or maybe everyone, tough to know. "For what, he says." He shook his head. "Well sport, for finding the drugs and money of course."

Jim tried his best to look innocent. "What drugs?"

DEA agent #1 walked over to the UPS man and took the box he was holding. He pulled out a pocketknife and snapped it open. He carefully cut the seams of the box flaps open and pulled out a bundle wrapped in black plastic secured by duct tape. He sliced the package open and the smell of pot filled the room.

DEA agent #1 held the package under Jim's face. "Well, ace, these drugs for starters. Your girlfriend over there signed for them from Agent Brown Shorts not more than an hour ago. Your roommate sent them all the way from the sunny island of Maui. By the way, nice legs, Agent Roth."

"Thank you, sir. Lots of gym time," Agent Roth replied.

"It shows. Remind me later to get your workout routine."

"Yes, sir, it would be my pleasure, sir. It's mainly calf raises."

"Roger that, Agent Roth." He turned to the room. "Ladies, house cleaning time."

The swarm of blue jackets ripped apart the rooms. They were thorough. This was not their first drug search rodeo. An agent standing near me searched the glass candle holders and vases on the fireplace mantle. He turned over a candle in a tall glass cylinder emblazoned with a picture of Jesus. Two joints and a pack of rolling papers dropped into his hands. He pulled a brown paper lunch bag out of his back pocket and placed the joints in it.

He turned and smiled at me. "How you doin?"

"I'm great," I answered. "Best morning ever."

"No kidding. I would think you've had better." He nodded toward my duffle bag sitting next to the sofa. "This your bag?"

"Yes."

"Anything in there I should know about, or anything that can stick me, cut me, or bite me?"

"There's nothing in it besides clothes."

He opened my bag and sorted through the contents. He put both hands deep into my bag and came out holding a pack of rolling papers. They were not mine.

He held up the papers. "Bingo, bango. Your morning just got worse."

"Those are not mine. You know they're not mine."

He smiled, pulled out an evidence bag, and put the rolling papers in it.

My head screamed, *You son of a bitch. You just planted something in my bag!* Instead, I said, "Why are you doing this? Those aren't mine."

His smile turned into a chuckle. Without another word, he pulled me up and searched me so thoroughly it felt like a date.

The blue swarm went on for half the day. The big find was a false wall in the back of the absent roommate's closet. Behind the wall was a safe containing a good quantity of pot and cash. They carted the safe and all its contents outside to a waiting van. Note to self: Home safes are worthless and can be opened with a crowbar and minimal muscle.

One by one, they took us into the roommate's bedroom.

It was my turn.

"Come on, let's have a chat." DEA agent #1 walked me into the bedroom.

I sat on the clothing-strewn single bed in the middle of the aftereffects of a localized tornado. He picked up a notebook and a pen.

"What's your name, sport?" I hated him for using that nickname.

"Cameron Gilchrist."

"Address?"

"I have a PO box."

"Won't do, ace. I need a physical."

"I don't have one."

"Look here, champ, we won't get along if you don't cooperate. Getting along is important to your future. I'll ask one more time. Where do you live?"

"I don't have a place, that's why I slept here last night."

"Last chance."

"I guess you can use my mother's address." I gave it to him.

He asked for the mom's name and phone number, my social security number, and date of birth.

I gave it all.

"What were you doing here last night, Cameron Gilchrist?"

"I work with Jim at Harrison's over on Adam's St. I DJed last night and I work there again tonight. I needed a place to sleep and Jim offered up his couch," I gushed out, trying to keep my voice innocent and level. My eyes filled with tears, but I wasn't about to sob in front of the guy.

"How long have you been dealing for Mike?"

Oh shit. This guy thinks I'm a drug dealer. My heart skipped beats.

"I don't know Mike and I'm not a drug dealer. I don't even smoke pot, let alone sell it."

"The rolling papers they found in your bag are what, then? And I guess it's just an accident that you were sleeping a wall away from a stash of Maui's finest. And of course, it's just a coincidence that you were here when another brick was delivered. You were here to load up, weren't you, slick."

"I am not a drug dealer."

"Lookie here, sport, we know you're dealing for him, so how about you stop dancing me around, Cameron the DJ. I plan to get home by dinner, and you're standing between me and the wife's pasta."

We sat silent, locked in a stare. It was like that game where whoever blinks first loses. I couldn't think of any way to win the current high-stakes version of the contest. Drops of cold sweat were making their way down the middle of my back.

I blinked first. "What kind of pasta?"

"What?"

"What kind of pasta? You said your wife is making pasta. What kind?"

"Look at the set of balls on you. Don't you worry about that, sport. If I were you, I'd start talking about Mike and what you do for him. If you tell me something I don't already know, maybe you can go to work tonight."

I let that hang between us for a minute before answering.

"As I already said, I am not a drug dealer. I am just in the wrong place at the wrong time."

"Try again, sport."

"I bet there is nothing I can say to you to prove that I'm not a drug dealer. Can you think of anything?"

I waited for a response. Nothing.

"I mean, how does one prove that you're not something?" I shifted closer to him. "Since I can't prove that I'm not a drug dealer, we might as well use our time together to talk about something else. I mean, you're going to do what you're going to do. The fact that your agent planted rolling papers in my bag shows me you don't care if I'm guilty or innocent, so fuck it, we might as well talk about something else. You seem to like pasta, and I like pasta; ergo, what kind of pasta is she making?"

His eyebrows went up. "Ergo? Did you just say ergo?"

"I did. It means—"

"I know what ergo means, sport. Holy flying Christ on a broom, you might even have three balls."

The silence between us was loud.

I blinked again. "Nope, just two."

I sighed. He sighed. But…a slight smile broke on him.

"Try," he said.

"Try what?"

"Prove that you're in the wrong place at the wrong time. I'll give you a shot. Go."

"I've got nothing."

"Not even going to try?"

"No... that's not what I meant." I took a breath. "Look, there is nothing I can call my own besides the clothes in my duffle bag and a few crates of records. I don't have a home or a regular place to sleep. I have $11 to my name until I get paid tonight. I lost my car, so I take two buses and the speed line to get here and then I slug back, dragging heavy crates of records behind me, rain or shine, to work a few more days."

He crossed his arms. I could tell that I wasn't making a case so far.

"I've survived on the street, with little to no support, for longer than I thought possible. I've slept on the ground, in cars, on stranger's couches, and on pool tables. I've slept on the floors of DJ booths after everyone's left the club."

He yawned and looked at his watch.

"If I was dealing, wouldn't I have a place to sleep? Come on, what kind of a drug dealer would I have to be to only have $10 to my name? I don't even have money to eat most days. Trust me, if I was a drug dealer, I would be a good one, and I would make bank, certainly enough to have a bed and regular meals."

His face didn't change.

"I get it, you have a job to do, and your job is to get the bad guys, but we both know the rolling papers aren't mine. I've seen enough cop shows to know the hows and whys of it, but that doesn't make it right. You can ask anyone down here if I do drugs and they'll say no. Just ask Jim and his girlfriend if I've ever even been here before. Ask them if I know Mike. Ask them if I ever smoke pot. Check me in your database. I'm clean." I stopped and looked him straight in the eye. "That's all I got so, believe me or not, just do what you going to do."

He considered me like a collector considers a painting. Were the colors right, the brush strokes? Was the signature correct? He cocked his head slightly like a dog trying to understand its owners words. I didn't know if anything I'd said moved the needle toward freedom, but it was all I had in me.

After a few minutes he slapped his thighs, abruptly got up, and walked out of the bedroom. He left me alone in that room for hours.

Finally, Agent Planted-fucking-evidence-in-my-bag came in.

"Stand up."

I stood up.

He unlocked my cuffs.

"Get your shit and get gone."

I didn't move. What was happening?

"Get. Gone. Now."

I broke the laws of physics getting my shit and getting gone. I speed-walked the miles to Harrison's Bar, looking over my shoulder every few minutes, fully expecting to see the DEA, lights and sirens blazing, minds changed, coming for me.

I made it to Harrison's just as my shift started. I set up the DJ booth and got some music going. We opened for the early dinner crowd and the bar filled up with regulars.

Around 8:30, the hostess came back to the DJ booth with a tinfoil-covered paper plate in hand.

"Some guy dropped this off. He said to give it to DJ Cameron and said to tell you she made fettuccine."

I took the plate from the hostess. Taped to the top of the foil was a folded piece of paper. The note read:

> *Good luck to you, sport. I hope you make it. Ergo, stay away from drugs and dealers.*

The pasta was good.

So was the advice.

I should have listened to it.

Hell, we all should have listened to it.

31

DEUS EX MACHINA

"Can you fuckin' believe this bullshit?" Wiseguy #1 yelled at the TV.

"Fuck 'em, cuz," Wiseguy #2 said.

"Yeah, fuck them casinos," Wiseguy #1 said.

"And fuck the Casino Commission," Wiseguy #2 said. "They just know how lucky you are, and don't want you taking any more of their money."

"Gimme another drink," Wiseguy #1 said

"Sure, sure." Jim the bartender's hands trembled a bit as he set up another round.

The newscaster on TV screen continued, "The New Jersey Casino Commission said that the ban stems from an incident earlier in the year that resulted in two counts of aggravated assault. The Philadelphia native, allegedly with mob ties, is barred from all New Jersey casinos effective immediately."

From my DJ booth, I watched the Harrison's happy hour customers nervously settle their tabs and head for the exit. I wished I could join them in the exodus, but I had to start the happy hour music. Jim served up fresh drinks to the wise guys.

Summers in Margate, you couldn't swing a calzone without hitting a wise guy. They did their business in South Philly, but when the calendar clicked to Memorial Day, they headed to the shore in waves of pomade and sports cars to their second homes in Ventnor, Longport, and Ocean City. Margate was the party magnet town right in the middle. It was peppered with nightclubs, restaurants, and bars.

The two wise guys were getting angrier by the drink, and the tension in the bar was building. I knew one of the wise guys loved Stevie Wonder, so I put on a Stevie song, hoping to change the tone. Halfway into the song the waitress came over with a drink on her tray.

"This is for you." She nodded toward the bar.

I took the drink and looked over at the bar. The now smiling wise guys raised their glasses and said, "Salute."

I nodded back. "Salute." I took a sip.

"What is this?" I asked the waitress, not expecting the sweet kick of the drink.

"It's scotch and amaretto. It's called a 'Godfather.'"

Of course, it is, I thought. My insides clenched but my outside smiled as I drank it down.

Carl came out of the kitchen to the DJ booth.

"Hey, Cam, can you put on a long record? My dad wants to talk to you."

Carl walked me upstairs to the living quarters above the bar where Ken, his father, was holding court with some people I didn't know. I had only spoken with Ken a few times when he made one of his visits to the bar to check on how his sons were running things. Ken was tall like me, with a head of thick white-grey hair and a kind face. He had a comfortable, welcoming vibe. If he wasn't developing real estate, I could imagine him bartending in some small town in Ireland. He was the type of person you could see yourself sharing a drink, or five, with. Ken was always friendly to me, and I liked him from the moment we first shook hands. He made his money in real estate, and like some gregarious people who make a pile do, he decided to open restaurants and bars. Word was, he was working on a project somewhere inland in Southern New Jersey, converting his old real estate office complex into a hotel.

"Thank you, team." Ken stood up and the room followed suit. "Give me ten minutes with Cameron."

The room cleared.

"Have a seat," Ken said. "How are you doing?"

"I'm good."

"Are you?"

Was I in trouble?

"Yes, sir. All good. Great. Is everything okay?"

Ken smiled. "No need to call me sir. Ken will do."

"Will do, Ken."

"Carl tells me you're having a tough go of it."

"I'm doing okay."

"Carl tells me that you've been sleeping downstairs on the floor. Before that, I understand you were sleeping in your car?"

My chest tightened to steel. Hearing my reality said by someone I respected hurt in a new way. I knew what was coming next. It was three steps back time.

"It's alright, son, you don't have to answer. We all have hard times."

Ken got up and poured me a glass of water and placed it on the table between us.

"Thank you. I'm sorry I slept in the bar. I won't do it anymore." I took a sip. "I don't want to be a bother. I have other places I can go."

"No, that's not…You aren't in trouble. I have a job for you."

"A job, sir? Ken, I mean."

"I'm opening a complex that will contain a hotel, a restaurant, and a nightclub. If everything goes according to plan, we'll be opening October 13th. Friday the 13th, in fact."

I sat as still as I could, fearing that any movement would alter the current reality I found myself in.

"Are you interested in a job? A bigger job?"

"Yes, sir, very much."

"My boys tell me that you're great with people, great with the DJ thing, and you know how to keep the customers drinking. Most importantly, they tell me you're trustworthy. I need people I can trust."

"Thank you for the kind words."

"I need someone to run the entertainment for the entire complex. Interested?"

"I'll take it."

"Hold on, we haven't discussed the money. Never take a job before you know the pay."

"I'll still take it, but yes please, continue."

"I can pay your DJ fee for every night both clubs are open. You can DJ whatever nights you want, but I want you in the new place on the weekends. I'll pay you a salary on top of that to handle the advertising and entertainment bookings both here and at the new place. Are you up for the job?"

Am I up for the job? I am most certainly up for the job. I could get my own place after a month of that kind of money.

"Are you serious, sir?"

"Seems to me you could use a break, and if my boys trust you, then so do I. This won't be easy, though. I've got all my marbles in this operation, and I'm going to ask a lot from you. Are you up for it?"

"Yes. A thousand times yes and thank you."

"Great." Ken stood up and offered me his hand. I shook it. In that moment I felt my father in the room. "We have a deal. We open in the fall. Will you be okay until then?"

"Yes, sir. Thank you, sir."

"Two more things. One, that's the last time you call me sir. Seriously. Stop that."

I nodded a yes.

"Two. Since you'll be an important part of my team, I want you close. I've put aside rooms at the hotel for my sons, my head chef, and if you want it, one for you. No charge. I'll make it part of your deal. We can work out some dinners at the restaurant as well. How's that all sound?"

I thought about pushing back, saying it was too generous. I thought about slapping myself in the face in case it was a dream. If it was a dream, I'd just let it play out for a while longer.

"Ken, it sounds great. In fact, it sounds better than anything I've heard in a long, long time. Thank you."

"Great. You earned it. The hotel will be ready before the club. We'll let you know when your room is available and get you in it as soon as we can."

I made it back downstairs just as the record was about to end.

"Are you our new Director of Entertainment?" Carl asked.

"That's a fancy title for DJ, but yeah, I guess I am."

"Great. It's going to be hard work, and you'll be doing a lot more than spinning records. Working directly for my dad is tough."

"I'm ready."

"You'd better be. My inheritance is riding on this place. No pressure." Carl smiled, but I had a feeling he was serious.

I stepped over to the bar.

"Jim, three Godfathers for these gentlemen and me," I said.

"Comin' right up," Jim said.

"Thank you, cuz," said Wiseguy #1.

"Salute," said Wiseguy #2.

"Can I ask you guys a question?" I said.

"I plead the fifth," said Wiseguy #1.

"It wasn't me," said Wiseguy #2.

"I didn't even know the guy," Wiseguy #1 said.

"I swear I didn't know she was married," Wiseguy #2 said.

They ran out of one-liners.

"Yeah, yeah, sorry. Whatcha need?" Wiseguy #1 said.

"Do you believe in guardian angels? Things or people that watch out for you?"

"In our line of work, we call them Godfathers." Wiseguy #2 laughed.

"Abso-fucking-lutely. The stories I could tell you," Wiseguy #1 added.

Jim put the drinks on the bar.

Wiseguy #2 picked up his drink. "What should we drink to?"

I raised my glass. "To guardian angels."

"To guardian angels," Wiseguy #1 said.

"To Godfathers," Wiseguy #2 said.

"To Godfathers," we said in unison.

We drank.

I reached into my pocket and pulled out a few dollars to tip Jim. I separated the wrinkled dollar bill that David had laid before me in the woods like an offering. He might have been crazy, but he wasn't wrong. You must not give up hope. Sometimes you just have to hold on a little longer.

I slipped David's dollar bill back into my wallet. You never know, I thought.

They say that Friday the 13th is unlucky.

I guess we would see.

REVELATION

32

FRIDAY THE 13TH

"Good evening, ladies and gentlemen, and welcome to Harrison's!"

I cranked up the volume and dropped the needle on the record, letting the opening beats of "Point of No Return," by Expose, blast out from the club's state-of-the-art sound system. A roar went up from the crowd and, with a rush, the dance floor filled up to overflow.

I looked down on the club floor from my elevated DJ booth with a glass of champagne in hand. I was sporting a fresh haircut, the first one I hadn't done myself in quite some time. I was wearing new clothes and new shoes. I felt shiny. Before the night began, I enjoyed a lobster and steak dinner at the restaurant. Quite a change from trash can diving at the mall food court.

Better than the feeling of a full belly and new exterior was knowing that after I was done playing music, I had a place to sleep. The room at the hotel was mine if I pulled my weight at the complex. This had to be the luckiest Friday the 13th in recorded history.

Why did I feel like an imposter?

A line of women formed at the roped-off entrance to the DJ booth to say hello and to request songs. The most popular radio station in Philadelphia was doing a live remote from the club and the radio personality was trying to get my attention for an on-air interview.

He did a countdown with his fingers. Three, two, one, and we were on the radio.

"We're live here at Harrison's with DJ Cameron, and the place is hopping. Say hello to the Q102 audience, DJ Cam."

I froze. Just below the joyful buzz of the crowd, a low-frequency murmur played in my head. Since my turn of good fortune, it was there like a tiny itch I couldn't scratch. The murmur, born of a mother's constant criticism and a religion's continual end-of-the-world programming, would not let me live in the moment with any sort of true peace.

The murmur cranked up the volume to eleven.

Armageddon is going to take it all away at any second, you dirty sinner. You'll see.

I gulped down my drink and waved to the waitress to bring me another. It helped. I grabbed the microphone.

"This is DJ Cameron, and we're packed here at Harrison's. Come on down and say hi."

And just like that, I spoke live on the radio to tens of thousands of people. I wondered what those people would think if they knew what I'd been doing only weeks before. I wondered if any of the Q102 listeners had driven past me when I was panhandling with Boo Boo.

A few hours into the night, the energy of the music, conversations with willing women, and four double vodkas took the murmur down to a five. I was having fun. The attention of the crowd was having an effect on me. I felt good. I felt strong. I felt cocky.

Fuck you, murmur. I can just drink you away, so fuck you back to wherever you came from. I can be anything I want. Nobody has to know what I really am.

People were clamoring for my attention. I was no longer invisible. I was the center of the party. I was in control. With the right music, I could steer the mood of the people below me. With a twist of the volume control, I could elevate the room or bring it back down at my whim. With a few words on the microphone, I could get strangers chanting anything I wanted.

People were pushing their way into the DJ booth to get on the radio. It was chaotic, but I didn't care. I was swept up in it. Let 'em all in, and let that girl in for sure, and nice to meet you, and yes, I would love a drink. What's your name? Hi, Connie, I'm Cameron. Oh, yes, I guess you do know my name. You're lovely, where are you from?

"Cherry Hill. Where do you live?" Connie asked.

There it was. The previously dreaded question. The one I had avoided like a ninja avoiding the light.

"I live here at the hotel."

"That's so cool," Connie said.

I woke up the next morning in a tangle of hotel sheets. I didn't remember much past last call, but I vaguely remembered the walk from the club to my hotel room. Blonde hair poked out from under the sheets. I followed the hair back to its owner and found it was attached to Connie of the "That's so cool" fame.

Through my pounding forehead, I called up a blurred memory of kissing. I didn't remember much else. We were both naked under the sheets and our clothing was strewn on the floor like remnants of a yard sale. I slid to the bathroom to empty my bladder.

The bathroom had a soaking tub big enough for two, and as evidenced by the half-filled tub and used towels scattered about like defeated wet ghosts, we had taken a swim. Somehow, between last call and the walk to my room, we had obtained several bottles of champagne. One of the empties was floating slowly in a circle in the tub's water like a broken compass trying to find sober north. On the edge of the tub was a Whitney Houston album cover with a rolled up $20 bill. Coke residue was dusted across Whitney's forehead like crystal dandruff. Like the champagne, I had no idea where the coke had come from.

I considered myself in the bathroom mirror. What came back from reflection universe wasn't the Cameron I knew. It certainly wasn't the same man who had looked back at me from a mall bathroom mirror not that long ago. This was a different man, and I wasn't sure about him.

Fuck it, I thought, as I drained the last champagne from a bottle. Everything was good now. I had a place to sleep, money in my pocket, and a beautiful girl in my bed. What else did I need?

"Good morning, lover," my new friend said as her naked double joined me in the mirror universe. "Got any more coke?"

"No. But I know someone who might."

She smiled. I dialed. Sid answered.

"How much you want?" Sid said.

"Dunno, how's it come?"

"Buck, you crack me up. A gram is $85, and an eight ball is $250."

"What's an eight ball?"

"It's about three and a half grams."

"Is that a lot?"

"Depends."

"I only have enough for a gram, so I'll take that if I can."

"How about I get an eight ball, sell you a gram, and then I'll cut and sell the rest."

"How's that?"

"We take out your gram, then we mix in baby laxative with the rest. It increases the weight and, just like magic, you get a free gram."

Connie was lying on the bed, naked. She mouthed to me, "Does he have any?"

I nodded yes. She spread her thighs and licked her upper lip as her fingers trailed down between her legs. She moaned and arched her back. I was transfixed.

"Cam? Yo. Buck? You there?" Sid said.

"Yeah, yeah, sorry, I got distracted."

"You in?"

"I'm in."

I hung up the phone and joined Connie.

Yeah, everything was great now.

The mask was on.

I was DJ Cameron Alexander.

33

FRIENDS

The limo pulled up to the club and my crew piled in. It had been six months since the club opened, and I was taking advantage of my new income, popularity, and access to party supplies. The limo was stocked with bottles of Dom Perignon, Stoli Vodka, and mixers. In my pocket was an eight ball of coke. The last of the group jammed into the limo.

"Where would you like to go tonight, sir?"

"Miss Linda, please take us to the city."

"Any place in particular?"

"Not sure. Pick a bridge and go over it. We'll figure out the details when we get settled. Please and thank you."

"My pleasure, sir," she answered.

I preferred female limo drivers, and Linda was my favorite. She gave us a tip of her hat as I raised the divider. Someone popped a cork and filled glasses. I pulled out the coke and the party kicked into gear.

By the time we stopped at the Roxy on South Street, we had already hit two clubs, and the crew was feeling no pain. We lost two party crew members to the night and gained two replacements. Al and Sam were friends of one of my crew. They were sons of wise guys, and they made no secret of it. I had heard stories, but I was too altered to give much thought to the risks of hanging out with them. Truth was, having wise guys in our crew was exciting. They were celebrities of a sort, funny as hell, and they liked to pay for things.

Al knew the doorman at the Roxy. After some side hugs, we were hustled past the line. The club was packed. My two new friends made their way down the row of barstools and asked people to get up from their seats. Halfway down the bar, it hit me that they were making people move for my crew. It made me extremely uncomfortable, and I certainly hadn't asked them to do it.

One guy wouldn't move.

"Nah, I'm good," the guy sitting in the end seat said in response to being asked to give up his seat.

"Cuz, come on. Grab your drink and get up," Sam delivered with a laugh.

"Do you know who I am?" the guy said.

Sam's smile got bigger. Al laughed. If the guy only knew.

Sam was as tall as I was at six feet five inches. Our height was the only physical similarity. Where I was David Bowie thin, he was made of steroids and weight plates. With his prison physique, if he weren't working for the family, he could have played lineman for the Eagles.

His sidekick, Al, was a few inches shorter than me with soft eyes and a deceitful baby face. The guy's refusal to move caused Al's soft face to morph into angry angles as it took on the appearance of a shark. If you'd told me then that Al's eyes rolled back in his head when he ate, I'd have believed it.

The reluctant mover gave them both a long look and got up from the bar. He opened his mouth to say something. Probably something smart mouthed. He had that look.

Sam beat him to it. "Cuz, don't say whatever it is you're gonna say. Don't be a hero, and don't forget your drink." Sam picked up his drink and held it out to him.

The guy realized he was at a two-to-one disadvantage. He grabbed his drink and got up.

"Good boy," Sam said.

With a last, hard look at Sam, Al, and me, he faded away into the crowd. Our group now owned the seats at the bar.

"There we go, DJ Cam, all cozy now. I'm buying, who's drinking?" Al said.

The coke was gone, the club was closing, and it was time to go. Most members of my group had hooked up and gone off to do whatever with whomever. It was just the Al and Sam show and me. We made our way out of the club onto South Street to find Linda and the limo.

South Street was a colorful collection of shops, clubs, and restaurants. It had been a gathering place for Philly residents since the 1800s. In the '50s, it was an artist's haven. In the '60s, beat poets and the hippie movement took over. In the '70s, disco tried to come in, but punk kicked its ass out and South Street became a mecca for safety pinned, ripped shirted, roving bands of Mohawked punks. The street was trying to reinvent itself as a tourist destination. During the day, John and Suzy Normal from Idaho walked the street to see the weirdos, buy T-shirts, look in the window at Zipperhead and eat cheesesteaks at Jim's. After ten pm, the best way to describe South Street was "sketchy." After two am, it was best to move through the South Philly Street with purpose.

"South Street Diner?" Al asked.

"South Street diner sucks," Sam said.

"Yeah, but it's right around the corner and I need protein." Al flexed his sizable biceps.

"How about Melrose?" I suggested. "Linda can take us once we find her."

"Hell yeah, cuz, let's go there. Their meatball parm is smack-your-momma good," Sam said.

"Smack-your-momma good?" I asked.

"Yeah. It's so good you're gonna go home and slap your momma for never making you one," Sam said. "We'll make an Italian out of you yet, Cam."

"Yo, assholes!" came from behind us.

We turned. It was the reluctant mover from the beginning of the night. He was angry and he had found back-up. They were stirred up like a basket of vipers.

"Look who it is. Heya, cuz. How's ya night?" Al asked, without a hint of sarcasm.

"You wanna go?" Reluctant Mover said.

In South Philly speak, we had been invited to fight. The local code of honor demanded we respond that we did indeed "wanna go." I did not "wanna go," but it was the wrong time to mention my preference.

"Are you kidding me right now? Did you wait out here all night?" Sam asked.

"Nah, just a happy accident," he said. "You wanna go?"

Sam pumped out his chest. "Let's go, asshole."

Al smiled like he'd just won the daily number and flared his lats like a cobra.

Reluctant Mover, now Wanna Go guy had just written a check with his mouth and Al and Sam were going to cash it. What was he thinking?

Wanna Go guy reached behind his back and came out with a gun. He pointed it in Sam's general direction.

"How about now? Still wanna go, asshole?"

"Whoa cuz, whoa. No need for all that," Sam said.

I took a step backwards.

The gun was now trained on me. "Don't move, fucker."

"Not moving." I put my hands up.

Someone walking down the other side of South Street yelled "GUN!" and ran off down the street. A few late-night stragglers ran after him.

"Wanna tell me what to do now, tough guy?"

"Fuck you. You don't have the balls," Sam said.

I was thinking that he might have the balls, and I didn't want that confirmed. At least, not before I had a chance to have a "slap-your-momma-good" meatball parm sandwich. Maybe it was because I was drunk, high, hungry, cocky, or all four, but, before the part of my brain that stops me from stupid actions had a chance to comment, I stepped between Sam and the gun.

"Is this necessary?" I asked Gun Guy in a perfectly reasonable and, I hoped, calming voice.

"Who the fuck…? Get your ass back," he said.

"What's your name?" I said.

"You wanna date me or somthin? The balls on this guy," Previously Wanna Go guy, now Gun Guy said.

"Nah… I mean you're good looking and all, but I like girls." I tossed out a trial laugh. "Do you really want to shoot someone over a bar stool? I mean, it was a rude thing what Sam did, but do you want to bring down all of Philly on you and your families' heads because of it?"

"What does that mean?" Gun Guy said.

"Do you know who you just pulled a gun on?" I continued.

Gun Guy shifted nervously and looked to his friend. His friend returned the nervous look.

"I don't give a fuck who he is," he said.

"Yeah…maybe. Sam's last name is Diamonte. Maybe you heard of his father, Giancomo?" I said.

Their throats gulped in tandem.

"Put it down," Gun Guy's friend whispered. "Let's get out a here."

Sam smiled and waved at them like a Miss America contestant. "Nice to meet yas."

"Sure, I know the name. My father knows him good. So what?" Gun Guy said.

"Is your father a friend of ours? Who's he with?" Sam said.

That's wise guy speak for "Is your father connected and is he part of a crew?"

"He's with Abate."

"Why didn't you say you were family?"

"Because I'm not. That's my father's business. I'm a civilian," Gun Guy said.

"Then why the gun?" Sam asked.

"Cause shit happens," Gun Guy said.

"Well, that's true. Look, how about I say it's my bad and then you put the gun down and we go get breakfast?" Sam said.

"Put it away," Gun Guy's friend said, nodding violently.

Gun Guy lowered the gun and put it away. I let out the breath I didn't know I was holding.

"See that. All friendly like," Al said.

Gun Guy shook his head. "Sorry about that. I'm hotheaded. I shouldn't have done that. But you shouldn't be rude like you were."

"No, you shouldn't have. We good?" Sam asked with a chuckle.

A police siren sliced the night air. Someone had called the cops and, from the volume of the siren, they would be on us in seconds.

"Shit," Sam said. "Let's go."

We all took off running away from the sound. We flew down a side street and into an alley. The alley dead ended into the short side of its L shape at a back entrance to a restaurant. It smelled like garbage and cat. The five of us huddled in the dimly lit alley under a sign that read: *Ring bell for deliveries.* The doppler sound of a police siren passing filled the alley.

"Shit, that was close," Gun Guy said. He put his open hand out to Sam. "I'm sorry about earlier. I didn't know. I'm Anthony. We good?"

Everything happened at once.

Sam punched Gun Guy Anthony in the jaw.

Anthony stumbled back against the alley wall.

His gun flew out of his waistband, spinning to land at his friend's feet.

Sam punched Gun Guy mercilessly.

Gun Guy's friend picked up the gun and brought it up to aim at Sam.

I grabbed his gun arm and pushed down.

With a boom, the gun fired into the ground, inches from Sam's feet, sending up a shower of old cobblestone.

Time froze in the alley. Every mote of stink and brick dust locked in place like a frozen mist.

Anthony's friend broke the freeze, dropped the gun, and pulled free from my grasp.

He and Anthony rocketed out of the alley.

"Let's get 'em," Al said, bending down to pick up the gun.

"No, leave it," Sam said. "The cops are still out there. I'll handle it another way."

"Anyone hit?" Al asked.

"No," I said.

"I'm good," Sam said.

The reality of what happened hit me and beat the residual coke and alcohol out of me. My body quivered like a tuning fork. I tasted rising bile in my throat. Sam squared up in front of me and put his hands on my shoulders.

"Are you sure you ain't Italian? That was a real thing you did," Sam said.

"I just reacted."

"Yeah, you did." Al clapped me on the back.

"I owe you big time." Sam hugged me. "Just name it, and it's yours."

I was shaking. I stood there in that dim, stink-filled alley wondering how the night went from a party with friends to a near-death experience. It was then I realized that I wasn't shaking simply because I was afraid. I was also shaking with excitement. That scared me more than the bullets.

I liked these guys. I liked the fuck-it-all attitude that powered them. I liked that they demanded respect even if they were slow to give it. Most of all, I liked the power they wielded. But I also knew that if I continued down the path the events of that evening had paved, things were going to get complicated, and I wasn't equipped for the life that would bring.

"How about a chicken parm from The Melrose and we'll call it even?" I said.

"Not a chance, cuz. I owe you. Anything you need. Anything, anytime," Sam said.

We made it to the Melrose Diner. I'm sure it was the events of the night, but that chicken parm sandwich was the best thing I'd ever eaten.

After we ate, my limo dropped Sam and Al off at their cars.

"Seriously, cuz, what do you need?" Sam asked as he exited the limo. "Anything, just ask."

"I'm good but thank you."

"You got a favor in the bank. Anytime you need to cash it out, call me. Here's my number."

"Thank you. I'm sure I won't need it." I had no intention of calling in the favor.

"I hope you don't, but you never know, do you?" Sam said.

34

LAST CALL

In less than five hours, my best friend in the world, my brother from another mother, would be getting on a plane and leaving the country before they found him.

"Can you play "Jet Airliner" by the Steve Miller Band?" I asked.

The DJ dug through his milk crate of albums. "I might," he said.

"If you find it, can you send it out to Sid and say his friends will miss him?" I tossed $20 his way.

The Budweiser clock over the bar read 5:42 am. I squeezed in between two gray-whisker-faced regulars beginning their daily work of dispatching the withdrawal demons. Small glasses of beer backed by shots of something quicker looked to be the standard order of the members of the early-riser drinker club. Membership was easy, and everyone was welcome. Good luck quitting that club.

I ordered four shots of something quicker and took them to the table where four of us were commiserating. We chose the table closest to the back door, believing it was safest, just in case. But any feeling of safety was an illusion, and we all knew it.

The opening notes of "Jet Airliner" came over the cheap speakers hanging from the ceiling.

"This one goes out to Sid. Your friends will miss you," the DJ said.

Sid smiled. The four of us held up our shots. The five early risers at the bar turned in our direction and lifted their beers, gripped tightly by veiny, large-knuckled hands. They were happy to have a reason to drink besides their usual ones.

"To Sid," I said. We hoisted.

"To Sid," echoed over Steve Miller. We drank.

"Are you sure about this?" Greg asked.

"Not much of a choice," Sid answered.

"Where are you going?" Mike asked.

Sid just smiled, smartly not willing to give away his destination.

"Not going to say, huh?" Mike said.

By way of an answer, Sid pulled a sizable baggy of coke out of his pocket and dropped it on the table.

"Can't take this with me, so who's in?" he said.

We were all in and took turns escorting the baggy into the bathroom.

Not saying where he was going was probably the smartest thing Sid had done in months. I'm not sure how you manage to get almost everyone in two states looking for you, but Sid had done just that. He must have set some sort of record. At a minimum, Sid was wanted by the New Jersey State Police, the Willingboro Police Department, the Princeton Police Department, the staff and faculty of the Princeton High School, seventy-five Princeton High School seniors and their parents, some very angry Italians, and a bus company.

If I were Sid, I'm not sure who on the list I'd consider the biggest threat. Sure, the mobsters might break his legs, but parents of high school kids could be vicious. I could picture some irate parent ending him on sight with their BMW.

A few weeks before the sendoff party, I found Sid waiting for me at my hotel room after Harrison's closed. His forehead was damp with sweat.

"Did you see it?" Sid said.

"See what?"

"On the TV, did you see me?"

"Why would you be on TV?"

"I fucked up, Cam. I fucked up big time." He pulled out a bag of coke, dug in his nail, and snorted a small pile. He offered it to me.

"I'm good," I said. "Look, whatever it is, we can fix it. Whatever you need, I got you."

"Don't think so."

"What do you need?"

"For starters, thirty grand."

"What? Thirty what? Did you say thirty grand? As in three, zero, and then three more zeroes?"

"Yeah, Buck, you heard right. I *sooo* fucked up." His pupils were large and vibrating.

I poured us each a whiskey and pushed one of them into his hands. I didn't know how much coke he had done or how long he'd been up, but he needed to chill. Maybe the whiskey would help, maybe it wouldn't.

"Okay, let's sort this out. Spill."

Sid drank the whiskey and took a deep breath.

"You know the ski trips I've been booking for high schools and whatnot?"

"You've got one to Vail soon, right?"

"Yeah, soon." He barked out a laugh. "So soon that I should be in Vail right now."

"Why aren't you?"

"Long story, Buck, but the deposit money they gave me to pay for the flights and hotel is gone. I never sent it."

"What happened to the money?"

"I took the $10,000 deposit to Atlantic City."

"Oh no. It's all gone?"

"Yeah, all gone. I was gonna double or triple it and make everything good."

"But that's only $10,000. We can get $10,000 somehow and pay it back. I've got some you can—"

"Then I got another $10,000, you know, to win it back."

"More? Who gave you more? Casino credit?"

"Nah, they wouldn't approve me."

"Who gave it to you?"

"I don't want to say."

"Who, Sid?"

I hoped with all I was that he wouldn't say what I knew was coming.

"The Italians."

"Are you out of your mind?" I screamed. "Those guys don't play. You're into the mob for $10,000?"

"$20,000."

"What the fuck?"

"I went back for $10,000 more. Lost most of it at Caesar's."

"What were you thinking?"

"I know, Buck. It's bad."

"You gambled it all away?"

"I didn't lose it all. I took some of it and bought coke. I figured I could cut it and sell it and pay back some of the money."

"Where's the coke?"

"I got a suite at the Playboy and threw a three-day party. It was out of control. I sold some, but most of it went up stranger's noses and a bunch of it was stolen."

"Fuck, what's left?"

"I've got $900 and some coke."

"So, you owe the high school $10,000 and the mob $20,000?"

"Yeah, and one more thing."

"Come the fuck on. What else?"

"The Italians asked me to do a favor. They said if I did it, they would wash out part of the debt."

"What did they ask you to do?"

"They asked me to do a pickup at the airport."

"Drugs?"

"No, GI Joes and Barbie dolls. Yeah, of course drugs, but I didn't do it. I was on my way to do the pick-up, and something was off. You know that Spidey sense that tells you something's wrong? It was going off for real, and I knew I was the fall guy. You know the deal. Sacrifice the black guy to the cops while the tonnage is happily driving up Route 95."

"What happens now?"

"I've missed the first two payments, including vig, and I didn't show up at the airport. I figure I'm a dead man walking."

"Fuck, Sid. Fuck fuckity fuck!"

"I know. I'm an asshole."

"Why did you ask me if I saw you on TV?"

"The Princeton High ski trip was supposed to leave yesterday. Seventy-five kids and their parents were waiting at six am for me to take them to the airport. When I didn't show, they called the police. It was all over the news. They somehow had a picture of me and did a '*Have you seen this man who ripped off these poor kids?*' special report."

"The cops are looking for you, too?"

"Yup. I'm toast."

"Maybe you should turn yourself in? Might be better than being on the run."

"They can get me anywhere. You know the deal."

"I wish I had that kind of money. I'd give it to you."

"Thanks, Buck."

"Did you ask your folks?"

"Yeah, I broke it down for them. They would have to sell their house to get even a piece of that kinda cash. I can't let them do that, even if they were willing."

"What's your next move?"

"I need some time to collect myself."

We worked the problem from every angle. The only solution that Sid saw was a one-way ticket to somewhere. Anywhere. After hours of trying to come up with a fix, we couldn't keep our eyes open.

The phone woke me up.

"Hello," I answered.

"Where's Sid?"

Fuck, fuck, fuck.

His voice sounded familiar. "Who's this?" I said.

"Don't you worry about that. Where's Sid?"

Whoever was on the other end of the phone could be close. Somehow, he knew we were friends, and he knew exactly where I was. He could be at the lobby of the hotel. Was it the cops or the opposite of cops?

I gambled it was the cops and they were fishing.

"I don't know where he is." I covered the receiver and kicked Sid. I mouthed the words: Get out.

"Yeah, you do."

"No, I don't. Who is this? Do I know you?"

Sid was awake, scrambling to get it together.

"I'm gonna ask you nicely one last time—" I hung up and turned to Sid.

"You gotta go. Now."

The phone rang again. My answering machine picked up. After the beep, an angry voice came out of the speaker.

"Listen up and listen good. If you don't pick up, I'm comin' to see you and it ain't gonna be…"

"Sid, who is this guy?"

"That's Gordon's friend, Tony."

"The guy I met at the Coliseum? Shiny suit guy?"

"Yeah."

"Get outta here. I'll handle him."

Sid left. I picked up the receiver.

"This is Tony, right?"

Tony stopped his threatening rant mid curse.

I continued, "Tony, we met before. This is Cameron. I am…I was a friend of Gordon's."

"You knew Gordon?"

"Yeah. He introduced you and me. Remember, we met at the Coliseum, you gave me your business card and you said—"

"Any friend of Gordon's is family…yeah, yeah, I remember," Tony said, his voice softening.

Silence filled the wires. I knew in my soul that he was remembering Gordon.

"You're the kid that wanted to be a DJ, right?" Tony asked.

"Yeah, that's me."

"Sucks what happened."

"It does. Gordon was a good man."

"Yeah…" He let out a heavy breath. I could tell that he wanted to say more about Gordon. He didn't. "One of my boys gave me this number and said some DJ might know where Sid is, and I guess that guy is you. Where is Sid?"

"Tony, I swear to you, I don't know where Sid is right now. He was here when you called, but we thought you were the cops so he hightailed it out of here."

"The cops? What do they want with him?"

"I'm not sure."

"Come on, you know, and you know where he's goin."

"I don't. He didn't tell me. He was scared. I've never seen him like that in all the years I've known him. He told me he owes a lot of people a bunch of money."

"I'm the people he owes. Tell me where he is."

"I don't know. You gotta believe me."

"Even if you knew where he was going, you wouldn't tell me anyway, am I right?" He laughed. "You know what, don't answer that."

"I'll answer that. You're right. I'm loyal, and I don't talk, and I wouldn't tell you if I knew. He's my blood and I owe him, but I'm telling you straight up that I don't know where he is or where he's going."

"I respect the loyalty, but I gotta get my money. That jamoke made me look like an asshole. Twice."

In a very real way, I owed Sid my life. Without his mentorship, I may not have found the courage to break free from the control of the Jehovah's Witnesses. Without his advice and help I may not have made it through homelessness. I knew that Sid would lay down his life for me should it ever come to that.

"I'll take the debt."

Tony laughed. "Do you know what he owes me?"

"Twenty large."

"Yeah, plus vig."

"How much total?"

"Twenty-two right now."

"I've got five here right now. It's everything I got in the world, but it's yours and I'll make good on the rest."

"How are you gonna cover the rest? Is DJ'ing paying that kind of cabbage?"

"I'm doing okay. I'll find a way."

"It's not just the money. Sid was supposed to do a favor for some friends, and he never showed."

"Can you get your friends to let that go?"

"Ain't gonna happen."

"Can you give him some time?"

"You sure are asking for a lot, aren't ya?"

"I'm asking you, in Gordon's memory, to give Sid some time."

Had I gone too far? Asked for too much? Crossed a final line? I was juggling on a high wire with Sid's life, my life, and a chainsaw dipped in acid.

"How much time?"

"Two weeks."

"He's got five days if I get the five large today. That's a grand a day. Then I come looking."

"Thank you. I'm good for the rest."

"You'd be surprised how many times I've heard that from people. I guess we will see, won't we. And you owe me for the other thing."

"What other thing?"

"You owe me a favor, over top of the money."

"I understand." I didn't, but I said it anyway.

The coke was gone, and so were two of the four of us. The sendoff party was running out of things to be said or things that needed hearing. Our coke-driven lips had been running uphill in fifth gear for hours, and they were spent. The only thing left was the goodbye, and neither one of us wanted to let it in. Soon, the cab would pull up and it would just be me.

"Are you sure? Maybe you could make it right with the cops. With the parents?"

Sid ignored my question. We both knew he was out of options.

"One more shot for the long road, Buck."

We raised our glasses and drank them down, the fire of the tequila helping hold back the emotions that men are not allowed to express in public.

Sid got up from the table, lifting his bag of everything he had left in the world. In that moment it struck me that he was now homeless. The heaviness of it added to the pit in my core. We walked outside into the morning sun, the brightness of it cleansing away any fantasies of a last-second reprieve we may have secretly harbored.

We stood in the dirt of the bar's parking lot, waiting.

You would think one of us would have said something profound. Some reassuring or encouraging sendoff words. Some sort of hallmark card goodbye. *Something.* But we didn't. And it wasn't because we didn't have words. We both had those a plenty. We just silently agreed by friend telepathy that any words we chose couldn't possibly measure up.

The cab pulled up. Sid got in the back.

As the cab drove away, it kicked up a mini storm cloud of dust.

When the cloud settled, the cab was gone, as if some unseen force had crushed the cab and its occupants into dust, joining it with the storm.

I stood there, morning sun mocking me, until each grain of dust settled.

I wondered how many more people I loved would turn to dust.

35

MY EMPIRE OF DIRT

"Hit me," I told the blackjack dealer.

His head looked too big to be supported by his thin neck. His pinched face ended in pursed lips that edged up ever so slightly when he busted someone's blackjack hand. He dropped a ten of hearts on my thirteen and cleared away my cards and my bet. There went the last of my money.

I'd been at the table for thirty minutes and I had yet to take out the money Tony gave me. Each of my pockets held a rubber-band-wrapped bundle of $10,000, in fifties and hundreds. My hands repeatedly checked the bulges of cash in my pants.

"It was no sweat," Tony told me. "Anyone could do it."

I guess I wasn't anyone because I was sweating. Profusely. I reached into my pocket and let my fingers rifle the stack of bills. Yes, still there. They must have weighed a million pounds, because I couldn't bring myself to take them out.

Four days prior, Tony and I were sitting across from each other at the Melrose Diner in Philadelphia.

"Okay, kid, here's what your gonna do." Tony stirred his coffee. "This Friday night, you're gonna go to the Trump Plaza Casino, 'cause they're friends of ours. Play at ten different blackjack tables, buy $2,000 in chips per table. Don't get crazy. Play the table minimum for ten, maybe fifteen minutes. Don't lose much. Don't do anything stupid. Should only take you a few hours to convert the cash to chips. Once you've converted the twenty large, you head to the cashier and ask them to pay you out with a check. After the check clears, you write out a few checks to who I tell you. Anything you lose over five hundo, you owe me, so, like I said, don't go crazy. If you win while you're playing, that's gravy, and you can keep it. Easy, peasy, pudding pie."

"If I do this, then we're square, right?"

"No sweat at all."

"Sure, but if I do this, I'm square on the favor?"

"Yeah, sure, sure, but you're gonna like it. Then we can get you a betting account at the Trump Plaza, and then you can make us both some regular lettuce."

"No, I—"

The waitress appeared. "Can I get you handsome men anything else besides the coffee?"

"No, hun, we're right as rain," Tony said. "For you." He slid a $5 across the table under his index finger like he was delivering life-changing news.

"Just to be clear, this is a one and done thing," I said.

"Yeah, sure, sure." He dropped a brown lunch bag on the table. "Don't forget your dessert." He nodded at the bag. "There's twenty donuts in there."

I stared at the paper lunch bag sitting on the table next to my untouched coffee. The same kind of paper bag that the mom used to send with me to school. I imagined it filled with a wax-paper-wrapped turkey and cheese sandwich with the crusts cut off, an apple, and a bag of chips. The sight of one used to bring up fond memories. Not anymore.

I looked at the bag between us. It'll be okay, I told myself. It's just a one-time thing, and then the favor is done. Like he said. Easy, peasy, pudding pie.

I slid the bag over to my side of the table. The sound of the brown paper sliding across the Formica tabletop sounded like a knife being drawn against a throat.

Tony delivered an approving nod. "Atta boy, cuz. We're gonna make an earner outta you yet."

The dealer pursed his lips. "Bet, sir? Do you want to put a bet down?"

I was out of delaying cash. The next bet had to come from one of the bundles.

"Gimme a minute." I got up from the table. I was self-conscious of the packs of cash bulging out of my pockets as I walked to the restroom.

I stood at the bathroom mirror, looking at my sweat-soaked shirt. My heart was jabbing my rib cage like a pint-sized prizefighter trying to get out. I splashed some water on my face and tore off a paper towel to dry. I lowered the towel from my face. Tony was at my side like a magician's assistant popping out of a trunk.

A *"Ta-da"* would have been appropriate, but instead he said, "Everything okay, cuz?" Smile.

"Are you watching me?"

"You think you're the only one on deck tonight? I'm keeping an eye on all my kids." He tugged on the collar of his starched white shirt.

"How many people do you have doing this?"

"Don't worry about it." He smoothed down the lapels of his jacket. "You've been at that table long enough. Time to get a move on to another table."

"I didn't play your money yet."

"What? Why not?"

"I'm not cut out for this."

"Sure you are, kid. You just got a case of the nervous Nellies. Have a couple drinks. How about a bump?"

"No, I don't want to do this. I don't want to be this." I reached into my pockets and pulled out the stacks to hand them over. His smile evaporated like water on a hot pan.

"Are you fucking kidding me? Put that away." He looked around.

I stood there, $10,000 in each hand. "I'm sorry, I thought I could do this, but I can't."

"Ain't this a bitch!"

Tony grabbed me by my shirt and dragged me into the handicapped stall. He threw me up against the tiled wall.

"What the fuck?" I said.

"Shut your fucking mouth. Who do you think you are? This isn't a game." He poked me in the chest. "Don't be stupid. Now, go out there and do like I told you."

"I'm sorry. I can't. I couldn't even take the cash out of my pockets."

"You and that eggplant. Both of yas are worthless."

He stood back and pulled his jacket open, exposing a gun tucked into his waist.

In my mind, I had built Tony up into the kind of wise guy you see on TV. The type of mobster that has a heart of gold. The type that has a change of heart and does the right thing in the end. It wasn't a movie, and Tony wasn't a heart-of-gold TV wise guy. Gordon warned me.

"It's not that I don't wanna. I can't. I know I'll blow it somehow, and I don't wanna risk your cash. Look at me. I'm sweating rivers."

He stood silent, one hand wrapped around my collar, and the thumb of the other rubbing the grip of his gun.

"I'm sorry for the trouble, Tony."

He released me, smoothed down the sides of his suit jacket, and ran his hands through his hair.

"Is there anything else I can do? Something, I dunno, less public," I pleaded.

He moved back and forth in the stall like a caged tiger at feeding time.

He put his hand out. "Gimme."

I handed him the stacks. He pocketed them and left.

Was it over? Was I free? I fast walked out of the casino, back clenched, waiting for retribution.

Weeks passed and the muscles in my back had mostly relaxed when the phone rang.

"Time to go to work."

Fuck.

Tony continued. "Some guys are coming Friday at six am to put something in your room. You're gonna let 'em. Last chance."

The line went dead.

Friday at six am exactly brought three soft taps on my door. I opened it to find two big guys pulling a safe on a hand truck. One of the guys pushed past me and went straight to my closet area. He cleared out the area below the clothes rail. They rolled the safe over and put it on the closet floor and left.

The safe was old. The paint on the combination dial was faded and worn. I jiggled the handle. It was locked. I pushed on it, and it barely moved. Another tap on my door interrupted my exploration.

"A friend of ours sent me." In any other situation I would have thought the khaki-panted man at my door was an accountant.

"Gimme your room key," he said, not sounding at all like an accountant. "Ask 'em to give you another key. This one is ours."

I put the room key into his pudgy-fingered hand.

"I'm only going to say this once, so listen up. Someone is going to put something in this safe, and when they do, you wait outside. Whenever they need to use the safe, they will come in and use it. If you're here when they do, you wait outside. If you aren't, they're gonna come in anyway. Don't touch the safe. Don't tell anyone about the safe. And before you ask what's in the safe, a big pile of *none of ya business* is what's in the safe. We good?"

"How long?"

"How long what?"

"How long will it be here?"

"For as long as it takes."

"What about the maids? They'll see it."

"I dunno, maybe put a cardboard box over it and put sneakers on top or something. Clean the room yourself, whatever. They're just fucking maids. Figure it out."

Someone showed up to use the safe the next night.

"I'm with friends of ours, I'm Ray," he said when I opened the door.

"Yeah, let me get dressed and then I'll wait outside."

Ray was twenty-five pounds overweight with prematurely receding hair. What hair was left was slicked back. He was dressed in baggy sweatpants and a white T-shirt. Instead of sneakers, he wore tan leather shoes that looked expensive and were shined to a high gloss. The odor of dog emanated from him, and dog hair was all over his sweatpants.

"You're the DJ at the club, aren't you?"

"Yeah, that's me."

"You don't have to wait outside. It's good, it's good." He went to the safe.

"I'll be in the bathroom."

"It's good, it's good. I used to DJ sometimes, but there ain't enough money in it. I need to make big cash so I can buy salmon for my old man."

I heard sounds of the safe opening and closing. "You all done?" I asked through the closed door.

"It's good if you want to come out."

I exited to see him closing a beat-up brown leather briefcase. Dog hair was all over that as well.

"Salmon?" I asked, looking away from the briefcase and into his crooked-mouthed face. There was something unfinished about him. His face reminded me of an out-of-focus high school picture.

"Yeah. He had a heart attack, and they say you should eat salmon for the oils. That fish is expensive, so I gotta do what I gotta do, but it's good, it's good. I'm taking care of everything since he can't do tile work no more."

"I'm sorry to hear about your father."

"He's my pops. If he dies…" he trailed off.

"I lost mine to cancer when I was young."

"I'm sorry to hear that." He crossed himself. "If my father knew what I was doing it would give him another heart attack. Coming up he would always say, 'Clean hands, dirty money. Dirty hands, clean money.' This would break his heart."

Ray headed out the door. "See ya, DJ Cam. I left something for ya on top of the safe."

Sitting on top of the safe was a brown glass one-gram vial of coke.

Ray showed up every Saturday and Wednesday at six pm like clockwork and stayed a little longer each time. After a few visits, I was pouring us whiskeys and we sat and talked until I went to the club. He knew music, and he was a reader. Like me, he also liked to play chess. We had a game of chess that extended over his visits.

"Are you kidding me?" he said one Saturday. "The record business runs on this shit. Check, by the way."

"Check? Really? How did I miss that?" I contemplated the board.

"You left your rook alone. You shoulda moved it three moves ago. So, the labels give coke to the radio DJs to play their songs. They get coke for their artists. Remind me to tell you a story about the 84 New Music Seminar. I won't name names, but you play her records every night. She loves coke, and she ain't nothing like a virgin."

"What's the New Music Seminar?"

"Hold on. You're a DJ and you've never been?"

"Nope."

"Every single record label and all their artists jam into New York to meet and party for a week. The seminar is good, but the real action happens in the clubs and private suites. The next one is in a few weeks and you're comin' with me."

True to his word, we loaded into his car a few weeks later for the trip to Manhattan.

"Before we head up, I gotta make a stop. It's good?" he said.

"It's good," I said.

We parked in the garage of an exclusive high-rise just over the bridge in Philly.

Soon Ray was knocking on a door. No answer. He knocked again. Still nothing. He knocked harder on the third attempt.

"Jimmy. Open up, it's Ray." He tried the door handle. It was unlocked. "I'm coming in."

We walked into the living room of the converted warehouse loft. It had a fourteen-foot ceiling and floor-to-ceiling windows looking out over a million-dollar view of Philadelphia and the Delaware River. The place was furnished in contemporary style with original modern art on every wall. The colors of the place hit your eye like a kaleidoscope. I dreamt of one day having a place just like it. I wanted to check out the art, and I would have if there hadn't been a body on the sofa.

"Ah, shit." Ray sprinted over to the couch and shook the body's arm. "Yo, Jimmy. Wake up."

A glass pipe fell out of Jimmy's hand, landed on the hardwood floor, and slid to my feet. On the coffee table was a bag of coke, a butane torch, and a box of baking soda.

"Is he dead?" I asked.

Ray rubbed his fist on Jimmy's sternum. "Jimmy, come on, wake up!"

"I…We should go." I backed up to the door.

"Go get me some ice and a washcloth."

I went to the kitchen and grabbed a towel and some ice from the freezer, careful not to touch anything directly with my fingers.

I passed Ray the towel of ice. Ray undid Jimmy's belt and put the ice in Jimmy's underwear.

"Jimmy, wake up!" he yelled into Jimmy's face while rubbing his sternum.

"Is he dead?"

"Dunno."

"Shouldn't we call 911?"

"Are you stupid? Do you want to be found with a dead body, coke, guns, and whatever else is in this place?"

Guns? Now there were guns?

"Can't we leave and call them? Come on, let's get outta here and call an ambulance."

Jimmy sprung up to a seated position, sucking in breath. He let it out, sounding like a hissing relief valve on a water heater.

"There he is," Ray said, crossing himself.

Jimmy had a coughing fit.

"Go get some water," Ray said.

I obeyed, and Jimmy drank the water down like it was the last moisture on earth.

"Are you with the living?" Ray said. Jimmy nodded a yes.

Ray pulled a gun out of a waistband holster and put it to Jimmy's head. Jimmy went wide-eyed and froze.

"What I tell you about freebasing this shit?" Ray said.

"I'm sorry. I won't..."

"Don't say it. Don't you dare say you won't do it again. We both know you will, and I don't trust you no more." Ray pushed the barrel of the gun into the flesh of his forehead.

"I won't say it, I won't. Come on Ray, ease up," Jimmy said.

"Why? Isn't this what you want? Don't you wanna go? This way is faster. Sure, it will mess up your fancy sofa, but how about we just get it over with? Whadda ya say, fuckup?"

"Don't...I don't want that."

"Sure you do. If I hadn't shown up, you'd be dead right now, so what do ya say?"

Tears ran down Jimmy's face. I walked backwards and pushed my back up against the door, feeling behind me for the knob.

"I'm fucked up. I can't stop. I'm sorry, Ray. I tried to quit...can't. Just do what you gotta do."

"Where my money?" Ray asked.

"In the box."

Ray turned to me. The gun didn't waver. "Cam?"

I froze.

"Go to the dining room. In the cabinet there is a cigar box. Bring it to me."

If Ray pulled the trigger, I would be an accessory. Fingerprints! Had I touched anything? I used my shirttail to open the cabinet door and grab the cigar box. I brought it to him like he asked. Ray took a sizable pile of cash from the box and put it in his pockets.

Ray took the gun down from Jimmy's forehead.

"You and I are done," Ray said.

The front of Jimmy's pants went wetter and the smell of urine hit my nose.

"No more supply. You're dead to me. If I catch you selling a joint to your kid sister for a dollar, you are over."

"But Ray…" Jimmy was trying to compose a convincing smile.

The gun was back at Jimmy's forehead.

"Done. Capeesh?"

Jimmy nodded.

"Say it. Say, I won't do business of any kind or I will be ended. Say it."

"I won't do business of any kind."

"Or?"

"Or I will be ended."

Ray put the gun away. We left.

I didn't want to go with Ray to New York, but after what I'd witnessed, I was terrified to say anything.

After an hour of nothing but road noise, Ray said, "Sorry you saw that. That wasn't the way I thought things were gonna go. I was just there to pick up some cash."

"I thought you were going to do it."

"Nah, he needed a scare put in him. It's good I found out he's smoking the shit again. You can't trust a junkie. Remember that. Never trust a junkie."

"For a minute there, I thought I was going to be an accessory to murder."

"Nah, that would have been messy. The way he's going, he'll be dead in a month. It's all good. And I don't leave witnesses." He dug into his pocket and took out a vial. "Here, do a bump. It's good, it's all good."

Of all the things the trip was shaping up to be, it was not, by any stretch of the imagination, good.

What had I gotten myself into?

I did a bump of the coke.

36

BETWEEN THE SOUL AND SOFT MACHINE

I shut the equipment down and made my way to the bar to relax with my post-shift drink. I don't know how I missed seeing her earlier in the night.

She raised her wine glass to take a sip, the muscles in her finely defined jawline, exercised by a lifetime of kind smiles, giving life to her lips. Her movements were intentional, graceful, fated.

She didn't belong at Harrison's, or in New Jersey, or even the decade, but there she was.

Billy the bartender was wiping down the bar top in front of her and he must have said something funny. She laughed, and two dimples appeared. I was jealous that he'd made her laugh and seized by a desperate urge to kiss her. I caught myself staring. I looked down at my drink and pretended the ice in my glass was doing something amazing.

I raised my gaze. She was looking directly at me.

Her emerald eyes emitted intelligence, awareness, and promises. I forgot all the mistakes I had ever made and some of the ones yet to come. Just like that, I knew she was the Mary to my George Bailey, and that I'd lasso the Moon for her.

Her smile was airy and gentle, mine big, dopey, toothy. I couldn't help it. Her dimples got deeper as her smile widened. She pulled her long, brown hair back behind one ear, tilted her head down, and played with the rim of her wine glass, looking at me from under her bangs. She looked as if she was about to say something. Her eyes and mouth seemed to argue with each other, leaving her with a confused expression, like when you think you recognize someone. With a nearly imperceivable shake of her head, she changed her mind and looked away.

One of the club regulars, a muscle-bound personal trainer named Rich, came from the direction of the men's room and approached her. She stood up, grabbed her purse, and they walked together toward the exit.

Wait.

This isn't supposed to happen. No. This isn't right. The timelines are flexing and they will surely break from the fallaciousness of this combination.

My soul screamed, "Don't go with him! Please, for the love of all things, STOP."

She stopped. Had she heard my silent cry? For a nanosecond, I thought she was going to walk over to me. She went back to the bar and spoke to Billy. He handed her something.

Stupid me, she'd just forgotten to sign her bar check. She looked back at me a final time and left with Rich.

I took my drink down the long bar, taking a seat in front of Billy.

"Who was that?" I asked.

"Who was who?" he said while delivering a mischievous smile.

"You know exactly who I mean."

"Her name is Tina."

"Tell me everything you know."

"She isn't from here." Billy pulled some bottles of liquor from the rack and began wiping them down. "She came up from Georgia for her job. She's been here a few months."

"More."

"She is classy. She has a southern accent that will make a man crazy. She reminds me of an old timey movie star."

"What was she doing with Rich?"

"They were on a date. She isn't into him."

"Good. How do you know that?"

"Because." He took a folded bar check out of his pocket and spun it down in front of me on the bar.

Written on it in perfect cursive was:

I've never done this before.
I can't stop myself.
Tina (555) 771-1526

The first time Tina and I talked on the phone, we spoke for four hours. On our first date, we spoke for five more. On our first night together, we made love for two hours and talked in bed for eight. The sex was incredible, the sharing after, more so.

Conversations with women I'd dated before Tina were good, but after spending time with Tina, those previous conversations seemed like a radio when the station wasn't perfectly in-tune. There was always that little bit of static that distracted from the song. With Tina, the music was crystal clear.

We quickly discovered that we matched in ways we'd never looked for in a partner because we didn't think it was possible. From our first shared words, we wanted to tell each other everything, and we did. We dispensed with all filters and masks. Our honesty bordered on brutal, but it never was. It was vital, life giving, like the coldest water on the hottest day.

We were joined every day for two weeks and talked so much that we barely slept. Tina even missed a few days of work. Some nights we forgot to eat, only recognizing our bodies' hunger after our sharing was satiated for the night.

We shared a love of art, music, books, film, and philosophy. Like me, Tina wanted to do and see everything the world had to offer. She had a deep vein of kindness and wanted to change the world. The deeper we went, the more we vibrated like the two halves of a tuning fork. We found in each other an aligned combination of physical and intellectual passion. From day one, we were exclusive. We never stated it because we didn't have to. We didn't have a choice.

"Do you believe in fate?" she asked as we lay in bed together, after.

"I don't think so."

She sighed. "That's not very romantic bed talk. You're supposed to say yes and tell me how the two of us finding each other was fate." Her southern lilt played with my ears, driving me to want her again.

"Tina, since seconds ago, I believe in fate, and I am eternally grateful to the gods for bringing us together."

"Much better, now kiss me like it's the last time."

"Perish the thought. I will kiss you like it's the first time, always."

Each time we kissed, the atoms in the universe collapsed into the point where our lips touched. When we separated, the universe restarted, and the atomic structures returned to their previously boring state.

"Seriously, though, do you believe that our lives are already decided?"

"Maybe. I hope not. Otherwise, we're just fleshy robots living out a program. I'd like to think we have choice. I believe I do. Right now, I choose to kiss you."

I did.

"Fleshy Robots of Fate," I said.

"What's that?"

"It's our band name. What do you think?"

"This isn't supposed to be happening," she said, the warmth of her cheek radiating into my chest.

"Where did that come from? Why do you say that?"

"I left someone in Athens and we never completely severed it. I am only supposed to be here for a little while. This wasn't in the plan."

"Umm, okay. Well. Do you love him?"

"In a way."

"In what way?"

"Not in this way."

"What way is this way?"

"I feel like my soul knew yours before we met. Our bodies appear to be meeting for the first time, however, judging by how much I want yours right now."

"I want you."

"I think I'm…I'm falling…" she said.

"Why, Miss Tina, are you about to say you love me after only weeks?"

She looked up at me, the green of her eyes catching the reflection of the candles on the top of the dresser, like ornaments on Christmas Eve.

"Yes. I am."

"I've loved you from the second I saw you. Maybe even before," I said.

I'd said "I love you" only a few times in my life. The previous times I'd said it, I meant it. This time, the words "I love you" seemed pale and weak, like under-brewed tea. I wanted new words, new poems, new everything.

We kissed. The universe was us. There was nothing else.

She was amazing. And she loved me. How was it even possible?

We made love again. Laying together afterwards, I felt a mental pinch like an unseen ant biting my leg at a picnic.

Am I enough?

Tina and I had completely different upbringings. She was raised in a large, loving family. Her father was a professor and her mother a teacher. Education was paramount to her and her family. On that we agreed, although hers was formal and mine, shall we say, less so. But she never made me feel less than for not having a degree.

Tina was a magnet. Men wanted to be with her, and woman wanted to be her. Some women wanted to be with her too. Wherever we went, men were so focused on Tina that I was invisible. It made for some annoying encounters. At first, we made a game out of it, counting the number of times a man tried to talk with her, get her number, or ask her out.

"That's two so far tonight," I said while we sat at a bar one happy hour. "That one guy actually pushed between us to talk to you."

"Three. See that guy right over there?" She held up a business card. "He thought he was tricky and slipped this business card into my hand as I left the ladies' room."

"That's got to be his wife next to him. See the rings?" I said.

Tina was a two-drink maximum. After a third drink, Naughty Tina showed up. She was at two and a half drinks. For the most part, Naughty Tina was harmless. Not this night. She walked over to the couple.

"Hi, my name is Tina," she said to the man's wife.

She handed the business card to the woman. "Your husband dropped this."

The lady took the card, shifting uncomfortably toward her husband.

"Want to know where I found it?" Tina asked. "Right in my little hand. Now y'all are probably asking yourself, *How is that possible?* Well, I'll be charmed if he didn't put it in my hand when you weren't looking. Isn't that something? Y'all have a blessed night."

Tina flipped her hair and walked back over to me. "Let's get out of here, lover," she said loud enough for the couple to hear. "The people in here lack class."

She was fire. I loved her so much.

Naughty Tina was white hot when we got to her place. She began disrobing before we got inside. She pulled my clothes off and pushed me down on the floor. The sex was urgent, dirty, fervid.

"Don't you ever cheat on me. It's you and me. Forever," she said looking down at me. She dug her nails into my chest and scratched three deep scratches into me. Blood welled up.

"Tina, what the hell?" I rolled out from under her.

"Now, the other girls will see that you're mine."

"There are no other girls. Only you."

"Oh, come on Mr. DJ, I see how girls look at you."

"Tina, you're drunk."

"So."

"So, are you kidding me? You can have any man you want. If anyone here should be worried, it's me. I'm a nobody with nothing. You have a college degree, a great job, and a good family. I've got none of those things. It wasn't that long ago that I was sleeping under a tarp in the woods. Sometimes, I don't know why you're with me."

"Don't you ever say that again. I don't care about any of those things. I love your soul, and your heart, and the way you look at the world. We're soulmates, and you know that. I've never felt this way before. It scares me a little. I didn't think this was possible. But…"

"But what?" I said, feeling a sting.

"I'm all alone here. All of my family is back in Georgia. I don't have any friends here, only you."

"Yeah, only me."

"That is not what I meant. I miss my family so much it hurts."

"Then go see your family. Go meet some new people, make some friends. This is all fixable. And *only me* will be here to support whatever you need to do. It's you and me, forever."

"You and me forever and ever… I'm sorry I hurt your chest. I'm drunk. I'm sorry. Does it hurt?"

"I need some Band-Aids, or an ambulance. I'm bleeding all over."

"Hurry up and get a Band-Aid. I need you to make love to me again."

I hurried.

After, I couldn't sleep.

I lay next to her in the dark, watching the gentle rise and fall of her chest.

I couldn't lose her.

She was everything I wasn't. She was everything I believed I needed. Her light and love for me fought back the dark.

I had to become more. I had to get my act together. I had to make changes.

"I can't have it in my new place. I'm moving into an apartment, and I have a roommate that would freak out if he knew. You've got to take it out," I said.

Ray shifted from foot to foot uncomfortably. "I have to clear it with Tony."

"There's nothing to clear. I am out of the hotel room on Friday and the safe can't come with me."

"He's not going to be happy about it."

"Consider the favor paid, with interest."

"You got some kinda balls. Tony decides when it's paid."

"I don't care anymore. You both do whatever you need to do, but I won't be here Saturday."

"I like you, but you know this ain't a game of chess, right?"

"I can't do it anymore. My girl is going to leave me if I don't clean up my life."

"I'll talk to him, but no promises."

Friday at six am, two guys showed up to take away the safe. Ray stopped by after they left. His usual quirky smile was missing.

"Tony ain't happy. He says you owe him, and he wanted me to do something about it. I'm not gonna do that, but you need to go talk to him and square it. Good luck, DJ Cam. You're gonna need it."

37

A BANQUET OF CONSEQUENCES

"I made it!" Tina was doing little jumps and twirls.

"You made what?" I asked.

"I didn't want to tell you before, in case I didn't make the cut, but you're looking at one of the newest Philadelphia Eagles Cheerleaders."

"Wait, what?"

"It's official. I got the call today. I'm an Eagles Cheerleader! You may bow. Oh, and I get tickets to all the games. You will be my cheerleader while I cheer. Goooo Eagles!"

"When, what...how?"

"I applied and went through the process over the last two months. I wanted it to be a surprise."

"I am certainly surprised. Congratulations."

"Thank you." She did a little bow and a jump. "Practice starts in two weeks and fittings are after that."

She took a pose. "E-A-G-L-E-S," she cheered.

"That's great."

"You don't seem very excited for me. What's wrong?"

Truth was, I wasn't. I'd spent months dealing with the constant barrage of attention from other men toward my girlfriend. At first it was funny, but it quickly became intrusive. I couldn't compete with the doctors, lawyers, and millionaires that chased her. Now she was going to be on television every Sunday.

"I am excited for you. I'm just not excited for us."

"What does that mean?"

"You will be hanging out with football players and famous people. I can't compete with that."

"Do you think my love can be won in a competition?"

"No, but—"

"How can you doubt us? I'm closer to you than anyone else in the world." Tears welled up in her eyes. "It's you and me forever. Do you doubt that?"

"No. But sometimes I wish it was just us."

"It can't be just us. That isn't reality. Please don't ruin this for me. For us."

"I'm sorry."

"I thought you'd be thrilled. You said you would support me in my efforts to spread my wings."

"I did, but I didn't know that would include a football team."

"Ouch. Way to ruin it."

"I don't mean to. It's just hard to think of you still wanting to be with me with all the attention you'll be getting."

"I love you. You don't have anything to worry about."

I worried every minute. As the football season went on, I grew more jealous by the touchdown. Being an NFL cheerleader is more than showing up on game days. It's a second full-time job between practice, games, charity events, and signings. As her cheerleader activities and friend circle grew, our time together decreased.

Driven by my fears, the jealousy monster took over. If Tina went out with the girls, I questioned her, occasionally showing up at whatever bar they visited. When her phone rang, I had to know who it was. I even threw test questions at her new friend Liz to confirm things that Tina told me. The more popular Tina became, the tighter I squeezed.

Tina's parents came up from Athens, Georgia to visit. Tina was excited for me to meet them. She'd often said that she wanted a relationship just like her parents'. I was desperate to make a good impression, so I arranged a private dining room at Harrison's and asked the chef to prepare an extravagant meal.

Her parents were lovely. I could tell they didn't know what to make of me. By course number three, my brashness and direct ways had overpowered them, and it was clear that my campaign to impress them was having the opposite effect, but I doubled down. Pushing on with my attempt to win them over, I gave them a tour of the facility, stopping in at the club. I put on some music. They went on the dance floor and danced. Watching them together, I could see where Tina got her playful spirit. I hungered for what her parents had.

When we said our goodbyes, there was no talk of "Next time." No "Come visit us in Georgia." It was clear from what her parents didn't say that I was not what they wanted for their daughter. After their visit, something shifted between Tina and me. Everything felt off.

Tina was scheduled to leave in a month for an Eagle's exhibition game in London. In an effort to spend quality time together and reconnect before she went away, I booked us a week at a bed and breakfast in Cape May, New Jersey. We were packed and ready to leave in the morning. Tina's phone rang at midnight, waking us up.

"Hello... no, I can't... no, I'm leaving for a trip tomorrow," Tina said. "How about when I get back? Okay. Bye, bye."

"Who was that?"

Tina turned away.

"Who was it calling this late?" I asked.

"Rob."

"Rob who?"

"Rob Tillerson."

The name sounded familiar.

"Rob Tillerson from Channel Eight Sports?"

"Yes."

"Why is he calling you at midnight?"

"I don't know."

"You don't know? What did he want?"

"Umm, to talk I guess."

"How did he get your number?"

"I don't know."

"A Philadelphia TV celebrity calls you at midnight, and you don't know how he got your number? Come on Tina, that's ridiculous."

"He probably got it from the cheer captain, Kim. She's friends with him."

"Is the captain in the habit of giving out your phone number to anyone who asks, or just sportscasters?"

"I don't know how he got it. Please believe me."

I chose to believe her so we would have a nice week together before her trip. On some level, I knew my fears and insecurities drove us to this place. It was my fault. My fears were destroying the best relationship in my life.

The week in Cape May did not bring us to a better place.

The constant murmur played relentlessly in my head.

You aren't enough. You never were.

A few weeks after our trip, Tina went off to London to cheer at the American Bowl. While she was away, I called her hotel daily. She never returned my calls. I called her friend Liz to see if they'd spoken. Liz told me that Tina had met someone in London.

I was destroyed.

The murmur grew.

SEE…You are worthless. She sees it now.

"Liz told me what you did in London."

"I didn't do anything wrong in London. I didn't cheat on you."

"Then why did Liz say you did?"

"Because she's jealous of me and she's always wanted you."

"Bullshit. You're a liar."

"I'm not lying. I didn't cheat on you."

"Did you meet someone?"

"I met a lot of people, but I did not cheat on you. Meeting people is what cheering is all about. You know that."

"You don't love me."

"Do you really believe that Cam? That's not true and you know it. I loved you with all that I am. I have since we met. We're soulmates. You know that. Each second together was magic until I made the cheerleading squad. Until I had friends. Since then, you haven't believed in me, in us. It's not the cheerleading or other men that threatens us. It's your doubts. Your jealousy."

"Loved."

"What?"

"You said loved, not love."

"This is what I'm talking about. You've lost your belief in us. How could you do that? It's supposed to be you and me forever."

Tears were running down both of our faces.

Whatever we'd had was broken.

What had I done?

Eventually, Tina packed up and returned south to be near her family. Like a phantom limb, constant soul wrenching pain radiated from where she used to be. I did my best to move on. I failed. Everyone I met was a hollow facsimile, a shadow.

Time passed. My phone rang.

"Hi," Tina said. "How have you been?"

"Terrible. You?"

"Same."

"Are you dating anyone?"

"Yes. It helps. Are you?"

"Yes. She's not you, but she's very sweet and nice."

"I'm happy for you."

"Are you really?" I asked.

"No, that was a lie. I don't like her one bit."

Evening slipped into morning as we talked about us, the universe, and everything. It felt like it had in the beginning, and it was medicine for both of our fractured souls. That call led to another, and before long we were talking every day, sometimes falling asleep with the phone in our hands, waking up with the call still connected, to wish each other good morning.

Tina was traveling for a new job, and we made plans to meet at a conference she was attending in Washington, DC. During the three-hour drive from Philly, my heart beat like I was running a marathon, faster and faster with each mile that brought me closer to DC. It was like the pull of two magnets, increasing and increasing until a snap brings them together. Tina was my true north and I could feel her getting closer.

Seeing her in the hotel lobby, I felt a rush of regret for all my actions, all my doubts, my fears. We hugged, and I felt complete. She took my hand and led me to her room. Later, there would be time for talk; now, we had to touch each other, to make sure we were real.

We lay together in the ravaged hotel bed, sweaty, spent. As was usual with our passion, the sheets were pulled down on the bed and the comforter was on the floor. The dislodged sheet revealed handwriting in blue pen on the white mattress. The writing was faded and worn and looked like it had been there for quite some time. I pulled the sheets down further to reveal a hand-drawn heart with the words *Tina + Cam* written in the heart's center.

"Cute," I said, pointing to the mattress graffiti. "You know, you can get jail time for destroying a mattress. I hope you didn't remove the tag as well."

"I didn't do that."

"What? Come on. Sure, you did."

She shook her head no.

"Maybe in your sleep?"

"No, look at how it's faded. It's been there for a while."

"What are the odds that someone with our names stayed in this room and did that?"

"What are the odds of us?"

The murmurs stirred. "But we couldn't make it work, could we?"

I got up and put the bed sheets back on. I noticed the phone was off the cradle. I hung it up. It rang seconds later.

"Do you need to get that?" I asked.

"Can you please take it off the hook?"

"Is it your boyfriend?"

"Someone I'm seeing, yes. He won't stop calling."

Memories of calling her in London gripped my stomach. On the other end of that phone was a man feeling what I'd felt.

"Does he love you?"

"He says he does."

"I feel bad. I know how he must feel—the jealousy, the worry, the sick feeling in your stomach."

"Cam. Please don't."

"Tina, was I enough?"

Tina took my face in her hands. "You were always enough for me. I wish you would have believed that."

"I wish it could be just us."

"But it can't."

"I know, but a boy can wish."

"Nothing can ever change what we are to each other."

"Then we should be together, shouldn't we?"

She looked at me without answering.

"What are we doing here?" I asked.

"I don't know."

We didn't make love that night. We held each other until dawn reminded us that there was a reality outside the hotel room that couldn't be stopped, no matter how tight our grip on each other.

A cab arrived to take her to the airport. I loaded her bags into the trunk.

"What do we do now?" I held her close against me.

She pulled away. "Kiss me like it's the last time."

I should have stopped her from leaving. I should have followed her to the airport and got onto her flight. I should have screamed my love so loud to the sky that the angels would have no choice but to fly down to make it right. I should have dropped to my knees and begged her to give us another chance, given her a ring, or refused to let her get in the cab.

I did none of those things.

I kissed her like it was the last time.

As the cab drove away, we held each other's eyes through the glass of the cab's window until traffic broke our hold. I stood there for a long time not knowing what to do next.

I went back into the hotel and did three lines of coke in the lobby bathroom.

The murmur was loud. So loud.

I made the long drive home. It was agony.

I thought he had forgotten about me. Tony's voice came out of my answering machine, like a tiny devil that had taken up residence in its circuitry.

"Hey, smart guy. You still owe me. Time to go to work."

38

ARMAGEDDON

"Your music sucks." His sweating upper lip had an attempt at a mustache. It was a fail.

"Do me a favor and back up," I told him.

He stumbled back.

"Do you know who I am?" he said, stretching to his full height of 5′6″ in his baggy, brown, nine-to-five, banker suit.

"Lemme guess. You're the king of IllFittingSuitAstan?"

The insult passed over his receding hairline.

He moved toward me, his drink sloshing over the edge of his glass to spill on his shoes.

"I'm from the bank. We own this place now, and you gotta do what I say, so play something good."

"Maybe you missed it, but the dance floor is packed. I'm going to go out on a limb here and say that not only does my music not suck, it is, in fact, your taste that sucks."

The Harrison's complex had hit hard times. The club was making money, but the cost of carrying a failed restaurant and a nearly empty hotel weighed down the entire complex. The bank had removed the owner and his sons and taken over the operation of the complex. They assigned a property manager that had no idea how to run a club.

After the first year Harrison's was open, I started a successful Sunday night, under-twenty-one dance party, and the night regularly made a pile of cash. I brought in national dance music acts and was getting paid for each attendee, making thousands more dollars per week over and above my original deal. The management company ruined the Sunday dance parties by instructing the doormen to deny entry to people of color. Not surprisingly, this racist policy caused tensions at the entrance and fights regularly broke out. They ultimately shut the night down, cutting off a sizable portion of my income.

Now one of the bank's toadies was drunk and up in my face. He dressed and sounded like one of the Elders.

I was a few lines of coke into the night and not having it.

"Play something else, or else," Bank Man said.

I was done with threats.

I walked over to the rack of amplifiers and shut them off one by one. The music stopped with an ear-drum-cracking pop. The dance floor erupted in boos.

"You just burned the last income this place had," I said.

"Turn the music back on right now or else."

"I quit."

"You…you can't."

"Now you're the DJ, and you can play whatever you want."

My regulars came up to the DJ booth to see what was happening.

"Looks like we're going to the Coliseum early," I said to the crew.

"What happened?" one of them asked.

"I quit."

No one responded. They disappeared like cockroaches when the lights go on. Fuck them too, I thought. Fuck 'em all. I packed up my records and left.

The Coliseum did not fill up until 3:30 am, and I was early and furious. I sat at the empty bar and drank, hoping it would calm me down. The dealers were the first to arrive to fuel the last few hours of the party. One of the dealers I knew slid me a few grams of coke. I went to the bathroom and did a line off the back lid of the toilet. I felt dirty. I felt like a loser. I did another line.

I was angry at everything, but mostly I was angry with myself. I could have handled the bank asshole better than I did. I could have done quite a few things "better" lately.

"Get you another one, Cam?" the bartender asked.

"Thanks, Dan. I can't think of any reason why not."

"I've never seen you here this early. Where are your friends?"

"I wish I had an answer. As for why so early, I quit Harrison's tonight."

"Why did you do that?"

"Long story, but I won't be disrespected."

"Then you're in the wrong business."

"Dan, you've known me for a while. Am I a good man?"

He set my drink in front of me. "I only know what people say about you."

"What do they say?"

"The general consensus is you're an asshole."

"Do tell."

"I don't think you're any more of an asshole than most, but you've rubbed some people the wrong way. Even the crew you hang with talks shit about you." He shrugged. "Look, you've got a big ego, and I guess that's to be expected, but nobody cares how much money you make or who you know."

Dan walked down to the other end of the bar.

There it was. How did I not know this? Had I become incapable of introspection, or was I hesitant to look inside for fear of what I would find? Did I believe that the hangers-on I picked up were real friends? They were a poor analog for family and yet, somehow, I thought of them as such.

Who was I kidding?

I guess I was kidding myself.

Dan returned from the other end of the bar.

"At least one person doesn't think you're an asshole." He laughed and nodded toward the end of the bar. "The guy in the shiny suit wants to buy you a drink."

"Hey, smart guy. Why are you ducking me?" Tony said, oozing into the seat next to me.

"I've been busy."

"Time to go to work."

"I'm done with all of that."

"Yeah, so Ray mentioned, but there's a problem with that. You ain't the one to decide when we're square."

"I've paid you all the money and I've done enough to satisfy any favor Sid bailed on."

"You did, did ya? Not for you to say, smart guy."

"Maybe not, but I'm out. I'm making changes."

"Sure, you are. Look here, I got something for you that's right up your alley and you're gonna make the both of us a lot of cabbage."

"Not interested."

"I'm not asking, smart guy, I'm telling."

Dan put a drink down in front of me.

"That's on me," Tony said, leaning in closer. "Drink up."

The drink sat on the bar, ice spinning on the surface in an endless loop, drips of condensation running down the sides. A distorted reflection of my face looked back from the glass.

"Pick up your drink."

"No… I don't think I will."

"Pick up the fucking drink."

One of the ice cubes cracked with a pop, reminding me of the gunshot in the South Street alley.

Tony's eyes narrowed to slits. "Last chance, my man. Pick up the drink."

I got up from the bar. Tony grabbed my arm and twisted me around.

"You and that nigger friend of yours, you're both nothing, and you'll never be nothing. Do you know how many guys like you I've seen in my life? Don't be stupid. Pick up the drink."

"Get your fucking hand off me." I yanked my arm free.

Tony laughed. "You a tough guy now?"

"Worse. I'm a guy with nothing left to lose."

"Wrong, smart guy. You got one thing left."

He was right, but not in the way he thought. I did have one thing left.

I went home. I paged Sam. Two lines of coke later, Sam called.

"Who's this? It better be important."

"It's Cam."

"Cam, my man. What's up? It better be an emergency because you woke me up from a great dream."

"I'm sorry. It is."

"What do you need?"

"I need that favor."

I told him about Tony. I told him about me taking on Sid's debt. I told him about the safe, and the dealer, and how it had gone on for too long.

When I got to the end, he asked me, "What do you want me to do?"

"I don't want anyone hurt. I just want to be left alone. I want some peace. I want the time and space to become more than I am now. I want to be a good man like my father before me. I want to become what eight-year-old me knew he could become," I said, my coke brain racing ahead of my mouth.

Sam didn't respond.

"Are you still there," I said.

"Yeah, I'm thinking about things."

It might have been his tone, but I knew in that moment that he shared the same desires. He wanted more. More than the road that had been paved before him. After a few minutes of silence came the soft click of him hanging up.

What the fuck? What was that? Why did he hang up?

I paged him. No call back.

I did two more lines off a Dead or Alive album cover. The irony did not escape me. My throat was numb from the drip, and my head was spinning right round baby, right round, but not enough to shut the murmur *THE FUCK UP*.

It was screaming.

The end is coming.

It's payback time.

Where have all your friends gone?

Have some more coke. Have some more drink.

She's gone forever, and it's your fault.

You are all alone.

She never loved you.

He's gonna come for you.

Maybe one more line would do it. And another drink. I did another line and washed it down with vodka. No matter how many vodka and cocaine blankets I threw over it, the murmur was louder than ever.

Waves of doom were headed in and I was buried up to my neck on the shoreline. I'd been happier when I was sleeping under a tarp.

The mom was right. Armageddon would come any second and I would be destroyed by God's judgement, or by Tony's hand.

The Jehovah's Witnesses Elders were right. I was no good. I deserved everything that was about to happen to me.

Tony was right. I was a coke-snorting loser with no future.

My heart wanted out of my chest. I didn't blame it. I'd try to leave me, too. I wondered if this is what a heart attack felt like. I lay down on the bed, my heart pounding like a foreign body in my chest. I had to move. I got up and paced. I paced like animal who'd lost all awareness of the world outside of its cage.

My vision narrowed to a tunnel of red. I crumpled to the floor.

I was at the front door of my childhood home. The door was ajar. I walked through the kitchen and into the living room. Looking up from my father's favorite spot on the sofa was…me.

I screamed.

The other me looked up with a steady countenance. His face vibrated in and out of focus.

Stop, he said.

My scream resolved into a whimper.

What is this?

Remember.

Remember what?

His face phased between mine and my father's.

Before.

Before what?

Before.

Before what? I screamed.

Remember.

What?

Gone.

I'm not gone. I'm still here. I've lost my family, my friends, my love, my home, but I'm still here. I'm here. Look at me.

He faded away. The couch, the house, the universe joined him, collapsing into a point of grey.

The point of grey expanded into a fuzzy view of my bedroom ceiling. I lay rigid, not breathing. I tried to sit up. It felt like someone was sitting on my chest. A big someone. Was my heart even beating? Pain exploded in my chest, and my heart spun like it had been jumped with an old car battery wired to my innards by rusty cables. I sucked air like a breaching whale.

I lay still until my heart returned to a regular rhythm. I considered calling an ambulance. I didn't. Fuck it, I thought. If I die, I die.

Lying on the bedroom floor, I looked inward for the first time in years. I pulled aside the mask of ego I had donned. Layer by paper-mâché layer I went, allowing each one to deconstruct and float away like an escaped kite.

I saw it.

It was swirling in the mirror-black pool where it had lived for years, swimming, feeding, growing. I saw it as clearly as my father saw the mom's many years ago, while sitting on a mid-century couch in a Levittown living room.

All this time, I was wrong. Demons do exist.

Not the kind the mom thought she saw and heard, but the kind of demon that rides your back your entire life, wrapping its scaled hands around your neck, whispering in your ear, stopping you from breaking through or rising above, choking away remembrances of who you were and eating any seeds of becoming before they can take root.

Demons do exist, and mine had a name. Its name was fear. It was born of the pain and insecurities gifted to me by my mother, passed down by the callous hearts, harsh words, and striking hands of her mother, her mother's mother, and so on throughout generations of abuse.

My demon, fed from the early loss of a protector father, had sprung its razor-sharp talons and sunk them into my guts. It thrived, feasting on the fears instilled by a doomsday cult, painted over by lies, fake smiles, false hopes, and self-righteous judgments. It grew fat drinking from a firehose of insecurity brewed by losing home, friends, family, future. My twin fears of rejection and abandonment gave it armor like liquid steel.

I was not free from blame. It was my spawn, and I fed it plenty while denying its very existence. Instead of facing it, I put on a shine of bravery, bravado, and boastfulness. I buried it under reams of denial and pages of hedonistic pursuit. I wrote it off as no thing, giving it cover and room to grow. I allowed it to hide in the library of me, at times, foolishly borrowing against its strength.

Emergence was imminent. A few more feedings and the person I wanted to be would be gone forever. Like a candle burning its last wax, my light was sputtering, throwing ash to the sky like the last offering on an alter to an uncaring god.

I stood on shaking legs.

I fled.

I made the drive from Southern New Jersey to Levittown, Pennsylvania. I arrived in my old town and drove through the sections. I passed Bolton Mansion, where I'd found early courage. I passed George Washington Elementary School and the Big Pine Tree, where I'd seen evil and tasted real fear. I passed the field where I was set alight and the streets where I'd ridden my bike, racing against dusk with the fireflies of summer.

My car turned onto my old street as if guided by spirit magnets. The gas tank gave up the last of its fumes. The engine stalled, coasting to a stop across the street from my childhood home. I pulled the baggie of coke out of my pocket. It was as empty as I was.

How was I still alive? I probably wouldn't be for long. You can't just walk away from people like Tony, no matter who you know. His goons would find me. I no longer cared. Everyone I'd loved was either dead or gone. Maybe it was time to join them.

I'd survived a lot in the years since I'd called this house my home. Probably more than I had a right to. I got out of the car to confront the locus of my early construction. Maybe there was a trace of me to be found in its old wood. Something good, something redeemable.

I slumped against the car door, the gravity of the place making me too heavy to stand.

Where was the boy that was going to be an astronaut, a doctor, a scientist?

Where was the boy who'd vibrated with plans birthed from a flashlight lit book under a blanket?

Where was the boy who'd swam in rivers of words and danced under the light of a thousand distant suns?

Was there anything left of that me besides an echo?

There was nothing of him in the old house. Its wood and brick were long purged of him, given over to a new family of life and love. There was no room for both and no more answers to be found there.

I abandoned my car and started on the old route to the library. My walk turned into a run. I pushed my legs faster, trusting them to remember the shortcuts between houses, across lawns. Faster I ran, the wind drying the wetness of my tears, leaving behind a film of salt like a rouge of all past pain.

The demon tried to distract me with memories and promises of the drink, the drugs, the sex.

You are alone, so alone.

I wanted a drink. I wanted a line.

Where are you going? Nothing for you there…

I ran faster, the burn in my legs helping to quiet the voice.

So, so, alone.

Alone.

The library looked smaller yet felt larger than I remembered. I leaned against its wall to catch my breath, feeling the coarseness of the brick under my fingers, willing my heart to slow, lest it explode in my chest.

Grabbing the library door's handle was like shaking hands with a lost friend. The opening door brought the scent of paper and secrets, as familiar to me as my grandmother's perfume. I went inside.

Inside of me, the demon writhed in anger, striking at me with everything it had. It seethed in its pool, unable to escape. It glowed white hot, like an ingot of cheap iron, trying in vain to burn its way deeper into me.

I sat at my favorite table, wedged in at the end of two rows of books. I rubbed my thumb against its smooth wood.

I willed myself still.

I closed my eyes.

My breathing slowed.

In that safest of spaces, that holy of holies, a small blue spark of clarity and remembrance formed.

How had I forgotten?

I was not alone. I was never alone.

Even in the darkest moments they were with me.

I was armed with the power of every story I'd ever read, been told, or seen on screen. Authors and characters from across a thousand worlds over a thousand years stood ready inside me to do battle.

The poets and philosophers were drawing up plans. The fields of war were filling.

Joan of Arc was there, as were Buck Rodgers, Sherlock Holmes, and the Hardy Brothers. Bilbo Baggins, Holden Caufield, Luke Skywalker, and Han Solo entered. John Carter, Jesus, Dejah Thoris, Evelyn Cyril Gordon, and James T. Kirk joined. The field overflowed with the heroes of story and more joined every second. Overhead, a seagull named Johnathan flew faster than the light of the twin suns that shined down over the throng of my allies.

Leading my warriors was my father, resplendent in the humble clothes of a working man, a crown made of "elbow grease" and "can do" adorning his head. A simple man who made a life for his family but was taken before the quest to quell his own demons was complete. He nodded to me and raised his arms to the crowd as if to say, *"This and more is what you have forgotten. You have all you need. And you are not alone, for we are with you, always."*

In that rickety old chair, at that elbow-worn table, I remembered who I was to become. With the remembering came the way.

It was time to rise up and own my life. All of it. The lies, the insecurities, the jealousies, the ego, the fears, the drugs, the alcohol.

All of it.

I wasn't a victim. I did most of it to myself, and it had cost me almost everything.

I had been given chances. The universe had laid them before me like gifts of the Magi. I'd let my fear close the doors those chances opened.

No more. It would take work, but I would do it.

"Father, I will become more."

The demon tried one last time.

Look at you, you are nothing.

No. You lie.

I am Hero.

I am Legion.

I am story.

And I will not be stopped.

The librarian came through the rows of books, appearing to glide like an angel. She stopped at my table.

I smiled up at her. She smiled back, quizzical, concerned.

"Are you okay?" she asked.

"I will be. I just forgot who I was. I remember now."

The demon screamed.

39

EXECUTION OF BITTERNESS

"I forgive you."

My mother was sobbing on the other end of the call. So was I.

"I'm so sorry. The Elders said it was the best thing to do. I couldn't find you. I tried. I asked everyone, but no one knew where you were."

"It's okay. I'm okay. I forgive you."

"I'm sorry."

"It was a long time ago. Almost twenty-five years."

"Where did you go? What did you do?"

"I made it through. The story will take some time to tell. Who knows, maybe I'll write it all down."

"Do you need a place to stay?"

"No, Mom, I have a house. A big one."

"Thank Jehovah."

I ignored the irony of her statement.

"Do you want to talk to your brother?"

"Another time. I'd like the opportunity to get to know him."

"He would love that. I'm so sorry for what happened."

"You are forgiven. I've moved past it. I hope you can as well."

"Why did you call me, now, after all these years?"

"It was time. I also have news. I'd like to invite you and Sean to my wedding."

"Happy, Mrs. Gilchrist?" I asked.

To my right, framed by the colors of the lush mountains, her green eyes matching the pines, was Julia, my wife of just two weeks. I reached my hand across the middle console and took hers, raising it to my mouth and giving it a kiss.

She took her hand from mine and brought it up to give her rings another look. She'd done it often since our "I do's."

"I am, Mr. Gilchrist. You?" She took my hand and gave it a kiss.

"I am."

And I was.

The Swiss Alps filled our car windows ahead and to the sides. We were making great time, having left our week-long honeymoon in Venice only three hours earlier. Behind us, I felt the magnetic pull of Verona, Milan, and Lake Como. We didn't have time to stop in those cities on this trip. The pull of Verona was the strongest. Over the previous year, I'd reread some of my favorite Shakespearean works, and I wanted to visit the tourist traps of Juliet's house and its balcony. I knew they weren't real, but the idea of reading Romeo and Juliet in its shadow plucked one of my heartstrings. I was feeling especially romantic. But Verona wasn't going anywhere, and we had someplace to be. I was needed in Basel, Switzerland.

"I still can't believe your father and brother showed up to our honeymoon."

Julia laughed. "Please forgive them. They don't know any better. They've been talking about going to the Venice Biennale for some time now, and they thought it would be nice to see it and surprise us at the same time."

"It was definitely a surprise." I looked at Julia and grinned.

"They meant well."

"I'm sure they did, and it will make a great story. We can tell people your father came with us on our honeymoon."

"Let's tell it exactly like that."

By the time we made it through the Alps, there was barely enough time to check into our hotel in Basel before heading out again. A short drive into the country brought us to our final destination. Bottmingen Castle was built in the mid 1300s and featured an actual working moat. The only way in was over one of two bridges unless you brought your own rowboat.

At the beginning of the bridge, the bridal party was greeting everyone with three kisses, as was the local Swiss custom. At the head of the greeting line was my best friend, my brother from another mother, Sidney, resplendent in traditional Swiss wedding garb. To his side, looking like a star that went missing from heaven, was the love of his life and his soon-to-be wife, Caryn. They broke ranks, rushing over to us.

"Buck!" Sid pinned my arms to my side with his hug. "I'm so glad you're here."

"Me too, my brother, me too."

"*Gruezi* Cam and Julia." Caryn kissed us in greeting.

"Are you two ready to do this?" I said.

Sid smiled. "We are. We were just waiting on you, my brother. Come on, the aperitif is beginning."

As we walked, four abreast, arm in arm, across the bridge to the castle lawn, where a tuxedoed wait staff stood, champagne at the ready, I felt many things. I felt the love of a friend that would always be there for me as long as we both drew breath. I felt the waves of joy lifting my best friend as he prepared to deliver a promise to his partner, a promise that I knew in my soul, he would keep. I felt gratitude to the people I'd met along my journey who'd shown me kindness and given me a chance.

The four of us raised our champagne. Glasses clinked.

Sid and I locked eyes. I was proud of the two of us and what we'd crafted from the start we were given and the messes we'd made. Mixed in with the pride was a faint murmur that said, *You don't deserve this.* The demon was small and powerless, but on days like that day, when things were almost too good, it tried its damnedest to let itself be known. I shushed it and it went still. The thing I'd learned about demons is that while you can starve them down, they're sticky bastards, and their claws can take a long time to pry out.

Rising above all else on that day was a feeling of wonder. Looking back through the books of both of our lives, I found no ah-ha moments, no special survival techniques, no cliche hallmark card advice that took us from there to here. Despite some close calls, we'd come through with only scars.

After my phone call with Sam, I never heard from Tony again. I don't know if it was because of Sam's intervention or if there was some other reason. I'd run into Sam a few times after that night I called him in desperation, but we never spoke about the events of that evening and my ask.

A few years after our final encounter, I heard Tony had pushed someone to their breaking point. When the guy broke, he broke in Tony's direction with a baseball bat. Word was, Tony disappeared for good not long after that.

After facing my demon, I embarked on the most important quest of my life. With the help of others who'd gone before me, I made changes inside and out. When the fog lifted, I discovered I was good at things besides drinking, drugging, playing music, and ducking criminals.

While I was experiencing homelessness and finding ways to survive, I honed my ability to think and speak on my feet. Manipulating situations and people with nothing more than words developed into a core skill. No college course can teach this skill better than the curriculum of the street.

It was suggested to me that because of the way I could read people and talk, I might be good at sales. I tried it and I was. In the early selling days, I sold anything from clothing to diamonds to stereos to furniture. I read all the sales and psychology books I could find to hone my skills and sand down my rough edges.

After a few successful years of sales, I went looking for ways to maximize my time. What I really needed was a way to talk to people from the road and pay-phones weren't cutting it. I found a mobile phone store at the back of a business park and peppered the lone salesperson with questions for over an hour. Once I'd teased out of him everything he knew about mobile phones, I purchased an installed car phone.

Using that phone, I knew it contained the power to change the world. I went back to the mobile phone store and got myself a job. I started at the bottom and learned about the technology from the people who built the networks. Over the years, I built myself a career in wireless communications, combining my sales ability and the technical knowledge I picked up from looking over the shoulders of the network engineers. I found that I had a knack for translating highly technical solutions and the ability to communicate them to all levels of a business. Who would have thought a dropout with dyslexia would one day have audiences with CEOs of Fortune 500 companies?

Sid escaped the threats to life and limb and landed in Frankfurt, Germany with a few hundred dollars in cash and a cousin's address in his pocket. He then finagled a civilian job at a US military base supporting the base's retail store. After living a party lifestyle all over Europe and trying most vices known to humankind, he eventually calmed his wandering spirit, found a career in banking, of all things, and met Cayrn. Coming up, Sid often said that the two things he wanted in his life were to live in Europe and have a big family. I guess dreams can come true, but some of us walk through fire to get to them.

I looked at the castle, my best friend and his fiancé, and shook my head in disbelief. What were the odds that we would have made it through? Some folks I'd met on my journey hadn't, and I regretted not doing more to help them. I was working on that.

After I pulled out of poverty, I tried to locate Boo Boo to offer help, but he was gone. I spoke to the laundromat owner and the manager of the shelter he'd taken me to, and I visited the spots that he'd frequented, including the "safe" spots he showed me. No one had seen him. I'd like to think he found a home and is living a happy life with people who love him, but I know that's probably not true. The world swallows up people like Boo Boo. If not for the advantages I had, it would have swallowed me as well. I vowed to do better, to truly see other people and help where I could.

———

It was a beautiful ceremony, and I was honored to be Sidney's best man. He was certainly mine. Watching Sidney speak another language to his group of friends and family made me realize how much he'd been changed by his journey. I had never seen him so comfortable, so free. Working his way through the attendees, his smile was so big, I feared it would take his ears.

Sid's wedding reception was quite the affair, lasting a good twelve hours. I had time to get a little drunk, have a hangover, and get buzzed again before the party hit its full stride. As the reception was winding down in the early morning hours, I found Sid in the back of the castle's great hall, slightly drunk and partially obscured behind a post, standing silent and still. He was watching our wives dancing with Caryn's friends and family.

He wiped his eyes, looking down, hiding his tears.

"I wasn't crying, you were."

I laughed. "Lots of that today. Do you want to be alone?"

"No. I was just taking a moment."

"I get it." I put my arm on his shoulder.

We watched the celebration from a distance.

"Thank you for asking me to be your best man."

"Who else would I have asked?"

"You've made an entirely new life here. I'm sure any of your friends would have been proud to step up."

"Yeah, but they only know this Sid. You know the whole Sid."

"Are we talking about ourselves in third person now?"

We laughed.

"I have to thank you for something else," I continued.

"Whatever it is, you're welcome."

"I'm serious. Thank you for helping me through it when I was trying to break free from the Witnesses, and when I was on the street. The strength you gave me made all the difference."

"I wish I could have done more."

"You did all that was possible. Thank you."

"Nah. When you were on the street, I could have pushed my family harder or helped in some other way."

"No, you couldn't. You were going through your own stuff, and there was no way for you to know how bad it was for me. I didn't want anyone to know how it really was."

"Still, though."

"You did enough. Thank you."

We stood together, comfortable in the silence that only the best of friends can share.

"How'd we get here, Buck?"

"Not sure. Maybe fate. Maybe luck."

"You think it's just luck?"

"I've been giving it some thought. It might be something else."

"How so, Buck?"

"We got back up."

"What do you mean?"

"Whatever happened, no matter what came our way, no matter who or what knocked us down, even when we knocked ourselves down, we always got back up."

"Yep. We were always good like that."

"AND we were lucky as hell!"

Our laughter smoothed to silence, and we let it own us for a few.

"Sometimes, I wake up in the middle of the night terrified that I'll lose it all. What'll I do if I lose all of this? What do we do if all this doesn't last?" Sid said.

"Nothing does."

"I'm not sure that's the wedding day pep talk I was looking for."

"Sorry. I didn't mean it like that. It's just…if I've learned anything so far, it's that nothing lasts forever, so you better grab onto what you have with both hands. It can disappear like dust in the wind."

"Those are some better wedding day words, Buck. Not exactly Hallmark, but better."

"It's been quite a ride so far, hasn't it?" he added.

"It sure has."

"Seriously, look at her," he said, nodding at his new wife on the dance floor. "She is the best thing that's ever happened to me. I don't deserve her."

"Don't ever say that. Of course, you do. We both deserve to be happy. That's the old Jehovah's Witness programming talking, the old fears that it's all going to end at any moment. It's those thoughts that don't allow us to commit fully to life or live like we have a future. Don't let the fear demon get at you. Tell it to shut up. After a time, it will. Mostly."

"I don't know what I'll do if this doesn't work out. What if I screw up?"

"That's not going to happen."

"But what if I do?"

"You won't."

"But what…"

I turned him around so we were standing face-to-face. "Then you do what we've always done." I took him by both shoulders. "You get back up and do better."

A conga line of dancers was forming, led by Cayrn and Julia. Their joy made the leap from their hearts to their faces, and they glowed. They stopped mid-step and waved us over.

"Life is filled with a million Armageddons, and that's just the way it is." I gripped his shoulders tighter. "We've both found people who love us, and both scratched out places on this blue ball to call our own. Since we're standing in a castle in Europe, I'd say you've carved out a pretty good life. How about, at least for today, we both agree not to look too closely at everything? It's past time for both of us to accept the good things and just relax into it. Fear has cost us so much already."

The entire dance floor joined in our wives' efforts to get us to come over and join in the dance. An ocean of hands waved to us. In a sea of smiles, music, and joy, Sid and I shared smiles of our own with each other. Smiles built from thirty years of joy and pain, friendship, and love.

"Get Up Offa That Thing" by James Brown started playing.

"Shall we join them?" I asked.

"Yeah, Buck, let's dance."

40

SAN FRANCISCO - MONDAY, AUGUST 16, 2021, 2:12 PM

He was sitting on an overturned painter's bucket at the corner of Powell and Post in San Francisco. He couldn't have been older than eighteen. He had a tangle of dirty blonde hair, a thin black T-shirt, and street-worn Converse. He looked clean, but I knew, if I asked him, that he couldn't give me a permanent address.

Wedged between his knees was a dirty canvas backpack. He was hunched over, engrossed in a book gripped tightly in both hands, oblivious to the lemming motion of tourists around him. Tilted against his backpack was a cardboard sign that read, "Be Kind."

The ringing of the Powell-Hyde cable car bell brought his gaze up from the pages of his book and our eyes met. One hand released the book and the cover became visible.

"Is that *Glory Road* by Heinlein?" I asked him.

He smiled. "Why, yes, sir. It is. Do you know it?"

"I do."

I reached into my pocket and separated out the dollar that had lived in my wallet for almost forty years.

I handed it to him.

"Thank you, kind sir."

The light changed and I moved across the intersection. Halfway across, I looked back. He was smiling. He held up the dollar over his head and gave me a nod.

I nodded back.

AFTER

When I was about halfway through writing this memoir, Sid's wife contacted me from Switzerland to inform me that my oldest and best friend in the world had suffered a cerebral hemorrhage on his first day of a new job. They rushed him to the hospital and operated to stop the bleeding. They saved his life, but he was in a coma.

It was a long fight for Sid and his family, but as I finished the first draft, Sid woke up from the coma.

He will get back up.
We always do.

THANK YOU

Thank you, the reader, for giving something of great value. Your time.

If you enjoyed my story, please consider leaving my book a review on your platform of choice.

Reviews are extremely valuable to authors and I thank you for taking the time to support me and my memoir.

Free your mind.
Slay your demons.
Live your truth.

ACKNOWLEDGMENTS

Writing *The Truth About Demons* has been a journey of reflection, and vulnerability. This book wouldn't have been possible without the support, guidance, and inspiration of many remarkable souls.

To my father, Alexander Ronald Gilchrist. It is because of your protection, life lessons and love that I exist. I am proud to have inherited your sense of wonder, strength of mind and rebellious nature. You instilled in me the power to question everything and truly live free and I will share your story as long as I breathe.

To my best friend, and soulmate, Sidney Brown. You showed me by example how to be yourself in all of its imperfect perfection. You stood by me in my darkest moments and celebrated my triumphs. Your loyalty and love is a beacon of light in an often-dark world. I am forever grateful for you. Your soul has left a mark on this reality and its effects will continue on to infinity by the soul spark evident in your beautiful children.

To my partner, Amy. Thank you for your unwavering love and patience as I navigated the complexities of my life story. You selflessly gave me the space and time to put my truths on paper. Thank you for the millions of moments of "How do I spell...?", "What's a good word for...?", "Does this make sense...?", and my constant railing against the rules of comma usage.

A special thank you to friend, author and nexus of all things writing, Anne Moose. If a more altruistic soul exists, I will eat my first manuscript. Your graciousness, patience, and unwavering support have been nothing short of miraculous. You've been a guide, an editor, a sounding board, and an endless source of solid advice. Perhaps more important than the practical knowledge you've dispensed is your ability to connect people. Writing is a lonely affair but made less so by people like you.

A round of thanks to Gerald Webb, Bob Schmidt, Jill Strickland Brown, Courtney Murphy and others (you know who you are) who were the first to read my memoir and give me critical feedback that helped me sand down the edges.

To the countless readers, storytellers and the members and staff of the San Diego Memoir Writers Association who have shared their own tales of struggle and resilience. Your stories inspired me to keep writing when I thought I was out of words. Your courage is a reminder that we are never truly alone.

To librarians and teachers everywhere: You are the tour guides of knowledge, and from knowledge comes freedom, and with freedom comes life. You are truly society's heroes.

Thank you to the countless kind souls that provided comfort and kindness while I was experiencing homelessness. My time without an address was nothing compared to others I have met on the street. I hope you all found safe spaces and peace.

Lastly, to the demons I've faced along the way, thank you. You have taught me lessons I never imagined I'd learn. Now, away with you!

It is my hope that this book is a testament to the power of freeing your mind, slaying your demons and living your truth.

Story is life and I thank you all for being a part of mine.

With deep gratitude,

Cameron Alexander (Buck) Gilchrist

ABOUT THE AUTHOR

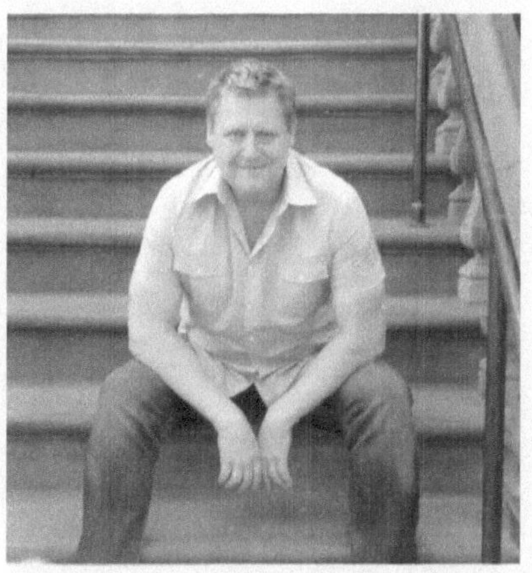

Cameron Gilchrist is an author residing in San Diego, California, a far cry from the suburbs of Philadelphia where he grew up. He is a self-proclaimed story addict and believes that we all have a story inside of us that needs telling.

Through the years, Cameron had multiple ventures including owning and running an art gallery, an entertainment company, a video production company and a career in solution engineering.

When not herding words into some semblance of order, Cameron can be found pretending to play guitar or perfecting a stand-up routine that will most likely never see a stage.

www.CamGilchrist.com

www.ingramcontent.com/pod-product-compliance
Lightning Source LLC
Chambersburg PA
CBHW021216130626
46554CB00004B/1244

* 9 7 9 8 9 9 1 4 0 2 9 2 7 *